T0272634

"In an age of relentless self-invention, I believe that many people are desperate to find an enduring story that makes sense of their lives. Historian Sarah Irving-Stonebraker is a superb guide to the religious and spiritual history that has shaped generations of our forebears over hundreds of years. *Priests of History* is an enlightening and compelling account of how re-engaging with the traditions, stories, and practices of the past can provide us clarity for our present times. In a confusing and divided age, this volume will give you hope for the future."

—JUSTIN BRIERLEY, author, speaker and broadcaster, creator of *The Surprising Rebirth of Belief in God* books and podcast

"A scintillating and much-needed plea to move beyond our shallow and simplistic cultural mood. Professor Irving-Stonebraker invites us to rediscover our place in history and the vitality of a worldview that is attentive to complexity and ambiguity, as well as open to learning from the past."

—PROFESSOR ALISTER MCGRATH, Senior Research Fellow, Ian Ramsey Centre for Science and Religion, Emeritus Andreas Idreos Professor of Science and Religion, Emeritus Fellow, Harris Manchester College, University of Oxford

"Drawing on both her own story of coming to Christ as a history professor and the stories of Christians through the ages, Sarah Irving-Stonebraker invites us to discover what for many of us is a long-lost inheritance. *Priests of History* encourages us to mine the riches of a Christian past that goes beyond our own lives and to learn from the insights and practices of brothers and sisters who are long dead but are still relevant. I knew Sarah back in her atheist days, and her story moves me greatly. I took particular delight in sitting at her feet and feeling her fresh and challenging rebuke of instruction to my own overly ahistorical life."

—DR. REBECCA MCLAUGHLIN, author of *Confronting Christianity*

"In a day when historical roots are forgotten or destroyed and contemporary fruits are weak or rotten, here is a truly fresh appeal to capture the God-given past. Sarah Irving-Stonebraker exposes the serious state of our 'Ahistoric

Age' and shows the wonderful benefits of an historic awareness. There are too many books 'like chaff that the wind blows away,' but I found myself thanking God for the weight of this volume and the rich gospel heritage that lies behind it. You will deeply value her convictions."

—SIMON MANCHESTER, Senior Minister, St. Thomas'
Anglican Church, North Sydney (1989–2019)

"Most today simply ignore history. Some twist history for partisan gains. Only a few sit underneath the wisdom of the past and learn to discern God's work in this fallen world still marked by his grace. Sarah Irving-Stonebraker is a reliable, inspiring guide for receiving that wisdom. The stories, examples, and arguments in this book will change you, whether you're already convinced of Christianity or still wrestling with its claims."

—COLLIN HANSEN, Vice President for Content and
Editor in Chief of The Gospel Coalition, host of the
Gospelbound podcast, author of *Timothy Keller*

"This book is not only an exciting overview of much modern history and historical thought, but it is an invitation to our ahistorical age to rediscover its own history. History offers us a lens through which to understand our own times and problems and also gives us a creative glimpse at ways forward out of the West's cultural malaise. Sarah Irving-Stonebraker's volume is one of the most learned, accessible, personal, and hopeful books in years to look at our current generation and talk constructively about history. In the process of reading this book, we will come ultimately to a deeper awe of the God who is not just the God of the universe but the God of history."

—JOHN ANDERSON, former Deputy Prime Minister of Australia

"*Priests of History* shines a piercing light on the damaging ahistoricism of much contemporary church culture: we have forgotten how to listen to the past. I hope and pray that this unique and precious book will help many Christians to comprehend the ill effects of ahistoricism and encourage us to learn from two millennia of mistakes, insights, and everything in between."

—CHRISTOPHER WATKIN, Monash University,
Melbourne, author of *Biblical Critical Theory*

"If you're like me, you're guilty of presentism. You uncritically see yourself as the free-floating, self-made, smartest person in the universe. But this perspective is intellectually dishonest, naïve, and existentially unfulfilling. We will consequently all benefit from Sarah Irving-Stonebraker's wonderful book *Priests of History*. This book shines the light on our historical situatedness. It will make us humbler and wiser simultaneously—enabling us to learn, understand, and prosper."

—SAM CHAN, head trainer and mentor, EvQ School of Evangelism, City Bible Forum, author of *Evangelism in a Skeptical World*

"Sarah Irving-Stonebraker makes the case for historical study as an indispensable part of the Christian—indeed, the human—experience. In this wide-ranging and imaginative book, she exposes just how dysfunctional our modern relationship with history has become and models how to engage the past with humility, curiosity, and moral conviction."

—MOLLY WORTHEN, historian, University of North Carolina at Chapel Hill

"In this original and engaging book, Sarah Irving-Stonebraker offers a compelling diagnosis of our present 'Ahistoric Age,' arguing persuasively that Christians must recapture a lost historical sensibility."

—PETER HARRISON, Emeritus Professor of History and Philosophy, University of Queensland, Professorial Research Fellow, University of Notre Dame, Australia

"*Priests of History* is an erudite and spiritually enriching account of the need for historical appreciation in an ahistorical age. Interspersed with autobiography, illustrated with history, and informed by much Christian wisdom, this book beckons us to see the power of history for our individual and corporate Christian lives. It is a tonic for our time!"

—REV. DR. MARK EARNGEY, Head of Church History, Moore Theological College, Sydney

PRIESTS *of*
HISTORY

PRIESTS *of* HISTORY

STEWARDING THE PAST IN AN AHISTORIC AGE

SARAH IRVING-STONEBRAKER

ZONDERVAN REFLECTIVE

ZONDERVAN REFLECTIVE

Priests of History
Copyright © 2024 by Sarah Irving-Stonebraker

Published in Grand Rapids, Michigan, by Zondervan. Zondervan is a registered trademark of The Zondervan Corporation, L.L.C., a wholly owned subsidiary of HarperCollins Christian Publishing, Inc.

Requests for information should be addressed to customercare@harpercollins.com.

Zondervan titles may be purchased in bulk for educational, business, fundraising, or sales promotional use. For information, please email SpecialMarkets@Zondervan.com.

ISBN 978-0-310-16107-3 (audio)
ISBN 978-0-310-16113-4 (international trade paper edition)

Library of Congress Cataloging-in-Publication Data

Names: Irving-Stonebraker, Sarah, 1980- author.
Title: Priests of history: stewarding the past in an Ahistoric Age / Sarah Irving-Stonebraker.
Description: Grand Rapids, Michigan: Zondervan, [2024]
Identifiers: LCCN 2024011400 (print) | LCCN 2024011401 (ebook) | ISBN 9780310160908
    (hardcover) | ISBN 9780310160915 (ebook)
Subjects: LCSH: Christianity and culture. | Church history. | BISAC: RELIGION / Christianity /
    History | RELIGION / Christian Living / Spiritual Growth
Classification: LCC BR115.C8 I66 2024 (print) | LCC BR115.C8 (ebook) | DDC 261.5—dc23/
    eng/20240402
LC record available at https://lccn.loc.gov/2024011400
LC ebook record available at https://lccn.loc.gov/2024011401

Cover design: Thinkpen Design
Interior design: Sara Colley

Printed in the United States of America

24 25 26 27 28 LBC 5 4 3 2 1

For my children: Madeleine, Charlotte, and James.

May you find your home in the historic Christian faith
and follow the Lord Jesus all the days of your life.

A people without history is not redeemed from time.

—T. S. Eliot, *Little Gidding*

Contents

Foreword

A t the outbreak of World War II, C. S. Lewis made a wry and pointed observation in a sermon at St Mary's Church, Oxford. "Good philosophy must exist," he said, "if for no other reason, because bad philosophy needs to be answered."[1] Lewis frequently pointed out the high levels of bad philosophy in Britain during his time, and he believed Christians had a sacred duty to remedy this situation. They could respond not by mere "Christian apologetics" but by superior thinking about all intellectual matters. Dr Sarah Irving-Stonebraker, herself a onetime academic at Oxford, has answered Lewis's challenge by writing a powerful call to superior thinking on the matter of *history*. A rephrasing of Lewis's point seems relevant: *Good history must exist, if for no other reason, because bad history needs to be answered.*

Sarah's argument for taking history seriously is first and foremost a call to truth in a post-truth world. We have entered an "Ahistoric Age," she tells us, in which we are nearly incapable of speaking meaningfully about the past, except perhaps as part of the "culture wars." Commentators today (and some professional historians) are certainly apt to use historical stories to score moral or political points, whether about sex, science, racism, religion, nationalism, the West, or whatever. Truthfully, some of this "presentism," as Sarah calls it, is valid. However, a great deal of it is selective and wrong. In contrast, good history, of the sort championed in these pages, will offer clarity and

---

1. C. S. Lewis, *The Weight of Glory and Other Addresses* (New York: HarperOne, 2001), 58.

correction. It will refuse to wield factoids as weapons of war; rather, it will invite the voices of the past to speak for themselves, as if at their own trial. Sometimes we—the modern jury—may find our ancestors guilty as charged—and there's a lot of such guilty verdicts nowadays! Yet at other times our forebears will prove *us* guilty of slander and evidence tampering.

Reviving good history in this Ahistoric Age is a path to humility, a point made repeatedly throughout this book. When we know something of epoch-changing figures like the scientific giant Johannes Kepler (1571–1630) or the social reformer Florence Nightingale (1820–1910)—as well as the many other figures described in this book—our own meagre achievements and sense of self-importance are placed into perspective. This is good for the soul, especially in a culture that claims to be at the apex of history! In some ways (medical and technological), we *are* at the pinnacle of history—but in other ways, we are certainly not. We could only arrive at this sobering judgment, however, by reflecting on history. We are also equally humbled when history holds up a mirror to what is ugly in our shared humanity. When we learn about the shameful deeds of the past, we should not wonder, "*How could they have done such a thing!*" but rather realise, "*I wonder what my blind spots are!*" and "*What will future generations say about us?*" Historically minded people are haunted by these thoughts. They find themselves less interested in judging their ancestors and are acutely aware that their era may one day be spoken of in the way popular culture regards inquisitors and slaveholders.

Furthermore, studying history can cultivate sympathy towards diversity, enabling us to see things from the perspective of people whose thoughts and lifestyles greatly differ from our own. This is a point Sarah clearly makes throughout her book, especially in chapter 5. Reading deeply about, say, the sixth-century Byzantine Empire or the ninth-century Saxons is a bit like spending a month in Rangoon or Turkestan. At first, we may marvel: "*How strange they are!*" Nevertheless, with time we may come to appreciate the wisdom of their idiosyncrasies and, therefore, the contingency of some of our own distinctives. There is nothing like spending time with people who are unlike us—to "walk a mile in his moccasins," as Mary T. Lathrap put it in her 1895 poem "Judge Softly"—to develop empathy (even affinity) toward the *other*. Likewise, Sarah's own specialised study of seventeenth-century European scientists led her, as an atheist at the time, to a fresh appreciation of a theistic vision of nature. That insight was an important step in her own journey of faith. Less dramatically, I have been studying the Roman Empire for three decades. Although I am very pleased that I live *here* not *there*, I have over the years come to see something noble at the heart of ancient Rome, which contemporary society has lost: the widespread conviction that duty and discipline are frequently more important, and more beneficial, than personal emotional fulfillment. I like to think that walking a while in Roman sandals has made me a little less "judgey" than I once was. Thus, reading history can foster a sympathetic outlook—"develop our character," as Sarah puts it—not just towards the faceless figures of the past but also towards neighbours and rivals right in front of us.

History can inspire us to achieve great things, partly because the heroic figures of the past provide a model of bravery and holy ambition. For instance, I think of the brave martyrs Perpetua and Felicitas; Fabiola of Rome, the founder of the West's first public hospital; the medieval educator Alcuin of York; or the abolitionists William Wilberforce and Frederick Douglass. Happily, Sarah introduces her international audience to some Australian greats, such as the tireless Indigenous activist and Yorta Yorta man William Cooper. Such people show us what is possible when a single human being is possessed by a timeless truth. Our first response to these individuals may (and probably *should*) be humility, as I mentioned earlier. But examining world-changing events like the birth of public healthcare or the end of the Atlantic slave trade can help us believe that, despite the enormous challenges facing us, dramatic change is still possible. Who needs superheroes when we have such a pantheon of historical greats? Being "priests of history," as Sarah puts it, in part involves lifting up history's titans and emulating their greatness. After all, there is much still to be done in our broken world (including further work on the issues of healthcare and slavery).

Additionally, studying history can enhance objectivity. This is a controversial claim; the misuse of history has made many people wary of appeals to historical *truth*. Unfortunately, many historians have lost credibility by participating in fierce culture warfare. Nevertheless, at its best, the discipline of history is "scientific" because it primarily deals with facts as it considers archaeological remains, surviving coins and inscriptions, and the numerous literary works produced in the period under investigation. None of these things is devoid of propaganda, of course: ancient coins, buildings, and documents are always human creations. But they are also factual inasmuch as they reveal something real about their time and place. We know, for example, that the Roman emperor Tiberius wanted people to see him as a "son of divinity," for those words were stamped on his coins. Also, we know that the first Christians met for worship in homes, partly because ancient sources tell us so and partly because the earliest church yet found (in Megiddo, Israel) is a renovated Roman villa. Naturally, good historians are always worrying about bias—in the sources and in themselves—but they begin their research with the surviving evidence and constantly strive to submit their accounts of the past to that evidence. Despite postmodern claims to the contrary, historians are trying to describe what was once true and real. Being a "priest of history," then, demands that we aim at objectivity about the past, even while recognising that all intellectual endeavours have a *human* element.

Finally, history invites us to draw from a much deeper well of human experience and wisdom than from what can be accessed in our fleeting moment. In his classic work *Orthodoxy*, the British intellectual G. K. Chesterton described "tradition" as a kind of democracy: "Tradition means giving votes to the most obscure of all classes, our ancestors. It is the democracy of the dead. Tradition refuses to submit to the small and arrogant oligarchy of those who merely happen to be walking about."[2] What Chesterton said of tradition may also be said of history. Studying history is a democratic enterprise; it is the great opinion poll of humanity. Consulting the insights of our wisest

---

2. G. K. Chesterton, *Orthodoxy* (Nashville: B&H Academic, 2022), 66.

ancestors—whether Aristotle on the art of rhetoric, Augustine on human desire, or Catherine of Siena on ecclesiastical authority—will make us better decision makers in the present. Here, the connection between "tradition" and history is rather close. As Sarah points out in chapter 12 and elsewhere, many of the church's best thoughts are preserved in the traditional prayers of the (Anglican) *Book of Common Prayer* or the (Presbyterian) *Book of Common Worship*. Praying these prayers allows the Christian wisdom of the centuries—not just yesterday's YouTube sermon—to shape our spirituality and moral character. Pity those who listen only to their "blip" in history—but blessed are those who give ear to the voices of the ages!

Sarah's book calls on Christians to be good stewards of the past, for the sake of the present. Patient readers will learn in these pages not to wield history as a weapon, nor to claim historical facts as a kind of secret knowledge. Instead, they will learn humility, empathy, wisdom, and the joy of seeing God at work through all times and places. To be a "priest of history" is to drink deeply from the great well of human experience—and the human experience of God—and then to share the refreshing waters with our thirsty, Ahistoric Age.

John Dickson
Jean Kvamme Distinguished Professor of Biblical
Studies and Public Christianity, Wheaton College,
Illinois, author of *Bullies and Saints*

Introduction

Winter was a lonely season in Oxford. Almost all the graduate students went home for Christmas—some to the rest of England, some to Europe, and some to North America and beyond. That year, I did not return home to Australia; instead, I remained in Oxford turning my doctoral thesis into a book and spending my days in the library after my morning run. Even though the temperature was below freezing, the sky was clear and bright one morning as I ran along the gravel pathways of University Parks, bordered by the River Cherwell on the east and the spires of the old colleges in the distance. I settled into a day's work in my college library, sitting at my usual desk that overlooked the quadrangle. By noon the day was becoming grey. Sleet began to fall, as if the sky were smarting from the cold.

Growing up in a secular home in Australia, I had been an atheist and a critic of religion for much of my life. I was especially hostile to Christianity. My stereotyped assumptions about Christians relied on fundamentalist caricatures: anti-intellectual and self-righteous. I was a high achiever, which felt rewarding; I ultimately realised my childhood dream of studying for my doctorate in history at the University of Cambridge. After my studies at Cambridge, I was appointed to a Junior Research Fellowship at Oxford University. And so I came to find myself on this midwinter's day at my usual desk in the college library. But I felt restless and strangely empty.

Ostensibly everything was going well for me, and I certainly was not depressed or unhappy. I was young, successful, and ensconced at

Oxford, where I had always wanted to be. I was pursuing my dreams and was free from almost all obligations to anything outside of myself. How could I be restless if I had everything I wanted? That winter's afternoon, however, I was distracted by a discomforting realisation: every achievement merely landed me at the bottom of another ladder. Yet these ladders were entirely self-created.

I had few external points of reference as I went about pursuing my desires and aspirations. I had no larger narrative that might give me a normative vision of human flourishing, a transcendent grounding for morality, or even a means of addressing life's ultimate concerns. Indeed, as an atheist, I believed that there was no such thing as ultimate meaning and nothing was transcendent. I was proudly authentic, but ultimately rootless.

My restlessness was intellectual as well as personal. A few months into my fellowship at Oxford, a couple of friends and I attended a series of lectures given by the renowned atheist philosopher (and fellow Australian) Peter Singer.[1] As I will discuss at the end of this book, these lectures became an important turning point in my journey to Christianity. But on that winter's afternoon in my college library, the intellectual and personal restlessness came together. Was this world all there was?

I stood up from my desk and turned around, deciding to wander through the shelves and lose myself in the books. At that moment, I realised that my desk happened to be in front of the theology shelves. Tentatively, I pulled out a book of sermons. Sceptical but slightly curious, I opened the cover.

The Ahistoric Age

Years later, I am now a Christian and an associate professor of history. The path of my conversion from atheism to Christianity is woven

---

1. These were the 2007 Uehiro Lectures at the Oxford Uehiro Centre for Practical Ethics, Oxford University. See https://www.practicalethics.ox.ac.uk/uehiro-lectures-2007.

throughout this book. What strikes me now is the extent to which I was living an *ahistorical* life during my mid-twenties at Oxford. As I mentioned earlier, I had no grounding in any larger narrative; my life was primarily a quest for self-discovery, self-fulfilment, and personal happiness. I did not see myself as a part of any enduring historical communities that might help frame a deeper purpose for my life. In fact, I would have been deeply suspicious of such an idea.

These sentiments will be particularly familiar to those of us who belong to the millennial and Gen Z generations, but I suspect people of all ages will recognise much of this ahistorical tendency. It is part of a worldview, that is, a framework of assumptions that shapes how we orient ourselves towards, and interact with, the world. A number of scholars have produced insightful studies of various aspects of our contemporary worldview in Western societies, including the idea of "expressive individualism," which emphasises authenticity, self-expression, and the reduction of moral judgements to matters of personal taste or preference.[2]

As a historian, I am attuned to the ways we deal with the past and, more broadly, with time. The contemporary secular worldview in the West particularly strikes me as *ahistorical* at heart. The premise underpinning the idea that our lives are a matter of self-invention is that there are no enduring stories shaping our identities and providing normative direction to public life. There are no traditions, histories, or inheritances that provide a compelling or agreed-upon vision of the good life; there are no transcendent stories or larger narratives.

Consequently, we have entered what I call the "Ahistoric Age" in the Western world. We have largely ceased to think of ourselves

---

2. Charles Taylor, *Sources of the Self: The Making of the Modern Identity* (Cambridge, MA: Harvard University Press, 1992); Robert N. Bellah, Richard Madsen, William M. Sullivan, Ann Swidler, and Steven M. Tipton, *Habits of the Heart*, 2nd ed. (Oakland: University of California Press, 1996); Philip Rieff, *The Triumph of the Therapeutic: Uses of Faith after Freud* (Wilmington, DE: Intercollegiate Studies Institute, 2006); Alasdair MacIntyre, *After Virtue: A Study in Moral Theory*, 3rd ed. (Notre Dame: University of Notre Dame Press, 2007); Carl R. Trueman, *The Rise and Triumph of the Modern Self: Cultural Amnesia, Expressive Individualism, and the Road to Sexual Revolution* (Wheaton: Crossway, 2020); Brian Rosner, *How to Find Yourself: Why Looking Inward Is Not the Answer* (Wheaton: Crossway, 2022).

as historical beings. Western societies have almost completely lost the ability to engage meaningfully with the past. In the past decade or so, we have come to know less than ever about history, and both individually and collectively we are losing the ability to grapple with history's ethical complexities without descending into culture wars. Underpinned by the idea that life is at heart a matter of self-invention and fulfilment, the Ahistoric Age holds that the past has nothing to teach us.

I am concerned that in the attempt to appear "relevant," the church has largely acculturated itself to the ahistoric worldview by jettisoning the historic ideas and practices of Christian formation. This is creating unintended and concerning consequences, leaving us unmoored from our history and struggling to live distinctive Christian lives.

Christians in the Ahistoric Age: The Problem

The church is struggling to resist acculturating itself to the Ahistoric Age. There are three major consequences of this acculturation. The first consequence is that many Christians increasingly struggle to make sense of history and do not know how to inhabit their own story as God's people. As a university professor, I have noticed the worrying trend that younger Christians seem to know little about the history of Christianity and are ill-equipped to deal with its complexities. They often have difficulty understanding what it means to be part of the church as a historical people and how the past can form us and disciple us in fruitful ways. Partly for this reason, they also feel that the past has nothing helpful to teach us.

Growing numbers of Christians are seeking fulfilment by placing their ultimate hope in politics, social causes, or a myriad of varieties of non-Christian spiritualities. This is intimately connected with a broader shift away from the church's focus on sanctification and holiness that historically lay at the core of biblical Christianity and gave Christians the resources they needed to navigate life. As David

Brooks recently observed, the numbers of people looking to politics as a source of fulfilment and meaning are increasing partly because the "flickering candle of Christian formation" has become "so dim."[3] Given that we are unmoored from our history, this phenomenon is unsurprising; many Christians are even drifting away from formal church membership altogether. In recent years extensive research has documented the rise of the "nones," that is, the religiously unaffiliated.[4] In fact, according to Pew Research, this category of people stood at 26 percent in 2019, whereas it was only 17 percent a decade earlier in 2009.[5] By 2023, this number had grown to 30 percent.[6]

The increasing politicisation and polarisation of history is another concerning phenomenon. The culture wars reduce history into simplistic ideology: we are compelled either to affirm or cancel historical figures, treating the past either with triumphalism or shame and guilt. Is the church simply falling victim to the culture wars and the facile politicisation of history, unable to deal fruitfully with the past and therefore abandoning it altogether? Surely, Christians ought to be equipped to deal with history in a more nuanced and fruitful way.

We urgently need a set of intellectual resources to think through the purposes and uses of history as well as the difficult issues the past raises. Many thoughtful Christians will recognise that history requires this degree of care because we are familiar with the rigour required in our responsibility to pass down the apostolic tradition through the

---

3. David Brooks, "The Dissenters Trying to Save Evangelicalism from Itself," *New York Times*, February 4, 2022, https://www.nytimes.com/2022/02/04/opinion/evangelicalism-division-renewal.html; Russell Moore, "David Brooks Wants to Save Evangelicalism," February 17, 2022, in *The Russell Moore Show*, podcast, https://www.christianitytoday.com/ct/podcasts/russell-moore-show/david-brooks-evangelicalism-politics-new-york-times-oped.html.

4. e.g., Jim Davis and Michael Graham, *The Great Dechurching* (Grand Rapids: Zondervan, 2023), and Ryan P. Burge, *The Nones: Where They Came From, Who They Are, and Where They Are Going* (Minneapolis: Fortress Press, 2021).

5. "In U.S., Decline of Christianity Continues at Rapid Pace," Pew Research Center, October 17, 2019, https://www.pewresearch.org/religion/2019/10/17/in-u-s-decline-of-christianity-continues-at-rapid-pace/. On the "nones," see Ryan Burge, *The Nones: Where They Came From, Who They Are, and Where They Are Going*, 2nd ed. (Minneapolis: Fortress, 2023).

6. Peter Smith, "Highlights from AP-NORC Poll about the Religiously Unaffiliated in the US," AP News, October 4, 2023, https://apnews.com/article/religion-ap-poll-nones-survey-111e9f5bbcaaa47ea522f1aae9c24df9.

generations from the earliest period of the church (2 Thess. 2:15) and adapt to the challenges of the contemporary age by careful meditation on, and engagement with, the Scriptures (2 Tim. 3:16).

Many of us who have studied history at university, or who simply love reading about history, know that the past is so much richer than a shallow set of ideological propositions. History can evoke our wonder and fascination. History can also show us the darkness of the human heart and remind us of the God who acts in history to redeem his people. Reading the books of the past and engaging with important ideas enlarges our horizons of imagination and experience, our ability to understand God's creation, our moments of blessing and human flourishing, and our awareness of the depths of human sin.

As adults in the church, how do we disciple and mentor our younger Christian brothers and sisters? We need to teach them how to draw upon the church's rich historical tradition in such a way that they can not only deal meaningfully with the past, but also draw from it the resources to prevent the church from becoming acculturated to our post-Christian society.

A second consequence of the church's acculturation to the Ahistoric Age is a growing rootlessness and spiritual malaise among its people. In some parts of the church, there is a kind of existential boredom. A concerning Barna study found that "only 20 percent of Christian adults are involved in some sort of discipleship activity—and this includes a wide range of activities such as attending Sunday school or fellowship group, meeting with a spiritual mentor, studying the Bible with a group, or reading and discussing a Christian book with a group."[7] I find myself having conversations about this phenomenon with Christians from all generations and walks of life. We seem to be losing a sense that Christians are set apart as a distinctive community that practices spiritual disciplines which for centuries have shaped how we embark upon the difficult task of becoming conformed to Christ's image. The church seems to be disconnected from its past, existing merely in the present.

---

7. "New Research on the State of Discipleship," Barna, December 1, 2015, https://www.barna.com/research/new-research-on-the-state-of-discipleship/.

This disconnection from, and almost disdain for, the past can make some Christians particularly enamoured of popular culture, embracing it almost uncritically. For instance, a person with an eye for analysing contemporary culture would notice that many worship services seem to be performances meant to entertain passive consumers. Sometimes the service leader even pumps up the congregation for the latest church event or vision statement and receives audible whooping in response. Sermons in these church services are casual and lighthearted pep talks containing extended witty anecdotes, inside jokes, and ironic cultural references.

Part of this spiritual malaise flows from how many churches have evacuated their worship of a sense of God's holiness and transcendence. This is confusing and unhelpful to those Christians who yearn to be in wondrous awe of God. All too often, churches give such believers the latest trends with an entertaining sermon. For example, a friend of mine who became a Christian at the age of twenty confessed to me that the church service he attends feels like a coffee shop and that people often seem to be there just to enjoy the performance. Members of the congregation would sip their coffees during the service and scroll through apps on their phones, consuming beverages, media, and worship all at once.

Are Christians just rootless consumers living in a perpetual present? The loss of the sacred and transcendent character of God is a symptom of just how acculturated we have become to the secular ahistoric worldview: if there is no God, all things are ordinary. There is nothing divine and nothing transcendent, and the past is irrelevant.

A third consequence of the church's acculturation to the Ahistoric Age is that we uncritically embrace elements of non-Christian culture. At a recent conference, a Christian lawyer specialising in intellectual property law remarked to me that she was uneasy about the extent to which her church seemed to be embracing the business and marketing models she was familiar with from her professional life. She was concerned that her evangelical church conceived of itself as a "brand" and had recently undergone what it openly termed "rebranding." The church's services were driven by a business model that prioritised numerical growth above everything else and centred on the desires and expectations of consumers. She felt that her church risked turning following Jesus into a lifestyle option.

The friend I mentioned earlier, who became a Christian at twenty years of age, wanted to understand what it meant to be part of the community of God's people into which he had been saved. "Who are we, and how do I actually live as a Christian?" he wanted to know. His church's response unfortunately reflected its rootlessness and genuine inability to teach what the Christian life might actually look like in practice. He was told, "Now that you are saved, just be who you already are." But unless the church can explain and model what putting on the "new self" looks like in practice (cf. Eph. 4:24), the idea that Christians just need to "be who you are" slides all too easily into "be yourself"—the catchcry of our contemporary secular culture and its idol of autonomy. Discipleship is reduced to expressing our "true selves" to God authentically.

It is not difficult to see my friend's church's acculturation to our Ahistoric Age. He was effectively told that Christianity should be cheerfully inserted into his existing life, much like a form of self-help therapy, and that his authenticity and self-expression was paramount. He was not given any sense that he was adopted into a historic people of God who for centuries had formed their disciples to live lives radically distinct from the world. The Christians around him had lost the historical knowledge and grounding to point him to the habits and practices of formation that would make serious discipleship possible. So, what can we do about all this?

Priests of History

This book is about the Ahistoric Age, its effects on church, and what Christians might do about it. Drawing upon my expertise as an academic historian and my experience as an atheist who became a Christian, *Priests of History* examines what history is and why it matters. I argue that engaging with history ought to be a central part of Christian formation and discipleship.

This book is both a critique of culture and a positive vision for a way forward. I will present a framework for how to approach history as Christians, both in the academic sense and in the way that Christians deal with the past outside of the academy. Drawing upon the biblical injunction to serve God as a "royal priesthood" (1 Peter 2:9) and the Reformation emphasis upon the priesthood of *all* believers, and inspired by the seventeenth-century natural philosopher Robert Boyle's vision of the scientist as a priest of nature, I will suggest that Christians are called to be priests of history. They do the priestly work of "tending and keeping"—watching over and cultivating—the past.

History is a rich storehouse—a "vast treasury," to quote Isaac Watts—if we are wise enough to know how to use it. By tending and keeping the past, Christians can not only strengthen and revive our spiritual and intellectual formation, but we can also equip ourselves to communicate the truth, goodness, and beauty of Jesus Christ to a confused and rootless world.

PART I

How We Lost
Our Connection
to History

ONE

What Is the Ahistoric Age?

Over one and a half millennia ago, a convert to Christianity from Carthage in North Africa turned the biblical lens onto the late Roman Empire and produced one of the most searing cultural critiques ever written. Augustine of Hippo's fifth-century work *The City of God against the Pagans* laid bare the deepest ideals the Romans lived for, in particular their cherished ideal of glory. In fact, the glory of Rome was so taken for granted that people were oblivious to, and unquestioning of, its underlying assumptions. Augustine exposed the Roman idea of glory as merely a glory of the self and a lust for domination. Rather, true glory, as Augustine argued, was the glory of Christ, which modelled precisely the *opposite* virtues of Rome: self-sacrifice, humility, and service to others.

The City of God revealed underlying characteristics of the culture and society of which the Romans (both Christians and non-Christians) were barely conscious. Augustine articulated the relationship between Christians and society with such insight and profundity that *The City of God* became one of the most foundational and influential texts in the history of political thought. Augustine used the metaphor of the city to reveal the hidden structure of society. People lived in one of two cities: the city of God, which was oriented toward love of God, or the earthly city, which was directed toward love of the self. The two cities were so entwined that they would only be made fully evident on the final day. Augustine wrote:

Accordingly, two cities have been formed by two loves: the earthly
by the love of self, even to the contempt of God; the heavenly by the
love of God, even to the contempt of self. The former, in a word,
glories in itself, the latter in the Lord.[1]

Augustine of Hippo (354–430)

Can we see our own society and culture as clearly as Augustine
saw his? There are characteristics and tendencies of our societies which

---

1. St. Augustine, *The City of God* 14.28.

we can only dimly perceive and do not yet properly understand. Ahistoricity is one of the most defining characteristics of the contemporary West, yet we are only barely conscious of this and certainly do not entirely understand it.

In January 2018, the statue of Captain Cook in Melbourne, Australia, which had stood for decades in peaceful repose, was suddenly vandalised and emblazoned with the words "we remember genocide." When this episode occurred, many people had a momentary sense that it indicated something curious and strangely novel about how our culture related to the past.[2] What exactly was going on?

In order to properly understand the world in which we live, Christians must follow Augustine's example and critically assess our cultures and societies. We need to comprehend their underlying features, not least because these are often the most entrenched aspects—so entrenched, in fact, that we are often oblivious to them just as fish are oblivious to the water in which they swim. In short, we need to understand our culture so we can engage with it properly, for we can only make disciples—of ourselves and of others—if we know how to live in the world but not be "of" it (John 17:14–15). Let us begin our journey to understand the Ahistoric Age.

What Is the Ahistoric Age?

I have coined the term the "Ahistoric Age" to identify the way in which contemporary Western societies have largely lost their meaningful engagement with, and connection to, history. Calling this a "loss" may seem counterintuitive at first. Ostensibly, there is a highly politicised approach to history in which people appear to care passionately about history's symbols and what they represent—for example, in the recent

---

2. "Captain Cook Statue Vandalised Ahead of Australia Day," BBC, January 24, 2018, https://www.bbc.com/news/world-australia-42813211/. A further instance of vandalism occurred in January 2024; see Hannah Ritchie, "Captain Cook Statue Vandalised in Melbourne on Eve of Australia Day," BBC, January 24, 2024, https://www.bbc.com/news/world-australia-68090094/.

protests about and tearing down of statues across the Western world. Yet at the same time the average individual knows less than ever about history and is losing the ability to discuss and disagree peaceably about the past. I do not intend to imply that ahistoricism is the *exhaustive* feature of contemporary Western culture. That is, to say that we live in an Ahistoric Age is not to say that ahistoricism identifies everything about the culture in which we live. Far from it. Rather, my point is that ahistoricism is one of the most important and defining features of contemporary Western societies.

There are five major characteristics of the Ahistoric Age:

1. We believe that the past is merely a source of shame and oppression from which we must free ourselves.
2. We no longer think of ourselves as part of historical communities.
3. We are increasingly ignorant of history.
4. We do not believe history has a narrative or a purpose.
5. We are unable to reason well and disagree peaceably about the ethical complexities of the past—that is, the coexistence of good and evil in the same historical figure or episode.

The ahistoric characteristics of contemporary Western societies are the result of long-term historical developments. To understand the Ahistoric Age, therefore, we need a concise historical outline of these long-term transformations. In the brief overview that follows, there will be some overlaps with broader subjects such as "modernity" and what some historians and philosophers have called "late modernity." However, there is a wealth of literature on these broader questions and these concepts do not concern us here *per se*. Rather, our historical outline is limited to the very specific transformations and historical processes that have produced the current dominant Western attitude toward time, the past, and our engagement with history.

How Did We Get Here?

Our societies in the contemporary West hold that it is possible to make sense of life and the world without reference to God; they largely reject the transcendent grounding of life. This phenomenon emerged gradually throughout the past several hundred years. As the philosopher Charles Taylor noted, in the year 1500 it was virtually impossible *not* to believe in God. Today, however, the prevailing belief of secular societies is that the cosmos exists because of random chance. There is no creator God and no ultimate purpose to the universe, to human life, or indeed to time. As Richard Dawkins put it in *River Out of Eden*, "The universe we observe has precisely the properties we should expect if there is, at bottom, no design, no purpose, no evil and no good, nothing but blind, pitiless indifference."[3]

By contrast, in the pre-modern West—Christendom is the accurate term—people understood themselves to be living in a chapter of God's transcendent story. The present age was understood to be "passing away," not merely because our pre-modern counterparts recognised how fleeting human life was, but also because the present era anticipated the return of Christ on the final day to complete his plan to recreate the broken and fallen world. As Isaiah 25:6–8 says of that last day:

> On this mountain the LORD of hosts will make for all peoples
>   a feast of rich food, a feast of well-aged wines,
>   of rich food filled with marrow, of well-aged wines
>   strained clear.
> And he will destroy on this mountain
>   the shroud that is cast over all peoples,
>   the sheet that is spread over all nations;
>   he will swallow up death forever.

---

3. Richard Dawkins, *River Out of Eden: A Darwinian View of Life* (New York: Basic Books, 2014), 133.

> Then the Lord GOD will wipe away the tears from all faces,
>   and the disgrace of his people he will take away from all
>   the earth,
>   for the LORD has spoken.

The earthly world, therefore, pointed—much like a book of sym-bols—to the divine order which was beyond it; the immanent always sat within the eternal and transcendent. If you look at a medieval depiction of the cosmos, for example, you will see a beautifully ordered picture showing the earth sitting in the middle of concentric circles of the elements (fire, earth, water, and air), with the unchanging starry heavens forming the outer ring. This was a cosmos imbued with classi-cal assumptions, primarily derived from the philosophers Aristotle and Ptolemy, about the imperfection of those things (especially humanity) that undergo processes of change and are finite. The created world, with its change and decay, is juxtaposed against the eternal change-lessness of the heavens and God himself.

The idea of the divine ordering of the cosmos framed the thought of philosophers and theologians in the pre-modern world. Their major interest was the *purposes* for which human life, and indeed the entire created order, existed. Christian philosophers and theologians reframed the Greek philosophical concept of *telos* so that the language of purposes permeated medieval and early modern philosophy. A good illustration of the medieval approach to understanding the natural world is a compendium of beasts, known as a bestiary. Bestiaries are magnificent books and a fascinating adventure to read; their pages are exquisitely illuminated with gold leaf and rich, colourful illustrations of all manner of animals, from foxes to bees to dragons.

Whereas a modern encyclopedia entry for a fox, for example, would focus on its observable characteristics, such as the classification of its species and its behaviour, skeleton, habitat, and so forth, a medieval bestiary describes the purposes and significance of each animal to the moral instruction of sinful humanity. One of the bestiaries compiled in c. 1225–1250, which is held in the Bodleian Library at Oxford University, represents the fox like this: "The fox is the symbol of the

Medieval cosmos by Petrus Apianus, 1545.

devil, who appears to be dead to all living things until he has them by the throat and punishes them."[4] What a contrast there is between the medieval bestiary, which preoccupies itself with God's meaning and purpose, and modern scientific description!

In the pre-modern world, God's ordering and purposes applied not just to the nonhuman natural world but also to humanity. For instance, English author Sir Thomas Elyot, a diplomat in the court of

---

4. Bodleian MS 764, reprinted in facsimile for the Folio Society (London: Folio Society, 1992).

King Henry VIII, explained that God had created various hierarchies
to bring order both to the human world and the rest of the creation.
In his *The Boke Named the Governour*, Elyot wrote:

> Hath not he set degrees and estates in all his glorious works. First
> in his heavenly ministers, whome, as the church affirmeth he hath
> constituted to be in devers degrees, called hierarchies. [...] But
> to treate of that, by which naturall understanding may be compre-
> hended. Beholde the foure Elements, whereof the body of man is
> compacte, how they be set in their places, called spheres, higher or
> lower, according to the sovereigntie of their natures. [...] Beholde
> also the order that God hath put generally in all his creatures, begin-
> ning at the most inferior or base and ascending upward.[5]

Elyot, like the authors of medieval bestiaries, was primarily concerned
with God's transcendent ordering of his creation.

Over the centuries, however, this worldview was transformed
by a constellation of economic, geopolitical, social, and intellectual
processes. The eighteenth-century European Enlightenment and then
the emergence of what historians call "modernity" witnessed profound
changes to the philosophy and organisation of government. From
the late eighteenth and early nineteenth centuries, the West saw the
Industrial Revolution, the rise of cities, the mechanisation of the economy, the creation of a consuming middle class, an attendant demand
for increasing political representation, the growth of the franchise, and
convictions about the rights of individual political subjects. All the old
institutions—of the church, government, social order, and economy,
and so forth—were rapidly changing. Karl Marx famously described
the sense of upheaval in his memorable phrase, "All that is solid melts
into air."[6]

What has all this got to do with how people thought about the
past? Along with the transformations that gave birth to industrial

---

5. Thomas Elyot, *The Boke Named the Governour* (1531; London: Thomas East, 1580), 2–3.
6. Karl Marx, *The Communist Manifesto*, ed. Gareth Stedman Jones (London: Penguin, 2002), 223.

modernity in the West, ideas about time—the past, present, and future—fundamentally shifted. The best way of understanding this is the process of secularisation.[7] The German sociologist Max Weber used the term which is most often translated into English as *disenchantment* to describe the way in which the world was slowly evacuated of the sacred and transcendent.[8] The transcendent framing of time and existence was slowly replaced by a flat or horizontal worldview in which the only things that exist are natural and immanent—in other words, things that belong to the material, empirically verifiable world. Within this disenchanted worldview, the only purpose to time is the one that exists *within* this material world. In other words, there is no ultimate, God-given purpose or meaning to time or human history.

Here is a good illustration of this transformation: in the study of the natural world, the question of "final causes"—the purpose or goal for which something exists (think of the fox, which reveals the cunning nature of evil)—was replaced by the conviction that the natural world could be understood on its own terms and without reference to divine purposes. In other words, nature came to be understood in terms of *how it works* rather than *what it means and what its purpose is.* This shift was central to the emergence of modern science.[9]

Secularisation also had ramifications for political and social questions as it began to challenge the idea that the social order, from marriage to political authority, was grounded in reference to God's intended purposes for, and ordering of, humanity. In the sphere of political philosophy, theories of politics began to explain the origin, purpose, and authority of government largely in terms of natural (as opposed to divine) processes. In fact, from the late eighteenth to the mid-nineteenth century a whole new intellectual

---

7. The most well-known and comprehensive account of secularisation is Charles Taylor, *A Secular Age* (Cambridge, MA: Harvard University Press, 2007).

8. See Max Weber, "Science as a Vocation," in *The Vocation Lectures,* trans. Rodney Livingstone and ed. David Owen and Tracy B. Strong (Cambridge, MA: Hackett, 2004) and Max Weber, *The Protestant Ethic and the Spirit of Capitalism,* trans. and ed. Talcott Parsons (New York: Scribner, 1958).

9. Robert Boyle, whom we will meet later in this book, argued this point in his *Disquisition on the Final Causes of Natural Things* (London: John Taylor, 1688).

field called the *human sciences* emerged, covering such subjects as sociology, psychology, and anthropology. This field was premised on the conviction that the naturalistic methodologies of the natural sciences could be applied to the study of humanity. Even before the advent of the social sciences, however, early modern philosophers increasingly began conceiving the foundation of government not in terms of a divine decree or *covenant*, but a secular *contract*. Thomas Hobbes, John Locke, and later Jean-Jacques Rousseau, all drew upon this idea in different ways.

In short, central to modernity's mindset was the idea that we can grasp human life, the natural world, and the social order without any external reference to God and his transcendent ordering of creation and time. However, these developments were gradual and nuanced. Boyle, Locke, and Hobbes, for example, were thoroughly shaped by theology, and they spent much of their time engaged in biblical and theological arguments which in no small part helped shape their contributions to philosophy, political thought, and what we now call science.[10]

The advent of modernity had profound implications for Christianity. One significant current of thought which eventually became known as liberal Protestantism emerged. Broadly speaking, this approach was an attempt to accommodate Christianity to the modern world in various ways—for example, by discarding miracles, the virgin birth, and so on. It finds its origins in the period of eighteenth-century Romanticism, and particularly in the thought of Friedrich Schleiermacher.[11] For Schleiermacher, religion was a distinct category of the human condition which was rooted in individual experience. The emphasis upon individual religious experience as the locus of truth, rather than on the Bible and the way it has been interpreted, meant that liberal Protestantism began deemphasising historical

---

10. See Jeremy Waldron's *God, Locke, and Equality* (Cambridge, UK: Cambridge University Press, 2002), which explores the theological underpinnings to Locke's understanding of equality in his seminal *Two Treatises of Government*; Sarah Irving, *Natural Science and the Origins of the British Empire* (London: Routledge, 2016 [2008]); and Peter Harrison, *The Fall of Man and the Foundations of Science* (Cambridge, UK: Cambridge University Press, 2007).

11. Friedrich Schleiermacher, *On Religion: Speeches to Its Cultured Despisers*, Cambridge Texts in the History of Philosophy (1799; Cambridge, UK: Cambridge University Press, 1996).

traditions and confessions in favour of highly personal feelings and emotion.[12]

So far, we have been outlining some of the major, long-term processes that transformed how we think about time and the past as humanity entered what is called modernity. Although there is ongoing discussion about whether we now live in a *postmodern age*, in my view the concept *late modern* better underscores how the tendencies of our current age actually accelerate the developments of modernity.

Late modernity (starting approximately in the 1970s) is characterised by highly developed and globalised consumer capitalist economies increasingly based upon information technology and knowledge. Society is understood to be comprised of atomised consumers who are economically, socially, and culturally mobile, so it is not surprising that late modernity has facilitated hyperindividualistic modes of living. The prevailing ideal of the good life reflects this mobility and fluidity: we must be free to be ourselves and create the life we desire. Unsurprisingly, this is also the age of identity politics, in which much political engagement is based around people's identities and their sense that these identities have been oppressed and need to be liberated.

In late modernity, we perpetually feel that we need to emancipate ourselves. Our major cultural preoccupations can be summed up in this question: *How can I be my true self?* There is no real authority outside of ourselves in the project of authentic self-creation. Nothing can tell me who I truly am—not the church, not the state, not my family, not history, not biology, and so forth. Being is not given to us by God; rather, we create ourselves relentlessly. This process is being accelerated by the advent of digital technologies and the internet. Nothing is eternal, transcendent, or sacred even though people still restlessly yearn for something which is ultimate.

In late modernity we are just autonomous, atomised individuals creating our authentic selves; we are trying to live our best lives and look only horizontally around us in the process. What does history

---

12. On the rise of liberal Protestantism and its effects, see J. Gresham Machen, *Christianity and Liberalism* (1923; Grand Rapids: Eerdmans, 2009).

have to teach us if this is who we are and what life is about? Why would we need or see any virtue in genuinely engaging with the past? In all these ways, late modernity undermines meaningful engagement with history. Our culture is now, in a word, *ahistorical*.

When Did the Ahistoric Age Begin?

It is almost always difficult to identify a starting date for any historical era. What year did the European Renaissance, the Enlightenment, or the modern era begin? This difficulty does not mean, however, that we do away with the idea of historical eras altogether. We are still able to speak meaningfully of these historical periods because they exhibit characteristics that mark them out as distinct in various ways. It is still helpful to speak of the Renaissance, for example, even though its dates are somewhat approximate.

Because the Ahistoric Age is a phase of late modernity in which we are currently living, our own immersion in this period presents an added difficulty. This is an issue in contemporary history more broadly, and the historians' rule of thumb is that we generally have more perspective after at least two decades have passed from the period in question. Nevertheless, I hypothesise that we can identify the early twenty-first century, particularly from about 2010, as the beginning of the Ahistoric Age.

From around 2010 onwards, the five characteristics of ahistoricism listed earlier became dominant in Western societies. These characteristics have deep historical roots, and they have underlaid Western societies for many decades, intermittently manifesting themselves. However, soon after 2010 these five characteristics of ahistoricism intensified and coalesced. This is in no small part due to the digital revolution and the advent of social media, as the iPhone became widely available on multiple telecommunication carriers in the United States between 2010 and 2013.

A number of scholars, including Jonathan Haidt and Greg Lukianoff, have observed that soon after 2010 society and culture in the West were significantly transformed, particularly on university campuses. Haidt is a social and cultural psychologist, so his interest is not in history as such. Nonetheless, he noticed that something significant has been happening in the past decade or so. As he put it in an essay in *The Atlantic*, "The past ten years of American life has been uniquely stupid."[13] Haidt (and others) have argued that the digital revolution, particularly social media with its algorithms promoting content most likely to provoke outrage, has contributed to the enormous populism in, and polarisation of, politics and culture. The clearest illustration of these trends is how social media has facilitated the culture of publicly shaming and cancelling people. What happened to J. K. Rowling when she expressed her view that people who menstruate are called women is a revealing illustration.[14] This time period has also witnessed the emergence of a culture of "safety" on university campuses promoting the idea that students are fragile and need to be protected from offensive ideas because—according to this mindset—offensive ideas can be harmful and oppressive.[15] Moreover, speech can now be defined as a form of violence.[16] The kind of public discourse engendered by the digital age has consequently eroded our trust in governments, institutions, and even other people.[17]

I am not suggesting a simple or singular cause-effect relationship between the rise of social media and the Ahistoric Age, but I would argue that the digital revolution and the rise of social media have acted like sparks to ignite the flame of ahistoricism in two ways.

First, social media accentuates the ahistorical sense that life is all about relentless self-creation. We have become preoccupied with curating our image on social media, and the constant flow of newsfeeds

---

13. Jonathan Haidt, "Why the Past Ten Years of American Life Have Been Uniquely Stupid," *The Atlantic*, April 11, 2022, https://www.theatlantic.com/magazine/archive/2022/05/social-media-democracy-trust-babel/629369/.

14. See the podcast *The Witch Trials of J. K. Rowling* for more details.

15. Jonathan Haidt and Greg Lukianoff, *The Coddling of the American Mind: How Good Intentions and Bad Ideas Are Setting Up a Generation for Failure* (New York: Penguin, 2019).

16. On the violence of language, see Haidt and Lukianoff, *The Coddling of the American Mind*, chapter 5.

17. On this issue, see the studies Haidt links in "Why the Past Ten Years of American Life Have Been Uniquely Stupid."

means that our posts need to be updated constantly. This is at heart an ahistorical way to live, because rather than receiving stories handed down to us and finding our place in society—that is, in historical communities—we are trained by social media to regard ourselves as highly autonomous subjects of our own creation and recreation. *Nothing* is to be handed down or given to us. In many ways, it is thus unsurprising that the generations most impacted by this social media and digital revolution have also become increasingly anxious and suffer from more mental health issues than previous generations.[18] We should note the possible effects of the Ahistoric Age here: these generations have been unmoored from their historic sources of identity—that is, from their history. They now carry the existential burden of creating their identity themselves.

Second, the digital revolution has helped create a public discourse that is not conducive to genuine discussion about history, which requires the ability to articulate profound disagreement while maintaining a civil conversation. Competing for attention, "likes," and "retweets" in (originally) the brevity of 140 characters exacerbates our tendency to pursue sensationalism over deep thought and nuance. This flawed discourse also hinders our ability to listen to the views of our opponent, and we consequently have difficulty articulating our own disagreement respectfully. Genuine conversations about history cannot flourish in this polarised atmosphere because it is so intensely politicised that historical discussions are reduced to contemporary politics.[19] We thus cannot express ideas freely and disagree well in this overprotective culture of safety, which seeks to protect people from presumed oppression.[20] Again, the rise of ahistoricism is a complex process with long and deep roots, but it is significant that the advent of social media and

---

18. See Haidt and Lukianoff, *The Coddling of the American Mind*, 157.

19. On the effects of this kind of culture on history, see Cambridge University professors Robert Tombs and David Abulafia's History Reclaimed project, https://historyreclaimed.co.uk/.

20. On the culture of safety and its impact on freedom of speech, see Greg Lukianoff and Jonathan Haidt, "The Safety Police: Is Free Speech Being Stifled on College Campuses?," *Saturday Evening Post*, August 15, 2019, https://www.saturdayeveningpost.com/2019/08/the -safety-police/.

the widespread use of the iPhone beginning around 2010 accompanies the intensification of ahistoricism's five major characteristics.

It is also significant that the period since 2010 marks a dramatic rise in the number of people who are moving away from historical Christian denominations. This involves a marked increase in those who identify as "nondenominational," as well as in those who have no particular religious affiliation and dislike organised religion—that is, the "nones." According to the U.S. Religion Census, nondenominational churches grew by about 25 percent (about 9,000 congregations) in the decade from 2010 to 2020. These comprise the largest segment of American Protestants, having about 3.4 million more adherents than the Southern Baptist Convention.[21] And, as I noted in the introduction, the number of the "nones" grew from 17 percent in 2009 to 30 percent in 2023.[22] These people are not atheists or agnostics. On the contrary, as Ryan Burge put it, "they still show up to a worship service a few times a year or maintain their belief in God."[23]

So, what is going on? I would argue that there is something deeply ahistorical about this phenomenon. The decline of long-established denominations is significant because each group has its own history, often with its own confessions, liturgies, musical traditions, forms of church governance, institutions such as seminaries and schools, and so forth. In short, the move away from historic denominations to nondenominational churches and the move away from organised religion to the "nones" both represent a rejection of history and historical communities.

21. See Daniel Silliman, "'Nondenominational' Is Now the Largest Segment of American Protestants," *Christianity Today*, November 16, 2022, https://www.christianitytoday.com/news/2022/november/religion-census-nondenominational-church-growth-nons.html/.

22. "In U.S., Decline of Christianity Continues at Rapid Pace," Pew Research Center, October 17, 2019, https://www.pewresearch.org/religion/2019/10/17/in-u-s-decline-of-christianity-continues-at-rapid-pace/; Ryan Burge, *The Nones: Where They Came From, Who They Are, and Where They Are Going*, 2nd ed. (Minneapolis: Fortress, 2023); Peter Smith, "Highlights from AP-NORC Poll about the Religiously Unaffiliated in the US," AP News, October 4, 2023, https://apnews.com/article/religion-ap-poll-nones-survey-111e9f5bbcaaa47ea522f1aae9c24df9/.

23. Ryan Burge, "Most 'Nones' Still Keep the Faith," *Christianity Today*, February 24, 2021, https://www.christianitytoday.com/news/2021/february/nones-religious-unaffiliated-faith-research-church-belief.html/.

Illustrations of the Ahistoric Age

Here are three brief illustrations that reveal how ahistoricism has reached a new intensity since 2010:

First, while the issue of how history is publicly commemorated has always been a matter of contestation and politicisation—people have vandalised and pulled down statues during moments of regime change and revolution ever since the ancient world—statue toppling in the West has become a distinct trend during peacetime only around the last decade. For example, there were no attempts to remove Prime Minister Edmund Barton's, Governor Lachlan Macquarie's, or Captain James Cook's statues in Australia before the past several years, even though the complex history of the British Empire was well-known.

It is important to note that the dramatic rise of attempts to deface and remove statues is occurring against the backdrop of genuine injustices in the present, particularly the ongoing issues of racism. Many, however, are newly emphasising the realm of culture as the sphere in which racism operates, which means that cultural symbols like statues, flags, and language become battlegrounds.

The second illustration that epitomises the peculiar intensity of ahistoricism in the past decade is the International Council of Museums's 2019 decision to redefine the very purpose of a museum. Its Standing Committee for Museum Definition decided that a museum was no longer concerned with the "collecting, preserving and providing access to the heritage of humanity" but, rather, needed to promote "human dignity and social justice, global equality and planetary well-being."[24] This redefinition by the major nongovernmental organisation for museums is part of a move to "decolonise" museums. "Decolonisation," which once referred to the geopolitical process of the winding back of empires, now describes a process that can affect

---

24. Kelsey Ables, "What Is a 'Museum'? A Revised Definition Looks Forward, Not Back," *Washington Post*, August 27, 2022, https://www.washingtonpost.com/arts-entertainment /2022/08/27/international-council-of-museums-redefines-museum/. The definition was previously updated in 2007, which was the first update since 1977.

culture and institutions. The purpose of a museum—once the conduit for heritage—is no longer to preserve the past, but is now explicitly and primarily to further a contemporary political agenda.

The concept of decolonisation has also been applied to universities, especially to their curricula; this movement began with the Rhodes Must Fall campaign in 2015.[25] Its proponents believe that "disciplines that are part of the academy have not been immune to the process of colonisation."[26] Accordingly, academics have the *responsibility* to engage in the project of decolonisation. As Rowena Arshad argued in *Times Higher Education*, "Concepts of academic freedom or disciplinary integrity have allowed some scholars to *distance themselves from any responsibility to engage with the decolonisation project.*"[27]

Third, Western societies' ignorance of history seems to have entered a new phase in the past decade or so. Significantly, the decline in history enrolments at the university level is roughly coterminous with this shift. For instance, 2010 marked the advent of a marked downturn in history majors in the USA.[28] An article and data published in 2018 in the magazine of the American Historical Association showed that history out of all the major disciplines has seen the steepest declines in the number of bachelor's degrees awarded since 2008. "Between 2016 and 2017, the number of history majors fell by over 1,500. Even as university enrolments have grown, history has seen its raw numbers erode heavily."[29] In Australia, my own experience reflects this. At Western

25. Kerry Pimblott, "Decolonising the University: The Origins and Meaning of a Movement," *The Political Quarterly* 91, no. 1 (2020).

26. Rowena Arshad, "Decolonising the Curriculum—How Do I Get Started?," *Times Higher Education*, September 14, 2021, https://www.timeshighereducation.com/campus/decolonising-curriculum-how-do-i-get-started.

27. Arshad, "Decolonising the Curriculum." Emphasis mine. For an example of a university's official approach to decolonising the curriculum, see Curtin University, "Decolonising the Curriculum," Staff Portal, https://staffportal.curtin.edu.au/learning-and-teaching/academic-practice/decolonising/.

28. Robert B. Townsend, "Has the Decline in History Majors Hit Bottom?," Perspectives on History, February 23, 2021, https://www.historians.org/research-and-publications/perspectives-on-history/march-2021/has-the-decline-in-history-majors-hit-bottom-data-from-2018%e2%80%9319-show-lowest-number-since-1980/.

29. Townsend, "Has the Decline in History Majors Hit Bottom?"

Sydney University, where I taught for ten years, the undergraduate history major subjects had enrolments of about 300 or more in 2012. In 2022, they were lucky to have 150.

The research data from the United Kingdom tells a similar story. The report *Trends in History in UK Higher Education* revealed that despite increased student numbers in higher education in the UK, the number of history undergraduates has been declining over the same period. In fact, history enrolments fell by 17 percent from the 2014/15 to the 2019/20 academic years. The number of history postgraduates also fell by 16 percent.[30] Elizabeth Tingle, a professor of history writing for History UK, the independent national body promoting and monitoring History in UK Higher Education, notes that the sharp decline in enrolments, particularly in the past half decade, "presents a sombre picture for historians."[31]

One could write an entire book about the issue of ahistoricism and its causes. But for our purposes, the coalescence and intensification of these key characteristics and tendencies over the past decade or so give us a good case for marking 2010 as a useful date to identify the beginning of the Ahistoric Age. Like Augustine, who laid bare the deep structures and idols of Roman society and culture, we must properly comprehend the deep tendencies of our own age. Therefore, Christians *must* understand the Ahistoric Age. This is the culture into which we must speak the truths of the gospel and in which we must try to live as Christ's disciples. Now that we understand this historical background, we can now explore the five characteristics of the Ahistoric Age.

---

30. See Gareth Brown and David Harvie, "Trends in History Provision in UK Higher Education," History UK, June 2022, https://www.history-uk.ac.uk/projects/trends-in-history/.

31. Elizabeth Tingle, "Student Numbers in History in UK Higher Education: Recent Trends," History UK, July 1, 2022, https://www.history-uk.ac.uk/2022/07/01/student-numbers-in-history-in-uk-higher-education-recent-trends/.

TWO

The Ahistoric Age in Society

In 1850, the British colony of New South Wales was awash with public debate about religious rights. Baron Lionel de Rothschild had recently become the first practicing Jewish person to be elected (as a member for the City of London) to the British Parliament's House of Commons. But there was a problem; Rothschild needed to swear an Anglican oath in order to take up his seat in the House of Commons. Since the sixteenth-century Protestant Reformation and the creation of the Church of England with the British monarch as its earthly head and governor, would-be public office holders in England were subjected to various religious tests, and non-Anglicans faced several civil disabilities.

A series of Test Acts, which began in the 1670s, required subjects to swear allegiance to the monarch and his or her headship of the Church of England. They also had to confess publicly the Thirty-Nine Articles of Religion, which formed the doctrinal basis of the Church. Thus, the Test Acts effectively prevented all non-Anglicans from holding public office or voting.

For just over a decade (beginning with his first election in 1847), Rothschild attempted several times to be seated in the House of Commons. In 1850, he walked into Parliament after his latest victory and insisted upon swearing his oath on the Torah. He did so. But when Rothschild refused to state that he swore his oath "upon the true Faith of a Christian," he was asked to leave. Rothschild would not be seated until the 1858 Jews Relief Act was passed, allowing him and other Jewish persons to omit the phrase.

21

On the other side of the world in New South Wales, the colonial press was brimming with indignation, support for Rothschild, and historical arguments. In November 1850, the newspaper *The People's Advocate and New South Wales Vindicator* published an article starkly entitled "RELIGIOUS TOLERATION." The article's author was the newspaper's editor, a political radical and convert to Catholicism named E. J. Hawksley. He used the plight of Rothschild as a point of entry into a detailed argument about the theological and historical grounding of the principle of liberty of conscience:

> What has man to do with the belief of his fellow-man? Nothing; his moral life, his social virtues or his vices, are naturally the concern of those who travel with him the pilgrimage of earth; but his religion, the doctrine which he professes, the rule of discipline which he observes—these are the ties which unite him not with man but with God.[1]

So began the article's journey into the theory and history of liberty of conscience, which involved inviting its audience to imagine a sweep of history from the ancient world to the current "enlightened times."[2] Hawksley's argument was richly historical. He referred to the tradition of doing unto others as stemming back to Jesus "eighteen centuries and a half ago . . . [on] the mountains of Judea."[3]

The Rothschild case was not unique. In the mid-nineteenth century, debate about religious rights and toleration abounded in Britain and her empire, and for good reason. A couple decades before Rothschild embarked upon his mission, the British Parliament had to decide if members of the Catholic Church could stand for election. The successful *Roman Catholic Emancipation Act* of 1829 was hotly contested.[4]

---

1. E. J. Hawksley, "Religious Toleration," *The People's Advocate and New South Wales Vindicator*, November 30, 1850, 8.

2. Hawksley, "Religious Toleration," 8.

3. Hawksley, "Religious Toleration," 8.

4. Sarah Irving-Stonebraker, "Catholic Emancipation and the Idea of Religious Liberty in 1830s New South Wales," *Australian Journal of Politics and History* 67, no. 2 (2021): 193–207.

One of the most interesting things about all this political discourse is how much it was founded upon appeals to history. When another colonial newspaper, *The Sydney Gazette and New South Wales Advertiser*, supported the emancipation for Roman Catholics, one of its editorials and articles referred to the Magna Carta and stated:

> [T]he people of England never knew what liberty was till it was won for them by Hampden and other conscientious Protestants . . . of the Long Parliament, and when the liberties of England were again lost through the unhallowed ambition of Oliver Cromwell, it was the Protestants (Whigs as they were then called) of 1688 who won them back again.[5]

This proudly Protestant position was, naturally, contentious and sectarian. Both Catholics and Protestants were keen to claim the history of the right of conscience as their own and disagreed, sometimes vehemently, about religious rights. But both sides appealed to history in their arguments. In the nineteenth century, history was one of the most important resources at your disposal if you wanted to contribute to public discourse and make a powerful argument.

Today, we still have arguments about rights. (In fact, it seems that contemporary Western societies are obsessed with rights.) But we rarely appeal to history, which has almost disappeared from our public discourse. On both sides of most contemporary issues, reasoned arguments have deteriorated into unfounded assertions. This phenomenon is exacerbated by the online world and social media, which tend to sensationalise arguments and reduce them to the size of memes or the length of tweets.

We often make assertions about various individual rights in contemporary public debates about ethical matters, and yet these claims are frequently made without any grounding in an understanding of where these rights come from. Historically, discussions about rights

---

5. Philadelphus, "To the Editor of the *Sydney Gazette*," *Sydney Gazette and New South Wales Advertiser*, August 18, 1832, 3.

were embedded in a larger story about what it means to be human, and about the origin of these rights in natural law and divine revelation.[6] But this larger story which would enable us to understand the human person to whom rights belong, as well as what rights are for, has been lost.

In Australia, for example, discussions about euthanasia are often couched in terms of a "right" of the terminally ill to access assisted suicide.[7] In fact, the laws passed in the states of Victoria and New South Wales were commonly referred to as the "Right to Die" laws.[8] However, the lawmaking process was conducted largely without considering any historical or moral philosophy that engaged with the profound questions of the value and dignity of human life and where human rights—including the putative right to die—might come from in the first place. The Australian Human Rights Commission's issues paper *Euthanasia, Human Rights and the Law*, for example, is an examination of legal ethics, but ironically makes no reference to natural law or to any of these larger questions.[9]

The philosopher Alasdair MacIntyre identified this kind of public discourse some decades ago in his seminal book *After Virtue*. He described how normative concepts like "rights" which we use

---

6. See John Witte Jr., *The Reformation of Rights* (Cambridge, UK: Cambridge University Press, 2007); John Witte Jr., *God's Joust, God's Justice: Law and Religion in the Western Tradition* (Grand Rapids: Eerdmans, 2006); and Brian Tierney, *The Idea of Natural Rights: Studies on Natural Rights, Natural Law, and Church Law 1150–1625* (Grand Rapids: Eerdmans, 2001) for a discussion on the development of these rights.

7. Some typical examples of contributions are this series of letters to the editor, "Dying with Dignity Should Be a Basic Human Right," *Sydney Morning Herald*, October 14, 2021, https://www.smh.com.au/national/nsw/dying-with-dignity-should-be-a-basic-human-right -20211012-p58zdl.html/, or this interview conducted by the journalist Peter FitzSimons, "John Barilaro Surprises on Right-to-Die Law for NSW," *Sydney Morning Herald*, September 19, 2021, https://www.smh.com.au/national/nsw/john-barilaro-surprises-on-right-to-die-law-for -nsw-20210917-p58shf.html/.

8. See FitzSimons, "John Barilaro Surprises on Right-to-Die Law for NSW" or Quentin Dempster, "Do You Have the Right to Die?," Australia Broadcasting Corporation News, November 28, 2011, https://www.abc.net.au/news/2011-11-29/dempster-do-you-have-the-right -to-die/3702050/.

9. Australian Human Rights Commission, *Euthanasia, Human Rights and the Law: Issues Paper*, May 2016, https://humanrights.gov.au/our-work/age-discrimination/publications /euthanasia-human-rights-and-law/.

today are "fragments of a conceptual scheme, parts which now lack those contexts from which their significance derived."[10] Those contexts had once provided shared moral ground to which people could appeal in their ethical arguments. When individuals no longer share a moral ground, ethical discourse slides all too easily into emotivism and moral reasoning deteriorates into assertions of individual preferences.[11] In other words, people tend to assert that what they *feel* is true. They consequently often accuse others who do not agree with them of being harmful and oppressive. This phenomenon, I suggest, is profoundly ahistorical. History once provided resources from which we could argue and common ground to which interlocutors could appeal. As we take a deeper look at the five characteristics of the Ahistoric Age, consider how they contrast with what we saw in the Rothschild episode and what they mean for the state of public discourse today.

The Five Characteristics of the Ahistoric Age

1. The Past Is Seen as a Source of Shame and Oppression from Which We Must Free Ourselves

As I write, there is a campaign in an Australian town to remove a statue of our first prime minister, Edmund Barton (1849–1920), because of his racist views. Instead of arguing that we can contextualise the past and critically engage with it—for example, by erecting a plaque pointing out Barton's views as well as his service to the nation as its first prime minister—the campaign's approach is to remove the statue of Edmund Barton altogether. A totalising and puritanical mentality underpins the insistence that Barton's statue ought to be removed, failing to recognise that historical figures, like all people, contain both good and bad. This campaign is a good illustration of

---

10. Alasdair MacIntyre, *After Virtue*, 3rd ed. (Notre Dame: University of Notre Dame Press, 2007), 1.

11. MacIntyre, *After Virtue*, 1.

the first characteristic of the Ahistoric Age: the prevailing idea that history is primarily a source of shame and oppression from which we must liberate ourselves.

This attitude towards the past is a manifestation of the broader cultural scepticism towards—and often rejection of—sources of authority outside of our individual selves. You can recognise this sentiment in the phrase "free to be me." It expresses the idea that to be truly ourselves, we cannot let any external authority tell us who we are or how to live. This view is concerned that authority and oppression are not just material and economic but also cultural. The past is no exception. The campaigners desiring to remove Edmund Barton's statue see oppression as cultural, and therefore the statue of Barton is a source of oppression.

This attitude is intimately connected with how contemporary Western societies define human flourishing: it is chiefly self-expression and self-actualisation. Recently, I asked my undergraduate students to describe our culture's sense of what life is all about. Their answers were some version of "finding and then being your true self." Our culture thus emphasises the highly individualistic self-creation of our identities and lifestyles. The cultural axioms of today, which we see everywhere from advertising for clothing to private schools, embody the idea that unleashing one's true potential is the key to finding happiness, which is defined as personal well-being through self-fulfilment. This hyperindividualistic and consumerist mindset is captured by the catchphrases "live your best life" and "you do you."

In their book *Soul Searching*, American sociologists Christian Smith and Melinda Lundquist Denton perceptively describe the culture of what they called "therapeutic individualism":

> Therapeutic individualism defines the individual self as the source and standard of authentic moral knowledge and authority, and individual self-fulfillment as the preoccupying purpose of life. Subjective, personal experience is the touchstone of all that is authentic, right, and true. By contrast, this ethos views the "external" traditions, obligations, and institutions of society as inauthentic

and often illegitimate constraints on morality and behaviour from which individuals must be emancipated.[12]

Contemporary Western culture claims that no authorities or communities outside of ourselves can demand anything from us, legitimately oblige our duty, or make some claim upon us that we cannot simply revoke at will. This phenomenon has a constellation of causes, but it is worth mentioning the role of consumerism in particular, which insists upon freedom from any obligations that might inhibit consumption.

In the past, people put value upon commitments, duties, and obligations, but we now tend to treat the world around us like a product to be consumed—such as in exchanging our identities or even attempting to alter our biology in accordance with our personal preferences. In short, this is a kind of unhinged liberalism detached from a conscious sense of its history and philosophical underpinnings. The language of "freedom" frames much of this thinking, although it is a very narrow conception of freedom expressed purely in negative terms as the absence of constraint upon our autonomy.

The historic Christian view of humanity as sinful has been replaced with a far rosier anthropology popularised in the Romantic era by figures like Jean-Jacques Rousseau. This view declares that the fundamental nature of each human being is essentially good. *Society* corrupts and dominates us, not a problem inherent in every human heart. Historical ideas, traditions, and institutions are absent of any ultimate purpose to time and any greater story. They are potentially a hindrance to my autonomy and individuality, and can only be understood in terms of my own preferences and tastes.

While these ideas about freeing individuals from constraints may be very familiar to us, few have described them as *ahistoric*. Our valorisation of the individual as the ultimate source of moral authority makes it difficult to see what the past might have to teach us. If we

---

12. Christian Smith and Melinda Lundquist Denton, *Soul Searching: The Religious and Spiritual Lives of American Teenagers* (Oxford: Oxford University Press, 2005), 173.

have freed ourselves from other forms of oppression, then we must likewise free ourselves from history, since it is associated with external forces and structures of society.

2. We No Longer Think of Ourselves as Part of Historical Communities

As we have just seen, our contemporary culture valorises the desires that underpin the individual human will and holds that this will ought to be able to sublimate almost everything to itself. Individual freedom of choice is paramount, surpassing issues of identity, life, death, biology, and so forth. I am not arguing that individual freedoms are bad things in and of themselves. Indeed, the dignity and worth of the individual, along with the importance of an individual's relationship with God, are central teachings of Christianity. Rather, the cultural moment we are living in has become hyperindividualistic because we have unhinged the individual from the story—the *telos*. Historically, Christian thought and its dialogue with and incorporation of classical philosophy provided the intellectual resources to reason through ideas about individual freedoms. Christians then could ask perceptive questions about why these freedoms exist, what limits could reasonably be placed upon them, and what duties correspond with them.

The hyperindividualistic focus of contemporary liberalism has consequences for how we think about history. The emphasis upon almost absolute personal autonomy and freedom turns us inward and undermines our belonging to communities that have a history. If I am primarily a self-determining person then there is little point to studying history, since history is constituted by stories external to myself—about processes, ideas, and communities in various forms (peoples, nations, classes, and so forth). I recently had an illuminating conversation with one of my undergraduates. He asked me, "Why would I study the British Empire? *It has nothing to do with my life.*" Upon hearing this, I was struck by how different his generation's attitude to the past is from mine. When I attended school in the 1990s, and university in the 2000s, I was taught to understand peoples, empires, nations, and so forth and *then* make sense of who I am and how to be a citizen in my society *in light of those larger stories*. But my student's question premised that we are primarily, if not exclusively, self-creating subjects.

Unsurprisingly, history seems irrelevant to these projects of self-creation. Every four years, the National Center for Education Statistics, part of the U.S. Department of Education, administers a history and civics test nationwide as part of the National Assessment of Educational Progress (NAEP). The most recent test was taken in January to March of 2022 by a nationally representative group of 15,800 students from 410 public and private schools across the country. The results showed a five-point drop in the average history score since the previous test in 2018.[13] The 2018 history scores, however, were themselves lower than the previous 2014 scores.[14] Moreover, as I mentioned in the previous chapter, over the past decade enrolment in history majors in U.S. universities has been declining more rapidly than in any other major. According to the study released by Professor Benjamin Schmidt for the American Historical Association, enrolments in history majors dropped by almost a third between 2011 and 2018.[15]

We find it difficult to understand what it means to be part of historical communities because they are neither the creation of, nor subject to, our sovereign individual choice. I believe that ahistoricism is inextricably bound up with the contemporary phenomenon of tribalism, particularly in politics and social media. I use the term *tribalism* to refer to the identities formed largely through social media that are united around common enemies; there are good people and

---

13. Donna St. George, "Students' Understanding of History and Civics Is Worsening," *Washington Post*, May 3, 2023, https://www.washingtonpost.com/education/2023/05/03/civics-history-education-naep-democracy/. See also Lauren Camera, "'A National Concern': Student Scores Decline on U.S. History and Civics," *U.S. News*, May 3, 2023, https://www.usnews.com/news/education-news/articles/2023-05-03/a-national-concern-student-scores-decline-on-u-s-history-and-civics/.

14. Natalie Wexler, "Why Kids Know Even Less about History Now—And Why It Matters," *Forbes*, April 24, 2020, https://www.forbes.com/sites/nataliewexler/2020/04/24/why-kids-know-even-less-about-history-now-and-why-it-matters/?sh=24c07d646a7a/.

15. Eric Alterman, "The Decline of Historical Thinking," *The New Yorker*, February 4, 2019, https://www.newyorker.com/news/news-desk/the-decline-of-historical-thinking/. See also Benjamin M. Schmidt, "The History BA Since the Great Recession," *Perspectives on History*, November 26, 2018, https://www.historians.org/research-and-publications/perspectives-on-history/december-2018/the-history-ba-since-the-great-recession-the-2018-aha-majors-report/.

evil people (or, often, victims and oppressors). Tribalism is marked by its illiberalism and its inability to be part of conversations with people who have opposing points of view. Scholars such as Jonathan Haidt have recognised that the surge of tribalism in the social media age began around a decade ago.[16]

Digital tribalism is profoundly ahistorical. Tribal identities emerge largely through the choices of otherwise unconnected individuals who are not part of any larger historical story. I might be a member of one tribe today, but in a few years I might be part of another. In a recent article in *The Atlantic*, Haidt observed that children educated over the past decade have little trust in what they are taught, because social media and the tribalism it exacerbates encourage parents to become outraged at anything in their children's history lessons or curricula. Young people today are "less likely to arrive at a coherent story of who we are as a people, and less likely to share any such story with those who attended different schools or who were educated in a different decade."[17] Faith in institutions declines along with faith in the stories those institutions tell. Tribalism, facilitated by social media, strongly opposes the passing down of historical identities.

In sum, the second characteristic of the Ahistoric Age is that we no longer generally think of ourselves as historical beings.[18] How can I be formed by, and be part of, historical processes or communities if I am a completely self-determining person? We have ceased to understand the point of studying history because it seems irrelevant to our projects of self-actualisation and enjoyment of life.[19] This insight leads us to our third characteristic.

---

16. See Jonathan Haidt and Greg Lukianoff, *The Coddling of the American Mind: How Good Intentions and Bad Ideas Are Setting Up a Generation for Failure* (New York: Penguin, 2019), esp. 57–59, 76.

17. Jonathan Haidt, "Why the Past Ten Years of American Life Have Been Uniquely Stupid," *The Atlantic*, April 11, 2022, https://www.theatlantic.com/magazine/archive/2022/05/social-media-democracy-trust-babel/629369/.

18. In fact, if we look at the increasing interest in personal ancestry, e.g., ancestry.com and the *Finding Your Roots* documentary, we seem to have a hunger for historical rootedness and belonging to historically rooted communities that we are attempting to satisfy in certain ways.

19. On a popular level, we can even see programming on *The History Channel* shifting

3. Our Societies Are Increasingly Ignorant of History

When I taught a class on the history of Australian politics at my former university, I asked my undergraduate students to name our first prime minister. Out of a class of twenty-five, only one person knew the answer. Historical ignorance is particularly pronounced in younger generations; recent research studies show that present-day Americans know less about history than their parents and grandparents. A 2019 study conducted for the Institute for Citizens and Scholars tested Americans' knowledge of their citizenship and history, asking questions about topics including the U.S. Constitution, why the Americans fought the British, the names of significant presidents, and historical figures like Benjamin Franklin. While Americans have always scored poorly on historical knowledge tests, the survey revealed a clear generational age gap. Those aged sixty-five years and older scored the highest, with 74 percent answering at least six in ten questions correctly. Those under the age of forty-five scored the lowest: only 19 percent passed the exam, with 81 percent in that age group scoring 59 percent or lower.[20]

In the early twentieth century, possessing a general knowledge of history was considered part of the essential education citizens needed to become contributing members of their societies. People needed to understand the history of their country and the defining events, ideas, and historical processes of the modern world. This knowledge equipped them to articulate the values of, and cast a critical eye over, the society and the world in which they lived. They were also encouraged to pass this information down to future generations.

In my own experience as a professor of history, I have observed that general knowledge of history is poor. When I taught European history, I found that most of my students knew very little about the major defining events and processes of the modern and premodern world. For example, many did not know there was a French (let alone

---

from more traditional historical documentaries to speculative shows about aliens, cryptozoology, and survival shows.

20. "National Survey Finds Just 1 in 3 Americans Would Pass Citizenship Test," Institute for Citizens & Scholars, October 3, 2018, https://citizensandscholars.org/resource/national -survey-finds-just-1-in-3-americans-would-pass-citizenship-test/.

American) Revolution, had never heard of the Protestant Reformation, and would look at me blankly when I spoke about Beethoven. They could not tell me much about the history of Britain and her empire. This was particularly concerning, given that I teach in Australia, a nation federated from former British colonies (and whose head of state is the monarch of Britain and the Commonwealth Realms).

When we are ignorant of history, we are unable to understand where the ideas we value today come from. There is a reason why every revolution tries to expunge the previous regime and sanction the way history is told. During the French Revolution, for example, the revolutionaries created a new calendar beginning at Year One (with renamed years, months, and days) after they abolished the monarchy in 1792. They systematically attempted to expunge—with iconoclastic vigour—all references to the past and to the Catholic Church, destroying church buildings, taking down bells, and removing the vessels used in the mass. To use the phrase of historian Michel Vovelle, this was "a clean sweep."[21]

Countless other examples proliferate across history. But even in our comparatively peaceful contemporary Western societies, we all too often do not know the heritage of the ideas we esteem. For example, my university students have their most animated and engaging discussions about the history of human rights. My students love the idea of human rights, and they make passionate statements in class about our need to defend these rights. Yet they know virtually nothing about where human rights came from historically. I find this odd and sobering.

Nor do our societies know much about the historical forces that shaped the world in which we live. Do we know much about the history of liberal democracy? Or of the history of the idea of a separation between religion and politics? Put another way, do we understand how modern liberal democracies emerged by constructing distinct realms for church and state? These are the historical categories which underpin pluralism and religious freedom. Do we know how and when modern

---

21. See Michel Vovelle, *The Revolution against the Church: From Reason to the Supreme Being* (Columbus: Ohio University Press, 1991), esp. 39–61.

science emerged? Do we know much of the history of modern nation-states or mass movements of fascism and communism that have purged millions from the face of the earth? Or of the Industrial Revolution and how capitalism emerged? These are only a few examples of the numerous historical influences upon our world. Yet we are increasingly ignorant of our history in this Ahistoric Age.

4. We Do Not Believe History Has a Narrative or a Purpose

The dominant secular worldview today holds that nothing transcendent—no ultimate story—gives time and human life purpose. Stanley Hauerwas astutely observed that in liberal societies "our primary story is that we have no story, or that the stories that we have must be overcome if we are to be free."[22] Christianity's transcendent story that addresses the big questions and gives us the grounding we need for ethical and moral categories has lost its normative status.

In the pre-modern world, as we saw in the previous chapter, the present moment was understood to lie within a larger story that not only had a past, but also had a future goal or *telos*. Historically, since the spread of Christianity in the West, this *telos* was the new heavens and the new earth. Christ will return. Though people did not agree on the details of when exactly this would happen—there were all kinds of arguments about eschatology—the Christian story held that Christ would return, and that his followers therefore had work to do on this earth before he returned. This provided a broad framework for understanding the present and future, as well as the past.

But in today's world, the dominant secular culture denies any ultimate story. The past is not part of the Christian—or indeed any—transcendent story that articulates a vision of where time is heading. The only significance of the past, therefore, is in relation to the present. This intensely philosophical characteristic of ahistoricism, while difficult to explain succinctly, is also deeply intriguing because of how

---

22. Stanley Hauerwas, *A Community of Character: Toward a Constructive Christian Social Ethic* (1981; repr., Notre Dame: University of Notre Dame Press, 2008), 149.

recently it emerged. Even non-Christian ideologies of modernity, such as Marxism, involved a metastory or metanarrative. These philosophies, though not Christian, still held a linear conception of time and history. History was heading towards its culmination, whether in the form of communism or some other utopian vision.

But having lost these metanarratives—Christian, Marxist, or otherwise—we no longer think history has any transcendent framing. In other words, time (and therefore history) is not heading anywhere in particular. Even those who subscribe to a highly optimistic view of science, known as scientism—the belief that science will improve human life indefinitely—do not have an actual vision of the purpose or end of this progress. What exactly does the fully enlightened earth look like? The prevalence of dystopian literature and culture in the twentieth and twenty-first centuries testifies to our awareness that progress without a goal may well, in the words of Frankfurt School theorists Max Horkheimer and Theodore Adorno, "radiate disaster triumphant."[23]

It is worth noting here that sometimes, often in contemporary public debate, people do use phrases that might seem to indicate a historical consciousness and sense of purpose to history, such as when they suggest their opponents are on the "wrong side of history." However, such phrases are a rhetorical sleight of hand; despite the speaker's use of an idea of progress, he or she is giving no theory of history whatsoever. Rather, the speaker is merely saying that the disagreement makes his or her opponents not only incorrect, but also morally inferior. This is merely emotivism. If we do not believe that time has a transcendent purpose, history is only significant if we deem it such. History is not part of any greater story and therefore has little to teach us. The past now only matters in terms of entertaining our curiosity, what it tells us about ourselves as individuals, or (as we saw earlier) as a source of domination from which we must constantly liberate ourselves. In short, history is not ultimately heading anywhere; it is now only important in terms of our present moment.

---

23. Theodor Adorno and Max Horkheimer, *Dialectic of Enlightenment* (London: Verso, 1987 [1947]), 3.

5. We Are Unable to Reason Well and Disagree Peaceably about the Ethical Complexities of the Past

Our societies are losing the ability to conduct civilised conversations and disagree with each other about the complex ethical issues that arise in history. In short, we have lost the tools of historical reasoning.

We yearn, for example, for the horrific wrongs of history to be recognised and properly understood. But we can only engage rightly with these kinds of issues—without our discussions deteriorating into shaming and cancelling people and the ideological polemic of the culture wars—if we have robust criteria for assessing justice and injustice, good and evil, truth and lies, and so forth.

In today's culture, much of the public debate about history concerns issues of how power was used. As we saw at the beginning of the previous chapter, unmasking structures of power begins not with the eighteenth-century Enlightenment as we might expect, but with St. Augustine's *The City of God*. One of Augustine's major claims in *The City of God* was that the Roman Empire *misused* power for its own glory. Indeed, Augustine also gave a story of what power ought to look like, embodied in the person of Jesus. For instance, Jesus implored his followers that they must not treat power and authority like the gentile rulers do, who, in Jesus's words, "lord it over them" (Matt. 20:25). Instead, Jesus says that even he, God incarnate, came into the world "not to be served but to serve, and to give his life a ransom for many" (v. 28). The Christian narrative provides the grounding for the idea that the proper use of power is through humility, self-sacrificing service, and the care of the most vulnerable.

History as the unmasking and critiquing of power was given fresh impetus during the Enlightenment, whose Kantian motto *sapere aude*, "dare to know," questioned the authority of all established institutions: the church, the monarchy, and so forth.[24] The potential implication is that only our own individual reason is necessary to attain knowledge.

---

24. Immanuel Kant, "What Is Enlightenment?," trans. Mary C. Smith, http://www.columbia.edu/acis/ets/CCREAD/etscc/kant.html.

Importantly, however, Kant was no relativist; he did argue for the necessity of the existence of God. But, gradually, over the past three hundred years or so, the use of critical reason—of which history is an example—to liberate ourselves from all authorities and pursue our personally-defined freedom has become unhinged from the overarching Christian story about the proper use of power and authority. Dispense with God and you dispense with the normative framework (the story) that enables us to know what power ought to and ought not to look like. Thus, power and the human will effectively become the only reality.

Indeed, the philosopher Friedrich Nietzsche recognised this phenomenon in several of his books, particularly *Beyond Good and Evil* (1886). We have largely lost the shared set of assumptions—about justice and the good, for example—to which we can appeal in our discussions. The more we unhinge the individual from the larger stories that give an account of the big questions, the less equipped we are to grapple with history. This has serious implications for how we understand and discuss the past, because without the metastory that helps us identify and make sense of good and evil, power and authority, and so forth, we are left with crude categories that impoverish our ability to wrestle with the coexistence—even in the same historical process or historical figure—of good and evil.

As we saw in our previous chapter, the Ahistoric Age reduces ethical reasoning to emotivism; we simply assert our wills and feelings. We fumble around with crude ideological categories rather than engage in a genuine conversation. Speaking from my academic experience in universities in the UK, the USA, and Australia, the problems we have in wrestling with the legacy of the British Empire are a key illustration. The campaign to remove Edmund Barton's statue is a good illustration: its proponents could not wrestle with that complexity, but merely wanted to abolish all reference to Barton altogether. This polarisation—often referred to as the culture wars—is one of the reasons why it is almost impossible to have a civilised debate and disagree with each other. This abolition of history fails truly to reckon with our past—both the good and the evil.

Our societies are confused about how to make sense of the good and evil in the past and about whether there is any hope for the future. On the one hand, many people sense that we are utterly superior to the past. What C. S. Lewis termed "chronological snobbery" is even more pronounced in today's digital world, which is focussed on the rapid updates and improvements to technology.[25] Some people also feel that we are morally superior to peoples of the past, who presumably have backward and narrow-minded views.

But at the same time, our culture is beset by serious pessimism and dystopianism because it does not have a story about where we are heading and has no sense that there is a purpose to human history. For example, a 2021 Pew Research Center study revealed that a rising share of U.S. adults who are not already parents say they are unlikely ever to have children. Among the reasons they gave for not wanting children was anxiety about ecological and humanitarian catastrophe.[26] Moreover, young people are increasingly advocating for vasectomies or sterilisation. To use the *Guardian* newspaper headline, they are "men getting vasectomies to save the world."[27] Similarly, think of the sheer despair and nihilism that underpins often horrifyingly violent dystopian television shows and video games, where nothing remains but the unleashing of the human will, producing unbridled darkness and chaos. Thus, the Ahistoric Age is filled with confusion and inconsistency. On the one hand, we feel that the past is inferior

25. C. S. Lewis, *Surprised by Joy* (1955; Croydon, UK: William Collins, 2012, reissued 2016), 240.

26. See "Growing Share of Childless Adults in U.S. Don't Expect to Ever Have Children," Pew Research Center, November 19, 2021, https://www.pewresearch.org/short-reads/2021/11/19/growing-share-of-childless-adults-in-u-s-dont-expect-to-ever-have-children/.

27. Simon Usborne, "'More People Is the Last Thing This Planet Needs': The Men Getting Vasectomies to Save the World," *The Guardian*, January 12, 2022, https://www.theguardian.com/lifeandstyle/2022/jan/12/more-people-is-the-last-thing-this-planet-needs-the-men-getting-vasectomies-to-save-the-world/. See also Robin Maynard and Barbara Williams, "Getting Sterilised to Save the Planet Is a Sad but Understandable Choice," *The Guardian*, January 14, 2022, https://www.theguardian.com/environment/2022/jan/14/getting-sterilised-to-save-the-planet-is-a-sad-but-understandable-choice/ and Elle Hunt, "BirthStrikers: Meet the Women Who Refuse to Have Children until Climate Change Ends," *The Guardian*, March 12, 2019, https://www.theguardian.com/lifeandstyle/2019/mar/12/birthstrikers-meet-the-women-who-refuse-to-have-children-until-climate-change-ends/.

to us since we have so much faith in human ability and technology. However, on the other hand, we are wracked with despair about the present and future.

In summary, Western societies have almost completely lost the ability to engage meaningfully with the past. The five characteristics of the Ahistoric Age manifest themselves like this: (1) The past is seen as a source of shame and oppression from which we must free ourselves; (2) We no longer think of ourselves as part of historical communities; (3) Our societies are increasingly ignorant of history; (4) We do not believe history has a narrative or a purpose; and (5) We are unable to reason well and disagree peaceably about the ethical complexities of the past. Having outlined the five characteristics of the Ahistoric Age in our society, we can now ask: What does the Ahistoric Age look like in the church?

THREE

The Ahistoric Age
in the Church

The church is always situated in a cultural context. Ever since the early church Christians have grappled with how to speak the gospel into culture and become all things to all people while remaining true to biblical teachings.[1] When I discuss the effects of ahistoricism in the church, I am not suggesting that we need to reject contemporary culture completely and simply re-embrace everything we did in the past, as if the past were somehow by definition superior. Rather, I am alerting us to some of the ways ahistoric attitudes are affecting the church so we can be aware of what is going on and be better equipped to engage with those issues.

Ahistoricism is by no means everywhere in the church. But where ahistoricism is present, it manifests itself in three broad attitudes towards the past: *irrelevance, ignorance,* and *ideology.* First, *irrelevance* posits that the way we did things in the past is simply not relevant to us anymore. We do not think of history or our traditions as a guide or helpful resource for us. Second, people are increasingly *ignorant* of history in general, as well as of the history, teachings, and practices of Christianity. Do we know the role Christianity has played in the founding ideas of our societies? Do we know how our core doctrinal beliefs and traditions developed, and are we aware of what they could

---

1. A key text in relation to this question is H. Richard Niebuhr's seminal *Christ and Culture* (1951; New York: Harper and Row, 1975) as well as D. A. Carson's *Christ and Culture Revisited* (Grand Rapids: Eerdmans, 2008).

offer us? And, finally, *ideology* is when we approach the past with an ideological attitude and framework, which we then use to judge the past.

These three attitudes often overlap and influence one another. Here are five outworkings of these ahistoric attitudes in the church:

1. Doctrinal drift from orthodoxy
2. Individualism and comfort
3. Entertainment and celebrity culture
4. A consumerist and marketing model
5. Corporate and depersonalised ministry models

I am not the first person to discuss these phenomena. But they are all, in various ways, facilitated by and connected to ahistoricism. In each illustration, we see different elements of approaching the past with the attitudes of irrelevance, ignorance, and ideology. Note that these illustrations only show tendencies operating in different places and to different degrees; it is not likely that one church will capture or embody all of them.

1. Doctrinal Drift from Orthodoxy

By doctrinal drift from orthodoxy, I mean the attempt to redefine or dispense with historic teachings and doctrines of the faith. Two attitudes underlie this attempt: an attitude of irrelevance and an ideological attitude that dismisses the historic teaching or approach as ignorant, oppressive, or prejudiced.

A prime example of doctrinal drift is the issue of same-sex marriage in churches. I do not intend to explore this issue in depth, and astute treatments of this question exist elsewhere.[2] I simply wish to point out that many people who desire to redefine Christian sexual ethics display

---

2. See Sam Allberry, *Is God Anti-Gay? And Other Questions about Jesus, the Bible, and Same-Sex Sexuality* (Epsom, UK: The Good Book Company, 2023); Sam Allberry, *What God Has to Say about Our Bodies: How the Gospel Is Good News for Our Physical Selves* (Wheaton:

an ahistorical attitude, namely, that the long tradition of Christian teachings is irrelevant. After all, all Christian denominations had a theological consensus about same-sex relationships for two thousand years. As Tim Keller pointed out, "Until very, very recently, there had been complete unanimity about homosexuality in the church across all centuries, cultures, and even across major divisions of the Orthodox, Roman Catholic, and Protestant traditions."[3] Keller also asks, "Why is it the case that literally no church, theologian, or Christian thinker or movement ever thought that any kind of same sex relationships was allowable until now?" One important piece of this puzzle, I would suggest, is ahistoricism.

Those who want to revise key doctrines often argue that the church needs to "move with the times." In *God and the Gay Christian*, Matthew Vines argues that there are instances in church history in which new information has prompted reinterpretation of Scripture. The "new information we have about homosexuality," according to Vines, warrants such a reinterpretation.[4] John Shelby Spong also made claims about the need to dispense with various issues of long-established doctrine, including the divinity of Christ and a theistic understanding of God. For Spong, there is no teaching of enduring historical importance that should not be reinterpreted in light of present experience. Spong posits that Christians must develop "a faith deeply connected to human experience instead of outdated dogma."[5] The subtitle of one of his last books is telling: *Why Neither Ancient Creeds nor the Reformation Can Produce a Living Faith Today*.

However, the idea that the church ought to reinterpret, or has always reinterpreted, doctrine to suit the times, especially to reverse

Crossway, 2021); and Rachel Gilson, *Born Again This Way: Coming Out, Coming to Faith, and What Comes Next* (Epsom, UK: The Good Book Company, 2020).

3. Tim Keller, "The Bible and Same Sex Relationships: A Review Article," Redeemer Presbyterian Church, 2015, https://www.redeemer.com/redeemer-report/article/the_bible_and_ _same_sex_relationships_a_review_article/.

4. Matthew Vines, *God and the Gay Christian: The Biblical Case in Support of Same-Sex Relationships* (New York: Convergent Books: 2014), 25.

5. John Shelby Spong, *Unbelievable: Why Neither Ancient Creeds nor the Reformation Can Produce a Living Faith Today* (San Francisco: HarperOne, 2019), quote from blurb.

long-established teachings, is overly simplistic, theologically impoverished, and historically inaccurate. There are some issues on which large numbers of Christians have developed their biblical interpretations over the centuries, but these are not cases of completely revising key doctrines to produce a position entirely at odds with the history of biblical interpretation. Nor are these instances of simply discarding the history of theology in light of new information or experience.

When Martin Luther wrote his *Ninety-Five Theses*, for example, he was advocating a return to a biblical understanding of salvation held by the early church from which the late medieval church erred in its fairly recent institution of indulgences and overemphasis on a causal relationship between penance and justification.[6] The church's understanding of slavery is another example, in which many abolitionists not only sought to recover a biblical understanding but also had precedent throughout history of Christians opposing slavery and actively buying the freedom of slaves.[7]

Moreover, for centuries Christians have been engaged in discussions about certain issues on which they continue to hold a variety of positions, such as the just war tradition and capital punishment. These, however, are not hills to die on, to use Gavin Ortlund's helpful metaphor.[8] In short, there can be different opinions on these issues within orthodox Christianity. But how might we determine which issues are hills to die on and which issues can support multiple orthodox positions?

It is enormously helpful to know how the history of doctrine and orthodoxy has developed over the centuries, as this can be an excellent resource to help us think through and discuss issues. It can also help us

---

6. See Matthew Barrett, *Reformation as Renewal* (Grand Rapids: Zondervan Academic, 2023), for an exploration of the nuances in the views of the Reformation.

7. See John Dickson, *Bullies and Saints* (Grand Rapids: Zondervan, 2021); Frederick Douglass, *Narrative of the Life of Frederick Douglass, an American Slave* (1845; New Haven: Yale University Press, 2017); Olaudah Equiano, *The Interesting Narrative of the Life of Olaudah Equiano, or Gustavus Vassa, the African. Written by Himself* (London: Self-pub., 1789); and William Wilberforce, *A Practical View of the Prevailing Religious System of Professed Christians* (London: T. Cadell, 1830).

8. Gavin Ortlund, *Finding the Right Hills to Die On: The Case for Theological Triage* (Wheaton: Crossway, 2020).

see which hills are worth dying on.[9] G. K. Chesterton's famous fence analogy is helpful here. Chesterton wrote that when we approach a fence or a gate erected across a road, a reckless person may say, "I don't see the use of this; let us clear it away." However, a more intelligent person would know that the "gate or fence did not grow there. . . . Some person had some reason for thinking it would be a good thing for somebody. And until we know what the reason was, we really cannot judge whether the reason was reasonable."[10] Likewise, when we approach the historic, orthodox doctrines of the church, an ahistoric approach will often say, "I don't see the use of this; let us clear it away." If we know our history, however, we can see how people came to that biblical interpretation. The doctrines held in the Apostles' Creed and the Nicene Creed are examples of "fences" built around Christian orthodoxy. We must know their history so we don't recklessly tear these fences down.

Biblical interpretation is a complex and weighty process. Arguing that ahistoricism partially underpins attempts to redefine key Christian doctrines today by no means implies the authority of historical teachings over the Bible, or that Christians never reinterpret passages of the Bible. When Protestants grapple with an issue of interpretation, the ultimate source of authority is the Bible. However, having the history of biblical scholarship is also beneficial, particularly on doctrinal matters. Consequently, we ought to be suspicious of those who dismiss two millennia of theological teaching on doctrinal matters like Christ's divinity as irrelevant. Historical grounding can provide a handbrake on rapid and profound doctrinal changes that undermine orthodoxy and sweep churches along the currents of culture.

We find a profound ahistoric attitude when we look at what lies at the heart of doctrinal drift in churches and especially on many

---

9. For an excellent introduction to the historical development of the faith, see Jaroslav Pelikan, *The Christian Tradition: A History of the Development of Doctrine*, 5 vols. (Chicago: University of Chicago Press, 1971) and Alister McGrath, *Historical Theology: An Introduction to the History of Christian Thought*, 3rd ed. (Hoboken, NJ: Wiley-Blackwell, 2023). See also John Henry Newman's seminal essay *An Essay on the Development of Christian Doctrine* (1878; Notre Dame: University of Notre Dame Press, 1989).

10. G. K. Chesterton, *The Thing: Why I Am a Catholic* (1929; London: Sheed and Ward, 1946), 29.

contemporary issues. One of ahistoricism's primary outworkings in the church is the claim that centuries of teaching on key issues of doctrine or Christian ethics can simply be dismissed because they are now deemed irrelevant; the past is just "outdated dogma," to use Spong's term.

2. Individualism and Comfort

As we saw earlier, Western culture today is preoccupied with individual well-being and comfort. For some years, astute observers have noticed almost exclusively therapeutic components of these ideas permeating parts of the church, effectively turning Christianity into a self-help program designed to make us feel better. While Jesus invites all people to place their burdens on him, an unbiblical overemphasis on comfort comes at the expense of a life of discipleship, which is often difficult and involves taking up one's cross, dying to oneself, following Jesus, living for him, and serving others.

When the emphasis shifts from costly discipleship to a therapeutic individualism,[11] the difficult issues (such as pornography addiction, domestic abuse, greed, materialism, serving the poor, and so forth) are rarely preached upon. Gone are the hard-hitting sermons about our sin and encouragements to spend our time, talents, and money in the service of others, even (and especially) when it is frustrating and costly. Individualism replaces hospitality, welcoming the stranger, making disciples, and serving the poor. My former pastor used a brilliant metaphor to encapsulate this issue: "Church is not a cruise ship. We are a lifeboat. We have a job to do."

However, when the church is a cruise ship the Christian faith is often reduced to a series of abstract propositions. In other words, the

---

11. The reference to costly discipleship is helpful because it reminds us that the tendency of churches to move away from true and faithful discipleship and biblical teaching towards cheap grace has a long history itself. See Dietrich Bonhoeffer, *Discipleship* (Minneapolis: Fortress, 2015). "Therapeutic individualism" is defined in the previous chapter by sociologists Christian Smith and Melinda Lundquist Denton, *Soul Searching: The Religious and Spiritual Lives of American Teenagers* (Oxford: Oxford University Press, 2005).

essence of the Christian life is merely to agree about who Jesus is and what he has done. As Paul Washer put it, "you think that just because you prayed a prayer once, then you're saved."[12] To make matters worse, these propositions are often not taught with nearly the same rigour as they were historically, which reinforces Christianity as simply a matter of shallow, abstract, and excarnated beliefs.

This version of the Christian life requires very little of us. We only need to show up on Sunday and be entertained by a performance, passively consuming a good dose of "don't worry, Jesus has done it all" platitudes (subtext: so, you don't have to do anything after you are saved). This kind of cheap grace is insidious because it involves half-truths. Yes, it is entirely true that no work of ours is required to earn our salvation and Jesus has, in fact, done everything necessary for us to be justified. Yet the idea that we do not need to do anything else once we are saved and justified is a far cry from biblical faith: "For just as the body without the spirit is dead, so faith without works is also dead" (James 2:26). Without the fruit of a saved and transformed life, we must question whether we were ever really saved at all.[13]

Our preoccupation with individual comfort and freedom from obligations is not only unbiblical, but it is also ahistorical. The Reformers, for instance, emphasised that the Christian is saved for good works and that good works "do spring out necessarily of a true and lively Faith; insomuch that by them a lively Faith may be as evidently known as a tree discerned by the fruit."[14] Luther's very first thesis in his *Ninety-Five Theses*, after all, was that "When our Lord and Master Jesus Christ said, 'Repent' [Matt. 4:17], he willed the entire life of believers to be one of repentance."[15]

---

12. Paul Washer, "2002 Youth Evangelism Conference," Montgomery, Alabama, YouTube video, 27:37, https://www.youtube.com/watch?v=2jsricffDrY/.

13. John Calvin, *Institutes of the Christian Religion*, ed. John T. McNeill, trans. Ford Lewis Battles (Louisville: Westminster John Knox, 2006), especially 3.2.12.

14. Article XII of the Thirty-Nine Articles of Religion, the *Book of Common Prayer* (1662; Cambridge, UK: Cambridge University Press, 2004), 616.

15. Martin Luther, *Luther's Works, Vol. 31: Career of the Reformer I*, ed. Jaroslav Jan Pelikan, Hilton C. Oswald, and Helmut T. Lehmann (Philadelphia: Fortress Press, 1999), 25.

By abandoning our teaching of the historic practices of discipleship and formation, we have created a vacuum and a sense of rootlessness. When we discussed doctrinal drift, we saw how ahistoricism can affect orthodoxy. Here, we see how ahistoricism can affect orthopraxy. Our rootlessness makes us more eager to embrace naïvely our own culture's obsession with individual comfort and self-expression. However, Christians often do not see the extent to which the church prioritises comfort and individualism because those things are so ingrained in our culture. We need history in order to stand outside of our culture and clearly observe it.

Here is an illustration: many streams of Protestant Christianity neglect the historic tradition of catechising new Christians and our children. Only recently have some Reformed thinkers sought to revive the wonders of this tradition.[16] Why did churches abandon the practice of catechism? In no small part, this is due to an underlying ahistorical assumption that the past is irrelevant and our traditions have little to teach us. For instance, I often hear that these traditions are nothing but "empty ritual." But, in truth, *all* rituals and habits have the potential to be empty, historical and contemporary alike. This knee-jerk reaction assumes that only our self-expression and *individual* belief is honouring to God. When Christians assume that long traditions like catechising are empty and irrelevant, they also presume that faith must primarily centre upon authentic self-expression before God.

When we cease actively to teach serious and costly discipleship and pass down the practices and habits of formation, we create an ahistorical vacuum that the idols of individualism and comfort are only too happy to fill. Ahistoricism turns Christianity into self-help and the church into a cruise ship.

---

16. See Timothy J. Keller, *The New City Catechism: 52 Questions & Answers for Our Hearts and Minds* (Wheaton: Crossway, 2017); J. I. Packer, *To Be a Christian: An Anglican Catechism* (Wheaton: Crossway, 2020); and J. I. Packer and Gary A. Parrett, *Grounded in the Gospel: Building Believers the Old-Fashioned Way* (Grand Rapids: Baker, 2010).

3. Entertainment and Celebrity Culture

Entertainment is a widespread feature of global and Western culture today, and is closely related to the rise of consumerism and leisure time. Entertainment affects the Christian life in a number of ways but becomes particularly problematic when it begins to shape worship. When this happens, worship becomes a finely tuned performance and the congregation nothing more than an audience. Worship is then casual, bordering on irreverence.

This entertaining atmosphere may seem benign or welcoming, and it is, of course, well-intentioned. But we need to consider whether it destroys our awe of God's holiness and his transcendence. For example, to draw from my personal experience, we ought to be concerned if the atmosphere during the celebration of the Lord's Supper is so casual that adults are chatting away while the bread and grape juice are distributed as pop music plays. Christians are effectively sitting back and enjoying the show. When entertainment infiltrates worship in this way, it undermines any sense of our need for serious self-examination and repentance as well as our recognition of the majesty and sovereignty of God.

What does the infiltration of entertainment into worship over the last few decades have to do with ahistoricism? Entertainment-driven worship is partly underpinned by the attitude that how we worshipped in the past is largely irrelevant to us now. Biblically, and indeed historically, worship was not entertainment; they are fundamentally different things. Churches that embrace elements of entertainment risk watering down, dispensing with, or replacing distinctly biblical practices that Christians have engaged in for centuries. These practices did not entertain Christians, but rather *formed* them in their faith.[17]

---

17. See Michael Jensen, *Reformation Anglican Worship* (Wheaton: Crossway, 2021) and Jonathan Gibson and Mark Earngey, *Reformation Worship: Liturgies from the Past for the Present* (Greensboro, NC: New Growth Press, 2018), for further reflections on the purpose of worship historically.

For example, the conclusion of a worship service throughout history prepared Jesus's disciples to go out and serve him in the world. The final words uttered at the service's end encapsulate the very purpose of worship. They summarise what this gathering of Christians has been all about. Historically, in most denominations the final words uttered were a specific *commissioning* or *sending* that reminded Christians of the great commission given by Jesus in Matthew 28:18–20. The words constituting this sending out into the world were often what is sometimes called the Grace: "The grace of our Lord, Jesus Christ, and the love of God, and the fellowship of the Holy Ghost be with us all evermore. Amen" (cf. 2 Cor. 13:13). Another form of words was: "Go in peace to love and serve the Lord." These words captured the truth that Christians are a people set apart from the world. Having concluded their worship by being reminded of God's saving work, they were sent back out into the world to serve the Lord their God.

By contrast, entertainment-driven worship often concludes with a cheerful and benign exclamation to just go and enjoy ourselves: for example, "Have a great week!" This approach strays so far from the biblical and historical tradition of sending us out into the world to make disciples that it turns the Christian mission on its head. When we are sent out, we Christians are being turned *away* from our sinful selves and our self-seeking pleasure and oriented *towards* service of God. But the words "Have a great week!" direct us *towards* ourselves and *our* personal enjoyment. This is precisely the opposite of what we ought to be doing. Yet if we are ignorant of our historical practices and traditions or assume they are irrelevant to us, we do not realise how we are reshaping the very nature and purpose of worship.

The sharing of God's peace is another example. This is a tradition dating to the early church. The apostle Paul often uses the words "grace and peace" to begin his letters, signifying that Christ's death and resurrection have brought us peace with God and with our fellow believers (Eph. 1:2). The early church's practice of greeting one another in grace and peace, often accompanied with a holy kiss, was attested to by Justin Martyr (c. AD 100–c. AD 165).[18] However, churches today often replace sharing God's peace with a time to turn to those around us and say hello to each other. While this alternative is good and well-intentioned, it is not as biblical as we might think. It misconstrues what the New Testament authors understood to be fundamentally distinctive about sharing God's peace. Meeting with brothers and sisters in God's peace is not the same as simply saying hello. Saying a friendly hello, after all, is how non-Christians also greet each other. But Paul's greeting the church with grace and peace is countercultural because it reminds us of what God has done and reiterates that we are bearers of the message of God's grace and peace to one another.[19] Such a greeting is all the more countercultural in our contemporary world filled with tribalism and unhinged individualism. Sharing the peace embodies the biblical truth that Christians are unified, reconciled, and one in Christ's body, being his instruments. Our act of joyous unity in the Lord reveals the idol of emphasising earthly hierarchies of status and affirms the truth of our equality and reconciliation in Christ Jesus.

In short, ahistoricism affects the church when we are ignorant of our history or dismiss it as irrelevant; we accordingly become oblivious to the impact of contemporary culture on the church. Indeed, "Have a great week!" captures how non-Christians would wish others to go about their lives for the next seven days. But being sent out into the world to serve the Lord is a different calling altogether. Knowing our history—about the practices of our sending and of sharing God's peace, for example—sharpens our vision by enabling us to recognise just how far we have embraced the unstated assumptions and idols of contemporary culture.

---

18. Justin Martyr, *The First Apology of Justin*, in *Ante-Nicene Fathers, Volume 1: The Apostolic Fathers with Justin Martyr and Irenaeus*, ed. Alexander Roberts, James Donaldson, and A. Cleveland Coxe (Buffalo, NY: Christian Literature Company, 1885), 185.

19. John R. W. Stott, *God's New Society: The Message of Ephesians*, The Bible Speaks Today (Downers Grove: InterVarsity Press, 1979), 27; Richard Coekin, *Ephesians for You* (Epsom, UK: The Good Book Company, 2015), 8.

When we view our history as irrelevant, we dispense with the way we have practiced these biblical traditions as well as the story and identity that we could pass down through the generations. Perhaps we dispense with the peace, perhaps we dispense with the sending, or perhaps we dispense with the reverent awe of remembering Christ's forgiveness for sins when we celebrate the Lord's Supper. Yet these practices could be especially valuable to us today in discipling and forming not only us, but also our younger brothers and sisters in the church. They are growing up in a rootless, radically atomised age in which they are consistently told to dispense with the past and go and invent themselves. The Christian message is a better story. It declares that we do not have to invent ourselves but rather we can be part of a people *with* a story. We know who we are because we are known by God and are invited into his historical people.

As I have stated from the beginning of this book, we should not simply reject the present and embrace the past. We do, however, need to know the effects of an ahistorical attitude, because when we dispense with our practices and traditions we create a void that our contemporary culture, particularly the pleasures of entertainment, is all too ready to fill. One of the more insidious effects of this ahistorical attitude and the rise of entertainment is the emergence of the celebrity pastor. There are some recent revealing explorations of this phenomenon and its disastrous effects.[20] When members of the congregation are rootless, they search for a sense of purpose, meaning, direction, and stability, which renders them particularly vulnerable to the power of celebrity pastors.

The celebrity pastor is also at odds with the historical calling and work of pastoral ministry. Historically, pastoring centred upon the rather unglamorous work of personally tending to, and caring for, the sheep in the congregation. The seventeenth-century English pastor George Herbert, who we will meet in a later chapter, gave a detailed

---

20. The podcast *The Rise and Fall of Mars Hill* is a powerful reflection on this issue in the United States, as is the warning of the scandals of Hillsong Church and Brian Houston in my own country. For an in-depth treatment, see Katelyn Beaty, *Celebrities for Jesus: How Personas, Platforms, and Profits Are Hurting the Church* (Grand Rapids: Brazos, 2022).

description of this kind of life in his work *A Priest to the Temple, Or The Countrey Parson, His Character, and Rule of Holy Life* (often shortened to *The Country Parson*). In this work, Herbert examined the importance of prayer, study, preaching, charity, family, catechising, visiting in person his flock, comforting, and administering the sacraments. In his section on preaching, Herbert explicitly states, "The Country Parson preacheth constantly, the pulpit is his joy and his throne. . . . When he preacheth, he procures attention by all possible art . . . by earnestness of speech. . . . By these and other means the Parson procures attention; but the character of his Sermon is Holiness; he is not witty, or learned, or eloquent, but Holy."[21]

More recently, Eugene Peterson's *The Pastor: A Memoir* described his life of traditional pastoral ministry, which was largely a reaction against the culture of viewing church as a business opportunity offering tantalising promises of a swell in church numbers and the fame of celebrity. Peterson remarked that adopting these strategies would have meant

> . . . turning each congregation into a market for religious consumers, an ecclesiastical business run along the lines of advertising techniques, organizational flow charts, and energized by impressive motivational rhetoric. . . . [It] violated everything . . . that had formed my identity as a follower of Jesus and as a pastor.[22]

4. A Consumerist and Marketing Model

Churches must always think carefully about how to relate to the surrounding culture and how to embrace the outsider. The command of Jesus to "Go therefore and make disciples" (Matt. 28:19) means that we are commanded to engage with outsiders, hoping that we

21. George Herbert, *The Country Parson, The Temple*, ed. John N. Wall Jr. and Richard J. Payne, The Classics of Western Spirituality (New York; Mahwah, NJ: Paulist Press, 1981), 62–63.

22. Eugene Peterson, *The Pastor: A Memoir* (San Francisco: HarperOne, 2011), 112.

can bring them into God's people. These are biblical considerations guided by the need to become all things to all people and to be a place where newcomers can feel welcome and loved. Churches also need to communicate what they do and believe to the local community. A problem arises, however, when a marketing mentality and a consumerist model of church become driving forces. A consumerist and marketing mindset assumes that we ought to accommodate what we do, particularly our worship, to fit the desires and expectations of the consumer. For example, a church might be so preoccupied about its "brand" and how to market that brand that it spends more of its time and resources developing its image than it does on running evangelism classes or helping the needy in the church or local community.

A marketing and consumerist mindset affects Christianity by making it attractive and appealing like a product. Practices which Protestants of numerous denominations have embraced for centuries are downplayed or replaced because they might make people feel uncomfortable. The Lord's Supper is a good example. Historically, Protestant churches emphasised that, as the Reformation's Augsburg Confession put it, "the Church is the congregation of saints [the assembly of all believers], in which the Gospel is rightly taught [purely preached] and the Sacraments rightly administered [according to the Gospel]."[23] However, as a number of recent articles have pointed out, in an age of consumer convenience Christians are tempted to engage with the church "quickly, easily, and preferentially." They thus think of the Lord's Supper casually, as if it is merely a quaint traditional add-on.[24] In fact, evangelicals in Australia frequently discuss whether they should celebrate the Lord's Supper on Easter Sunday because it seems too weird, awkward, or uncomfortable to outsiders.[25] While this

23. Philip Schaff, *The Creeds of Christendom, with a History and Critical Notes*, vol. 3: *The Evangelical Protestant Creeds, with Translations* (New York: Harper & Brothers, 1882), 12.

24. Eric Bancroft, "We Celebrate the Lord's Supper Frequently but Not Weekly," The Gospel Coalition, April 18, 2012, https://www.thegospelcoalition.org/article/we-celebrate-the-lords-supper-frequently-but-not-weekly/.

25. See, for example, Dominic Steele with Matt Varcoe and Luther Symons, "Planning

concern is well-intentioned, we need to consider whether the sacrament of the Lord's Supper can be properly administered if we think it is only worth doing in a manner that minimises its strangeness and solemnity. This capitulation to consumer satisfaction starkly exposes how ahistoricism makes us more susceptible to the idols of our current culture.

Another example of how consumerism has affected us is the abandonment of a prayer of confession. I know of a number of churches that routinely used to give this type of prayer yet no longer do. When we admit publicly and collectively that we are broken sinners, bowing our heads and knees humbly in prayer to God, we are profoundly unappealing to our contemporary culture.

Relentlessly importing new paradigms from the secular world which we hope will make us relevant and solve our problems is another illustration of the consumer mindset infecting the church. Of course, there is nothing wrong with carefully thinking through some insights from secular disciplines while holding them to biblical scrutiny. However, we need to exercise concern and caution if we find that we are spending time constantly reinventing the trellis and preoccupied with the latest theories from secular fields like business, management theory, marketing theory, and psychology. Each secular model or theory seems to have a lifespan, and every few years brings a different theory into vogue. A consumer logic of constant innovation underlies this phenomenon. It is just like the built-in obsolescence that our clothes and technology products rely upon—namely, that they are only good for a certain period of time before they need to be discarded and upgraded to the newer model. Indeed, built-in obsolescence lies at the very heart of consumerism. Ahistoricism thus renders us susceptible to being constantly enamoured of the next big thing: the next theory or model which could make our church grow or make us relevant.

To sum up, consumerism in its various manifestations is a clear display of ahistoricism. We view our past as *irrelevant*, or we are

Easter Gospel Impact," *The Pastor's Heart*, March 3, 2020, https://www.thepastorsheart.net /podcast/easterevangelism?rq=easter/.

ignorant of it, or we have an *ideological* view that the past is inferior to the latest fashionable idea. When we adopt these mindsets, we naïvely embrace consumerist contemporary culture, prioritising palatability over faithfulness.

5. Corporate and Depersonalised Ministry Models

When worship is replaced with entertainment and worshippers become little more than consumers, increasing pressure falls on pastors to shift away from the traditional historic practices of pastoring and embrace a results-driven model of leadership imported from the corporate world. The pastor thus becomes a kind of manager or CEO. To illustrate, a minister once commented to me that he now has Key Performance Indicators (KPIs) to fulfil, some of which were purely numbers-driven measures of his effectiveness based on quantitative data and not on whether members of his congregation were being cared for or becoming more mature disciples of Jesus. Eugene Peterson and others have written insightfully about these tendencies.[26] Here, I wish to point out the ahistoricism underlying much of this accommodation to the corporate world. This is another example of the move away from the historic practices of pastoring, which included caring for and visiting congregation members, developing in-person relationships with them, and holding regular in-person church gatherings. When pastors become CEOs, they no longer shepherd God's people; instead, they merely manage their staff.

This corporate and depersonalised approach to ministry and discipleship is often exacerbated by an uncritical embrace of technology which replaces in-person relationships and diminishes practices of formation. While technology is necessary (few churches should be without a website, for example), we need to be careful not to replace the practices

---

26. Eugene Peterson, *Working the Angles: The Shape of Pastoral Integrity* (Grand Rapids: Eerdmans, 1989); Eugene Peterson, *The Contemplative Pastor* (Grand Rapids: Eerdmans, 1993); and Eugene Peterson, *The Pastor: A Memoir* (San Francisco: HarperOne, 2011).

of spiritual discipleship and formation which we have relied upon for centuries. People in our society are already so atomised and lonely.[27]

When we depersonalise ministry and move what we do online, we do not foster relationships or disciple one another in nearly the same depth as we do in person. For example, when we move lay ministry training online (such as children's ministry training or adult Sunday School) or if we run our parenting or marriage courses online rather than having them in person, the parishioner misses out on the experience of training with others in the congregation. He or she can no longer share some coffee or a meal with fellow believers and the minister or lay leader, get to know them, and develop relationships with them as they do their training or course together. Profound opportunities for fellowship and discipling one another are thus lost.

A Barna study into the state of discipleship among Christians revealed the following situation:

> Millennials (and older adults, too) isolated by personal technology crave real-life, face-to-face relationships with individuals and small groups. The younger generation also desires wisdom—not just knowledge—to navigate changing times and culture. One-on-one mentoring is the ideal setting to deliver this type of guidance, fostering deep relationship that leads to transformation and serves as an anchor for continuing engagement with the Church. In a culture of isolation, discipleship relationships are an open door for spiritual transformation.[28]

Thus, the depersonalised model of ministry, led by its CEO manager, displays an *ahistorical* attitude to ministry and pastoring. This attitude is underpinned by a sense that the historic practices of ministry, fellowship, and pastoring are irrelevant or inferior. We also need to admit that we may be ignorant of these practices. As we saw

---

27. Patrick Parkinson, *The Loneliness of the Digitally Connected*, The Cambridge Papers, April 2022, https://www.cambridgepapers.org/the-loneliness-of-the-digitally-connected/.

28. *The State of Discipleship* (Barna, 2015), https://access.barna.com/studies/the-state-of-discipleship/.

earlier with Eugene Peterson and George Herbert, historically the pastor of the church cared for, guided, and preached to his congregation personally, with or without the assistance of others, and did not utilise corporate models.[29]

In short, like the water in which we swim, the spectres of unhinged individualism, comfort, entertainment, consumerism, and so forth are not always easy to discern, particularly when they become part of the church culture. However, if we are richly grounded in our history we have the resources to exegete, critique, and properly engage with our culture. History can sharpen our vision. It can turn our vague sense that something is awry into a critique we can articulate, chastening and reinvigorating our faith.

---

29. For more on traditional models of pastoral ministry, see Harold L. Senkbeil, *The Care of Souls: Cultivating a Pastor's Heart* (Bellingham, WA: Lexham Press, 2019); Gregory the Great, *The Book of Pastoral Rule* (c. 590; Toledo, OH: Aeterna Press, 2016); and Peterson, *Working the Angles*.

PART II

Why We Need History

FOUR

What Is History?

In 1927, a businessman brought to the Australian city of Melbourne a collection of indigenous sacred stones, or *tywerrenge*. However, word soon came out that the stones were possibly stolen and were of considerable religious significance to the indigenous Arrernte people of Central Australia. Amidst calls for the stones to be given to a museum, a public campaign to return them to the Arrernte people emerged. The leaders included several evangelical Christians, including David Unaipon, the Aboriginal leader from the Ngarrindjeri people; Harrington Lees, the evangelical Anglican archbishop of Melbourne; and the Baptist clergyman John Henry Sexton, who was also the secretary of the Aborigines' Friends Association. Together with Yamba, an Aboriginal man representing the Arrernte people, this group argued that the *tywerrenge* should be returned because Aborigines, like all human beings, were entitled to their sacred objects of worship. The group's key claim asserted that indigenous practices and places of worship ought to be afforded the same protection as Christian cathedrals.

This episode, although reported in a number of newspapers at the time, has been largely overlooked by historians.[1] Yet it is profoundly significant because it constitutes the earliest case of an argument for the religious rights of indigenous Australians. Evangelical Christians, both black and white, were the key leaders of this campaign. Unfortunately, as our forgetting of this occasion shows, many Australians lack a rich

---

1. See, for example, *Sydney Morning Herald*, August 19, 1927, 1; *The Observer*, September 3, 1927, 7; *The Register*, August 25, 1927, 11.

historical understanding of the development of religious rights even as we engage in heated contemporary public debate over that issue.

The fascinating case of the *tywerrenge* gives us a point of entry into understanding several aspects of what we do when we write history. The word "history" can be used in a variety of ways. When we say that human beings are engaged in studying or writing history, or that they know their history, we do not simply mean "the accumulation of all events in the past." For example, when I researched and wrote a scholarly article about the Arrernte people I was not simply compiling a list of everything that happened. I was interpreting the past and making sense of it. Historians do this by analysing sources of evidence in various forms; discerning patterns; seeking to understand the context of events and processes; developing explanations of what happened, why it happened, what its effects and significance were, and so forth; and drawing upon a variety of theoretical and analytical tools.

Historians have different areas of expertise and go about their endeavour in different ways. For example, I am an intellectual historian. Broadly speaking, I study the history of ideas in their historical contexts. When I studied the newspaper reports and archives relating to the episode of the Arrernte people's sacred *tywerrenge* stones, I was paying close attention to the language and the ideas that people were drawing upon. I was thus able to recognise that the analogy between sacred stones and a cathedral was a form of a religious rights argument from the natural law and natural rights tradition.

This brief illustration of the sacred stones also demonstrates that writing history is a complex endeavour. History sometimes frustrates our own attempts to impose contemporary categories, assumptions, or modes of understanding upon the past. It often provides us with surprising truths. Here were evangelical Christians arguing for the religious rights of indigenous people in relation to non-Christian sacred objects.[2] Here was a black indigenous leader (David Unaipon) who was avowedly Christian and drawing upon the long tradition

---

2. The sacred stones were part of the traditional indigenous religion, not Christianity. A significant percentage of Aboriginal Australians currently identify as Christians.

of natural law and natural rights to argue that his own people could pursue their conscience and had rights to sacred objects of their traditional indigenous religious practices. History is complicated.

We must understand how we can engage in the practice of history. In this book, I am arguing from a biblical position that all Christians are called upon to tend and keep history—to be priests of history. This does not necessarily mean I expect all of us to roll up our sleeves and dig into the archives or write professional or scholarly history. But it does mean all Christians can engage with history in our daily lives and pass down our heritage, especially through our intellectual and spiritual formation and discipleship.

The Discipline of History

All civilisations have wrestled in various ways to understand what it means to be human. We know our earthly lives are bound by time, yet humanity nevertheless yearns to overcome this transience. Throughout the centuries, music, art, literature, religion, poetry, and other forms of human creativity have wrestled with the ever-present spectre of our mortality, which threatens to render our fleeting lives forgotten and perhaps even meaningless. This is what makes history so fascinating; the past is at once strange and yet also compellingly familiar in the way it reveals our all-too-human struggles. For example, in Percy Bysshe Shelley's poem "Ozymandias" (1818) an obelisk boasts of the ancient Egyptian pharaoh Rameses II's power, yet thousands of years later it has decayed:

> I MET a traveller from an antique land
> Who said: Two vast and trunkless legs of stone
> Stand in the desert. Near them, on the sand,
> Half sunk, a shattered visage lies, whose frown,
> And wrinkled lip, and sneer of cold command,
> Tell that its sculptor well those passions read
> Which yet survive, stamped on these lifeless things,

The hand that mocked them and the heart that fed:
And on the pedestal these words appear:
"My name is Ozymandias, king of kings:
Look on my works, ye Mighty, and despair!"
Nothing beside remains. Round the decay
Of that colossal wreck, boundless and bare
The lone and level sands stretch far away.

Something feels haunting about the story of a great pharaoh who claims he is "king of kings" yet is ultimately defeated not by a mortal enemy but by time. In its broadest sense, history is humanity's attempt to make sense of the past and of time itself. In doing so, history seeks to give us a way of approaching the future. History lies at the heart of who human beings think they are, where they have come from, and where (if anywhere) they think they are going.

Different Approaches to History

Historical annals and chronicles existed in the ancient world, but arguably the first history was Herodotus's *The Histories*, written around 430 BC. Herodotus sought to preserve a record of great events and achievements. Though he was interested in causality, particularly in the context of the Greco-Persian Wars, his writing included no sense of the linear development of time. Other ancient historians such as Thucydides, Polybius, and Tacitus discerned cyclical patterns of change and decay with the rise and fall of civilisations and empires, which occasionally included a sense of development within certain institutions or societies. But these historians had no sense that history had a beginning or that it was heading towards a goal. This attitude was typical of the ancient world; in pre-Christian antiquity, most people believed that the universe was eternal.

The Judaeo-Christian conception of time, providentially ordered by God with its beginning in the creation and its end point antici- pated in the eschaton, inaugurated a new way of understanding and writing about the past. St. Augustine's *The City of God* was arguably the first text outside of the Bible underpinned by the understanding of history as part of the divinely governed linear unfolding of time. However, this view did not necessarily imply that history is a story of unmitigated "progress," since Augustine believed that humanity is sinful. Nevertheless, the idea that history is in some broad sense linear has been enormously influential ever since *The City of God* was written one and a half millennia ago.

There are different approaches to studying the past. History as a scholarly discipline and profession emerged in the early nineteenth century. These scholars sought to study the past akin to the way that the natural sciences examined the natural world. Historical writing of this period, such as that of the famous German historian Leopold von Ranke (1795–1886) emphasised the impartial and objective empirical study of sources and the inductive movement from particular observations to more general conclusions. Von Ranke, who became well-known for his phrase that history was concerned with the past *wie es eigentlich gewesen* ("as it really happened"), believed history was guided by God and his will.

The idea that history is guided by the outworking of a divine plan was secularised in a number of philosophies of history in the eighteenth and nineteenth centuries. Chief among these was the work of the atheist philosopher Karl Marx. In *German Ideology* (1846), Marx argued that a material conflict between economic classes is the engine of history. History progresses through what Marx called modes of production, which are how a society produces its material needs. Eventually, history would culminate in a secular communist utopia with a fundamental triumph over different forms of alienation. There would be a reconciliation, not between man and God, but rather between man and his labour, man and fellow man, and man and his "species being," by which Marx meant his fundamental humanity.[3] Marx's ideas and their subsequent development by thinkers in the

---

3. On Marx's ideas about alienation, especially alienation from man's species being, see Karl Marx, "Economic and Philosophic Manuscripts of 1844," in *The Marx-Engels Reader*, 2nd ed., ed. Robert C. Tucker (New York: Norton, 1978), 70–79.

Marxist tradition have had a diverse influence. One key approach that emanated from Marxist-influenced historians was the idea of doing "history from below," emphasising the stories of ordinary working-class men and women. E. P. Thompson's *The Making of the English Working Class* (1963) is a famous example of this approach to history, which brought to light something of the experiences, traditions, and culture of ordinary people.

In the mid-twentieth century, people began to rethink a number of fundamental ideas about how we approach the past. Soon after World War II, the British historian R. G. Collingwood published an essay entitled *The Idea of History*, in which he challenged the "social science" approach to history, with its attendant methods, and encouraged historians to reflect about the presuppositions they bring to studying the past.

In the last decades of the twentieth century, historians began to think more broadly about approaches to history, particularly the question of whose stories get told. They began to shift away from emphasising the stories of "great men." Historians interested in recovering the stories of those groups traditionally overlooked, such as women and black, indigenous, and colonised peoples, opened up new fields of history. To some extent, this took place against the backdrop of broad moves in the humanities towards what has been called "the cultural turn," which is a way of identifying the broad influence of ideas and theories associated with post-structuralism and postmodernism, though these terms can be misleading since they derive from philosophy. The work of the French philosopher and historian Michel Foucault was particularly influential in some areas.

Broadly speaking, these latest approaches to the past are interested in the nature of power and how it is closely related to the production of knowledge, meaning, and truth.[4] Postcolonial history is one example of an approach that pushed back against histories of European empires presenting imperialism as morally uncomplicated. This approach pays

---

4. See Peter Novick, *That Noble Dream: The "Objectivity Question" and the American Historical Profession* (Cambridge, UK: Cambridge University Press, 1988).

attention to the experiences of colonised peoples and decentred the focus of history, showing that the history of empires can be told as the history not just of the metropole but also the periphery. In other words, these are histories that do not merely focus on the imperial centre, but also pay attention to the geographic margins of the empire.

We must be cautious not to be simplistic or reductionist about these broad approaches to studying the past. We cannot assume that everything which came out of the latter half of the twentieth century ought to be lumped together or can fit neatly under a label. Intellectual influences can be diffuse. In my own field of intellectual history, some of the developments and methodologies that emerged from this recent period have been helpful in enabling us to understand how ideas developed in historical contexts, in which authors were often attempting to intervene in particular debates. For example, we do not properly understand John Locke's *Two Treatises of Government* unless we place that text in its immediate historical context. Locke was contributing to a political debate about the limits and legitimacy of government during the highly contentious time surrounding the Glorious Revolution. He published the *Two Treatises* after the Revolution in December 1689, seeking to justify the change in government. This approach to understanding texts and ideas contrasts with an alternative approach which deems historical context largely irrelevant and treats ideas as if they are akin to Platonic forms, floating above history.

Furthermore, Christian historians can—and do—study, for example, the history of seventeenth-century women's prose literature, or the history of indigenous responses to missionaries in the Pacific, or indigenous Australians without imbibing an entire theoretical approach to history that might be labelled with a variety of "isms," such as postmodernism. The fascinating story about the Arrernte people which opens this chapter is a good illustration. As John Fea pointed out, when we view history from God's eyes, "we get a very different sense of whose voices should count in the stories we tell."[5]

---

5. John Fea, *Why Study History? Reflecting on the Importance of the Past* (Grand Rapids: Baker Academic, 2013), 89.

Professor Sujit Sivasundaram, a Christian and professor of world history at Cambridge University, has written one of the leading studies of evangelism in the Pacific realm of the nineteenth-century British imperial world. He explored the role of missionaries in the production of scientific knowledge and revealed the ways in which the intellectual life of British expansion was not merely an elite phenomenon but also extended to ordinary people.[6]

As we would expect, some elements in the academic practice of history reflect the fashionable political and ideological preoccupations of contemporary culture, which we need to acknowledge. Since historians adopt a variety of approaches to the study of the past, we ought to commit to be careful, informed, and nuanced when we read histories as well as when we engage more broadly with the past.

Christians and the Discipline of History

Christians know that the ultimate history—the history that envelops all histories—is God's story of salvation. All the history we write, study, and practice is in some way part of this larger story. God created time with a loving purpose, and he revealed himself *in time*. This conception of God was unique in the ancient world. By contrast, pagan gods in other cosmologies, such as those of Sumer, Babylon, Greece, Rome, and India, were embodied in space. They were often worshipped in the form of natural or material objects; for example, the Canaanites set up poles to worship Asherah. These deities were often subject to the ravages of time through cycles of change and death. Indeed, the dying deity is a common trope in ancient mythology; witness the stories of Persephone, Dionysus, and Osiris. As we saw earlier, cyclical views of time dominated the ancient world, and these cultures did not believe that history was ultimately leading anywhere.

It is profoundly significant, therefore, that history has a purpose

---

6. Sujit Sivasundaram, *Nature and the Godly Empire: Science and Evangelical Mission in the Pacific, 1795–1850* (Cambridge, UK: Cambridge University Press, 2011).

and unfolds in a linear fashion, as St. Augustine argued in *The City of God*. God gave time its beginning, and the history of the universe unfolds according to his "immutable and eternal purpose."[7] The books of the Old Testament tell Israel's story and place that narrative in the larger story about God and humanity. Many key symbols of the Old Testament, including the garden, the covenant, and the temple, anticipate the historical purpose of the God who will come and dwell with his people.[8] Moreover, as Peter Jensen has recently pointed out, the divine name Yahweh in its biblical and Hebrew context refers to the "*past* in which he made his promises, the *present*, in which he is reminding them of his promises, and the *future* in which he will fulfil his promises. . . . History, not philosophy, is the key to understanding God."[9]

The overarching story of human history from the Christian perspective, despite the darkness and brokenness we see around us, is ultimately a story of hope thanks to Christ's death and resurrection. Hope is a temporal concept; it anticipates an expected event or fruition. Christ, the Alpha and the Omega—the beginning and the end—has overcome the power of sin and death. Jesus's resurrection forms the basis of this sure hope that human history will culminate when Jesus returns to reign over God's entirely just and perfect kingdom. The kingdom Christ inaugurates is both present and future. It has begun, but it will not be completed until Christ returns. This explains Jesus's words in John's gospel: "The hour is coming, and is now here" (John 4:23; 5:25). Jesus's resurrection provides hope not just on the world-historical scale of building his kingdom, but also on the level of individual human experience in the offer of salvation to all peoples through Jesus Christ. Paul can thus say, "For in hope we were saved. Now hope that is seen is not hope. For who hopes for what is seen?

---

7. St. Augustine, *The City of God*, ed. Boniface Ramsey, trans. William Babcock (Hyde Park, NY: New City Press, 2012–13), Book 12, especially 12.14–21.

8. N. T. Wright, *History and Eschatology: Jesus and the Promise of Natural Theology* (Waco, TX: Baylor University Press, 2019), 305.

9. Peter Jensen, *The Life of Faith: An Introduction to Christian Doctrine* (Sydney: Matthias Media, 2023), 104. Emphasis original.

But if we hope for what we do not see, we wait for it with patience"
(Rom. 8:24–25).

What does our understanding of this overarching narrative mean
for the Christian study of history? There are some excellent discussions about how Christians can and ought to engage with the practice
of history as a professional and academic discipline, as well as how
Christian students of history can think through their field of study
and vocation.[10] In fact, Christian historians take a variety of different
approaches to their discipline, and there are complex questions about
which they disagree. One of the central areas of disagreement, for
example, concerns whether historians can posit God's intention in particular historical events or figures. Can we pinpoint divine judgements,
instances of grace, or moments of divine intervention?[11] Thankfully,
there is nothing wrong with disagreement! When conducted well,
fruitful disagreement encourages lively discussion, sharpens our perspectives, and cultivates our humility and ability to listen.

Another important issue to consider is how Christians can draw
lessons from the past for the present. On one end of this spectrum is
"presentism," the narrow view that history matters merely in terms of
its significance for the present. Of course history inspires us, grounds
us, convicts us, and helps undergird our biblical identity. But this
does not mean that we should only study the past to derive lessons for
today.[12] On the other end of this spectrum is an antiquarian approach
to the past which embraces all things historical solely because of their

---

10. For recent discussion, see John Fea, Jay Green, and Eric Miller, eds., *Confessing
History: Explorations in Christian Faith and the Historian's Vocation* (Notre Dame: University
of Notre Dame Press, 2010); Jay Green, *Christian Historiography: Five Rival Versions* (Waco,
TX: Baylor University Press, 2015); John Fea, *Why Study History? Reflecting on the Importance
of the Past* (Grand Rapids: Baker Academic, 2013); David Bebbington, *Patterns in History:
A Christian Perspective on Historical Thought*, 4th ed. (Waco, TX: Baylor University Press,
2018); Vern S. Poythress, *Redeeming Our Thinking about History: A God-Centered Approach*
(Wheaton: Crossway, 2022); Mark Noll, "Traditional Christianity and the Possibility of
Historical Knowledge," in *Religious Advocacy and American History*, ed. Bruce Kuklick and
D. G. Hart (Grand Rapids: Eerdmans, 1996).

11. C. S. Lewis, "Historicism," in *God, History, and Historians: An Anthology of Modern
Christian Views of History*, ed. Thomas McIntire (New York: Oxford University Press, 1977).

12. An excellent recent discussion of this issue is John Fea, "In Search of a Useable Past,"
in *Why Study History?*, 25–46.

age. This approach misses the mark because it indulges in nostalgia and tends to fetishise the past. Consequently, we need to discern carefully how we approach history, since both extremes of this spectrum are dangerous. In chapters 5 and 6, I will propose that the creation mandate and our royal priesthood gives us a biblical and robust framework for approaching history.

Even though I am an academic historian and think the scholarly discipline and profession of history are important, in this book I am most interested in the question of how *all* of God's people are called to engage with history. I will draw upon a broad sense of history not merely as scholarship but also as what it means for the church to stand in the stream of history. What are we doing when we pass down traditions and spiritual practices, when we recover and communicate Christian intellectual heritage and theology, or when we educate ourselves and others about the past, sometimes lovingly disagreeing in the process? History, in its broadest sense, ought to be at the very heart of our Christian lives, both as individuals and collectively as God's people.

Memories of Memories: History and the Heart of Life

In his beautiful short story "That Distant Land," American author Wendell Berry has his character Andy Catlett reflect about his grandparents: "I loved to start them talking about old times—my mother's girlhood, their own young years, stories told them by their parents and grandparents, *memories of memories.*"[13] When our children ask us about who they are, we respond by giving them stories. We speak in "memories of memories" because stories—those memories—drive deeper into our hearts than any abstract proposition. They give us an identity. Jesus often told stories for the same reason.

---

13. Wendell Berry, "That Distant Land," in *That Distant Land: The Collected Stories* (Washington, D.C.: Shoemaker & Hoard, 2004), 311. Emphasis mine.

When my husband, John, and I had our first child, Madeleine, my parents and grandmother visited us in Florida, having flown from Australia. One afternoon, my husband's parents and grandmother, together with mine, joined us for afternoon tea, and John asked them all to tell stories about their lives and their families' lives, as far back as they knew. We wanted to take advantage of this special moment to hear their stories over our newborn daughter. John's grandmother's stories told of her childhood among cattle ranches and orange groves in central Florida, and my grandmother's stories were set in the rocky estuaries of Sydney Harbour and Pittwater. They told stories about our grandparents, our parents' grandparents, and our grandparents' grandparents. Across generations and across the globe, we were saying to our daughter, "This is who you are" and "This is where you have come from."

The stories were moving, but they were not nostalgic. Nostalgia yearns to relive the past. But our parents and grandmothers did not tell their stories to enliven a yearning for the past. They told some difficult stories of immigration, living in a culture of racism, and the Second World War. Rather, they sought to pass down heritage and a sense of belonging. Everything was not better in some mystical "great" past or golden era. That view of the past would be a type of historical romanticisation—a Disneyland-style invention of tradition, or what Jaroslav Pelikan called "*traditionalism*." "Tradition," Pelikan explained, "is the living faith of the dead; traditionalism is the dead faith of the living."[14] He also commented in an interview, "Tradition lives in conversation with the past."[15]

Those conversations with the past are at the heart of what we do when we engage with history in our day-to-day lives; we embed our identity in stories. Christians have been doing this ever since early church period. In 2 Thessalonians, written against the backdrop of the spread of the church beyond Judea and into the Mediterranean world, Paul implores the Thessalonian Christians to "stand firm and hold fast

---

14. Jaroslav Pelikan, *The Vindication of Tradition* (New Haven: Yale University Press, 1984), 65.

15. Jaroslav Pelikan, interview with *U.S. News and World Report*, July 26, 1989.

to the traditions that you were taught by us, either by word of mouth or by our letter" (2 Thess. 2:15). From the beginning, after Pentecost the saints devoted themselves to the apostles' teaching and to fellowship (*koinonia*), to the breaking of bread, and to prayers (Acts 2:42). This is what history is: we pass down memories of memories—stories and practices that tell us who we are in conversation with the past. We do this as families, and we have always done this as God's family in ways that reflect the gospel in the cultures of every language, tribe, and nation.

"White Sunday" is celebrated in all the churches of the Pacific nation of Samoa on the second Sunday of October. Its origins most likely stem from the London Missionary Society's instigation of the celebration of Pentecost in the mid-nineteenth century. Over time, the direct links with Pentecost were blurred and the day was moved to October, where it became a celebration of God's gift of children. Most Samoan children are baptised on this day.

On White Sunday, children dress in white and assume key roles in the church's worship, often leading the services as well as singing, leading prayer, reading, reciting or performing skits of Bible stories, and presenting what they have been learning in Sunday School. It is a day of laughter, singing, and joyous celebration. In expatriate Samoan communities in Australia and New Zealand, White Sunday is a key occasion to invite the extended community and friends to church and to the feast after the service. Parents work with the children's ministry to serve the food and run activities. The Presbyterian Church of Aotearoa/ New Zealand even has a special order of service for White Sunday.[16]

White Sunday is a beautiful way of passing down the beliefs and practices of the Christian life, embedded in Samoa's distinctive culture. Its story dates back to the missionary voyage of John Williams in 1830.[17] In this book, I will often use illustrations from my own

---

16. For an illustration of a White Sunday in the Presbyterian Church, see Ruth Caughley, "A White Sunday Order of Service and Play," Presbyterian Church of Aotearoa New Zealand, October 13, 2002, https://www.presbyterian.org.nz/for-ministers/worship-resources/special -services/services-for-special-occasions/a-white-sunday-order/.

17. On Williams's voyage and the relationship between his ethnography and theology, see Sarah Irving-Stonebraker, "Comparative History and Ethnography in William Ellis's *Polynesian Researches*," *Journal of Pacific History* 55, no 1 (2020): 1–17.

tradition, which happens to be Anglican, but I am not advocating that my own cultural traditions are somehow superior. Like White Sunday, there are stories, traditions, practices, and habits—memories of memories—that God's people all over the world pass down within their communities. When we know where we came from, we know who we are. Thus, we will be better equipped to step forward in faith and into the world.

FIVE

Why Does History Matter?

I n the first class of every semester, I talk to my university students about what we are about to study and why it matters. After all, history involves encountering people with whom we have very little in common aside from our humanity. I tell my students that during the semester we will probably come across some ideas, beliefs, and practices we disagree with or find strange and even offensive. I explain that part of studying history is trying to understand the lives of others from different centuries and societies. We will read multiple sources and gain diverse points of view in the hope of shedding light on what time has obscured. We are attempting to uncover the truth and to understand.

I then move to a deeper point: studying history develops our character. When we study history, we cultivate certain habits of mind that orient us towards truly listening to other perspectives and exercising an intellectual empathy to help us understand. We also learn to reason well. In contrast to the chronological snobbery of our time, we develop intellectual humility and yet do not avoid making moral judgements where necessary. In recent years, I have noticed that my students are increasingly drawn to this broader understanding of the role of history in developing our character. I suspect they find this perspective intriguing, appealing, and profoundly important in today's world.

Why History Matters Biblically

Let us start by outlining three broad principles that frame the biblical perspective on why history matters. First, history matters because God is the creator of history; it is his stage for his works of providence and salvation. God's plan of salvation—from creation through the fall, the incarnation, the resurrection, and ultimately the new creation—is carried out *in history*. In the Old Testament, for example, God takes a real historical people, the Israelites, for himself and chooses them as his "treasured possession" (Deut. 14:2). The Israelites come to know Yahweh through his mighty acts in history. Then in Christ Jesus, God himself entered into history. The book of Hebrews tells us that Jesus's life, death, and resurrection are the central events of history and the fulfilment of God's promise that he will dwell with his people: "Long ago God spoke to our ancestors in many and various ways by the prophets, but in these last days he has spoken to us by a Son, whom he appointed heir of all things, through whom he also created the worlds" (Heb. 1:1–2).

Jesus was born into a real village in first-century Palestine at a specific historical moment, which Paul reminds us was always God's intention: "But when the *fullness of time* had come, God sent his Son, born of a woman, born under the law, in order to redeem those who were under the law, so that we might receive adoption as children" (Gal. 4:4–5, emphasis mine). The Old Testament gave us glimpses of God's promise to enter history through the tabernacle, temple, and the weekly Sabbath rest, but now this promise is fulfilled and fully revealed in Jesus. In other words, the story of humanity from a biblical perspective is the story of God shaping history, becoming part of history in the incarnation, and ultimately bringing history to its conclusion on the final day. The church is a historical people saved in and through historical events, so when we engage with our history as God's people, we are engaging with a transcendent story. Moreover, the book of Revelation shows us that history has a cosmic significance because the events of history are related to a cosmic, spiritual war.

Second, the Bible instructs God's people to *pass down their history* and to *learn from it*. When God gave the Ten Commandments in Exodus, he declared who he was by reminding Israel of what he had done in history: "I am the LORD your God, who brought you out of the land of Egypt, out of the house of slavery" (Ex. 20:2). Moreover, the Israelites were to teach these things to their children (Deut. 6; 11). Psalm 78 retells this story so we might not forget God's mighty works. In the New Testament, Paul reminds the Corinthian church of their forebearers, the generation of Israelites that God delivered from slavery in Egypt and led through the wilderness. However, that generation disobeyed God despite their salvation and deliverance. Paul thus says that "These things happened to them to serve as an example" and "were written down to instruct us" (1 Cor. 10:11).

Third, the study of history is part of the responsibility that humanity is given to create and spread civilisation across the earth, ruling in God's image. "Thou madest him to have dominion over the works of thy hands; thou hast put all things under his feet," says Psalm 8:6 (KJV), echoing the creation mandate given in Genesis 1: "God blessed them, and God said to them, 'Be fruitful and multiply, and fill the earth and subdue it; and have dominion over the fish of the sea and over the birds of the air and over every living thing that moves upon the earth'" (Gen. 1:28). The act of tending, keeping, and cultivating the garden of Eden was to spread beyond it and across the whole earth. God intended humanity as his representatives to fill the earth with culture and civilisation rightly oriented towards him.

Understanding and passing down the history of human societies is part of God's design for how we tend and keep his creation and fill the earth with civilisation in such a way that glorifies him. This responsibility properly belongs to all human beings, since it was given to our first parents Adam and Eve in Eden. Because Christians are the only people who know God and have a relationship with him (Matt. 11:27 and John 14:6), they have a particular responsibility to tend and keep the past. This commission is not limited to those of us who are professional historians, however. First Peter 2:9 tells us that all of God's people are set apart as a royal priesthood. Because of Christ's redemptive work, all Christians now share in Christ's priestly status. Our union with Christ means the priesthood is no longer a separate caste of people. As we will see in the next chapter, the Bible calls all Christians to do the priestly work of watching, tending, and keeping the past. We are witnesses to the past by uncovering and cultivating the stories and ideas that comprise the history of the world in such a way that brings glory to God. This is a beautiful commission as well as a profound responsibility.

Why History Matters to Christians in the Ahistoric Age

We have seen how the Bible teaches us that history matters. In the Ahistoric Age irrelevance, ignorance, and ideology are the hallmarks of our attitude to history, and we are often oblivious to the way these tendencies infiltrate the church. In this context, therefore, stewarding history is even more important for Christians.

1. Historical Literacy Is Vital to Engage with Culture

History is deeply relevant for Christians in relation to their broader culture in two main areas. The first concerns our outward stance as we engage with our societies. Here, history sharpens our vision, giving us the tools to exegete culture. Our societies are wrestling with a multitude of vexing issues, and unless we understand their history we cannot properly engage with them. For example, in many parts of Western culture Christians are seen as "the bad guys," to use Stephen McAlpine's term.[1] In other words, Christianity has not only lost its normative status in articulating our societies' shared values, but it is now deemed a source of harm and oppression. This is a bewildering source of much consternation and discussion among Christians, and rightly so. If we understand how and why this change happened—that is, if we understand the history—we will be better equipped to respond.

---

1. Stephen McAlpine, *Being the Bad Guys: How to Live for Jesus in a World That Says You Shouldn't* (Epsom, UK: The Good Book Company, 2021).

One example involves issues surrounding race. If we want to understand what is truly going on here and, indeed, if we want to respond not in ignorance but with careful and informed humility, we need to understand history. The history of race relations in the United States and in my own country, Australia, is enormously complex. Understanding the history of race relations, including racism, does not mean we must embrace critical race theory. After all, biblical Christianity, not critical race theory, leads us to pray the words of the Litany, "Remember not, Lord, our offences, nor the offences of our forefathers."[2] History also enables us to see that the civil rights movement called the prevailing white southern culture in America to a more Christian and biblical standard. There is much to be learned from this history that will help both white and black Christians.

Esau McCaulley, associate professor of New Testament at Wheaton College, has shown that in a culture experiencing a profound struggle between "Black nihilism and Black hope . . . the Christian tradition fights for and makes room for hope in a world that tempts us toward despair. I contend that a key element in this fight for hope in our community has been the practice of Bible reading and interpretation coming out of the black church, what I am calling Black ecclesial interpretation."[3] McCaulley points out that there is not just one amorphous Black tradition, but at least three different streams, all of which have a history.[4] "Because of the legacy of enslavers using the Bible to oppress Black people there is a long history of Black secular criticism of Christianity. Black believers therefore have had to develop a *double apologetic*, answering questions posed by Black secularists *and* white progressives."[5] Unless we have some historical understanding, we will only see a fraction of the whole picture of the complexities of race and religion, the problems

---

2. *The 1662 Book of Common Prayer: International Edition*, ed. Samuel L. Bray and Drew Nathaniel Keane (Downers Grove: IVP Academic, 2021), 31.

3. Esau McCaulley, *Reading While Black: African American Biblical Interpretation as an Exercise in Hope*, (Downers Grove: IVP Academic, 2020), 3.

4. McCaulley, *Reading While Black*, 182.

5. McCaulley, *Reading While Black*, 183.

of racism in our cultures, and the enormous hope Christianity offers
to black and white people alike.

Secondly, history can help Christians by enabling historical
literacy to work alongside our biblical knowledge so we can engage
culture and articulate the gospel more effectively. For instance, many
of us find ourselves talking with friends or family about pertinent
but complex issues like the extent of our society's obligations to the
poor and the alien, the relationship between religious freedom and the
government, or the existence of human rights. We will be far better
equipped to talk about these issues if we know some history alongside
our biblical knowledge.

Let us take the idea of "rights," for example. This concept is a huge
umbrella covering many areas, yet the term *rights* is not mentioned in
the Bible. If we want to know how such a concept fits with biblical
teachings, we need to understand how it emerged historically. Indeed,
thanks to history we can point out that the very first recorded use of
the term "human right" was by the church father Tertullian in the
third century. Tertullian argued that "it is a fundamental human *right*,
a privilege of nature, that every man should worship according to his
own convictions."[6] But Tertullian did not have in mind the idea of
"rights" in the way we use this term today. Central to the development
of modern ideas of rights was the way medieval legal thinkers and
theologians such as Thomas Aquinas drew upon classical philosophical
ideas of rights and reshaped them around Christian teachings of the
universality of sin and the equality and dignity of all human life.

If we want to engage with ideas of *political* rights, we need to know
something of the Magna Carta and more recent history, as well as
the history of the denial of rights to women and citizens of colour in
different countries. That issue will inevitably come up in our conversations, and we need to be able to respond well, acknowledging when
sin was committed in Christianity's name but also pointing out that
biblical teachings about the *imago Dei* initially formed the basis of the

---

6. Tertullian, "To Scapula," in *Ante-Nicene Fathers, Volume 3: Latin Christianity: Its
Founder Tertullian (I, II, III)*, ed. Alexander Roberts and James Donaldson (Peabody, MA:
Hendrickson, 1994), 105. Emphasis mine.

concepts of equal and universal rights. In short, history equips us with the resources to speak into our culture with informed and articulate humility about some of the most important questions in life.

2. Historical Literacy Can Help Us in Evangelism

First, historical literacy enables us to articulate and present the invitation of the gospel clearly, not only as a message of individual salvation but also as an invitation to be grafted into—to *belong* to—God's family, a historic covenant people. When we become Christians, we are then adopted into this venerable family. God's church is not—and ought not be—like a contemporary "tribe" which is united merely by shared preferences and identity markers. As we saw in chapter 2, contemporary tribes ask very little of us because they are at heart just a consumer identity, a kind of "brand" which people choose in order to give themselves meaning and a sense of belonging. However, this kind of tribalism does not draw us into a historical community with obligations in our relationships with others; rather, it robs people of genuine community. In this cultural context, the historically rooted fellowship of the church can be profoundly attractive.

Indeed, the church is a *true* family. The truth of the gospel invitation which underpins membership of the church is lived out through general obligations and expectations to love, serve, and give to each other as brothers and sisters. We also live out the truth through specific age-old traditions and practices of meeting together, having fellowship, sharing the sacrament of the Lord's Supper, serving one another, showing hospitality, singing, praying, studying the Bible, and so forth. Unlike with a tribe, one can truly belong to God's people—the church—because these people have a *story*. This is profoundly attractive and countercultural. But if we are not grounded in our history, we will not be able to communicate or live this beautiful truth.

Second, understanding the historical development of some of the fundamental doctrines of the Christian faith helps us respond to people's questions and articulate the gospel more clearly. For instance, it is helpful to know the Apostles' Creed, the Nicene Creed, and something of the key documents that were central to the Reformed and evangelical traditions, such as the Thirty-Nine Articles of Religion, the Westminster Confession, or the Heidelberg Catechism. Knowing the basic history of the creeds is very beneficial when responding to questions about who God is, what the Trinity is, and whether each generation just modifies its beliefs about God because religion, as many people claim, "changes with the times." In a similar vein, knowing the history of one's own tradition, and indeed the history of the Protestant Reformation, helps us respond to questions about what Protestants believe, if they differ from Catholics, and so forth. For example, one of the most common questions my husband and I were asked when we ran an evangelistic course for our church was, "Why are there different denominations, and why are you Anglican and not Catholic or Baptist?"

Moreover, if we are able to understand the history of other Christian traditions and denominations, we are better able to respond to their differing beliefs. This is particularly true with Roman Catholicism; after all, Protestants share fifteen hundred years of history with Catholics prior to the Reformation. Also, understanding church history enables us to articulate to non-Christians the beliefs that all Christians hold in common, while also clearly outlining places of disagreement and difference. This is a helpful approach when talking with people who have some background or sense of affinity with a particular tradition.

Finally, as N. T. Wright has shown, understanding the historicity of Jesus and his first-century context is an essential but often overlooked part of natural theology and Christian apologetics.[7] Wright explains, "To study first century history with Jesus and his first followers in the middle of it is a necessary part of healthy Christian life theology and witness."[8] Knowing the compelling *historical* reasons to believe that Jesus really did rise from the dead is enormously helpful.

---

7. N. T. Wright, *History and Eschatology: Jesus and the Promise of Natural Theology* (Waco, TX: Baylor University Press, 2019).

8. Wright, *History and Eschatology*, 176.

3. Historical Literacy Can Help Us Move beyond Culture Wars

As we have seen, one of the characteristics of the Ahistoric Age is the reduction of history to ideology. Today, the term "culture wars" is often used to describe the way particular issues have been reduced to a simplified black and white debate in which certain positions are deemed so morally illegitimate that they are off-limits because they are considered harmful. Social media tends to exacerbate this situation, publicly shaming and silently or explicitly punishing people for their moral transgression. The culture wars can also affect disagreements about history. Is it possible to have a constructive engagement and disagree about the past without deteriorating into culture wars and cancel culture? Approaching history through the priestly responsibilities of tending and keeping the past enables us to recognise and repent of sin without falling into the traps of, on the one hand, seeing the past purely in terms of victims and oppressors, or, on the other hand, triumphally dismissing the idea that anything lamentable happened.

To see how history might help us, let us turn to a brief illustration. During the Elizabethan and Jacobean period in England, the renowned philosopher Francis Bacon (1561–1626) was one of England's most prominent statesmen, rising to the position of Lord Chancellor. Bacon wrote extensively in a variety of fields and published religious, moral, political, and legal tracts along with formative contributions to the origins of modern science. He was also interested in the nature and morality of English colonisation. During the sixteenth century, England began the process of establishing colonies (called "plantations") in Ireland. As a key supporter of the English state, was Bacon nothing more than an ideological apologist for colonisation? Should we reduce history to such ideological simplicity?

The historical truth is far more complex. It is certainly true that Bacon supported a powerful English state and the expansion of English power through colonial means into Ireland and into North America. But Bacon also had profound anxieties about how the English were conducting their colonisation of Ireland. In his essay "On Plantations," Bacon wrote the rather startling words, "I like a plantation in a pure

Francis Bacon (1561–1626)

oil; that is, where people are not *displanted*, to the end to plant in others. For else, it is rather an extirpation than a plantation."[9] Bacon is articulating a clear preference not to establish colonies if it means the dispossession of the indigenous people of the land. He is giving voice and argument to the anxieties of colonisation long before "decolonisation" or "post-colonialism" were even terms.

Long before I was a Christian, the first scholarly journal article I published while working on my PhD at Cambridge was on Bacon's colonial anxieties. Bacon was concerned about moral corruption, the dispossession of indigenous people, and the tendency towards greed in the context of the British colonisation of Ireland and America.[10] He advocated naturalising the Irish by incorporating them into the English commonwealth and wanted to establish just laws for them. Bacon sent a letter to George Villiers, the Duke of Buckingham, advising him to "make no extirpation of the natives under the pretence of planting religion: God surely will no way be pleased with such sacrifices."[11]

Bacon's understanding of what the English were embarking upon was framed by different traditions of thought, including classical republican thought as well as the Bible. He was particularly interested in the idea that God had endowed Adam with complete knowledge

---

9. Francis Bacon, "Of Plantations," in *The Works of Francis Bacon*, vol. 6, ed. James Spedding, Robert Leslie Ellis, and Douglas Denon Heath (London: Longman, 1863), 457. Emphasis mine.

10. Sarah Irving, "'In a Pure Soil': Colonial Anxieties in the Work of Francis Bacon," *History of European Ideas* 32, no. 3 (2006): 249–62.

11. Francis Bacon, cited in Irving, "In a Pure Soil," 260.

of the natural world, which made possible Adam's dominion (or "empire") over the rest of the creation. However, according to Bacon, humanity lost this encyclopaedic knowledge of the rest of the creation in the fall. He further explained in his work *Valerius Terminus* that recovering humanity's original empire of knowledge was part of the project of "restitution and reinvesting . . . of man to the sovereignty and power . . . which he had in his first state of creation."[12] The New World held the prospect of providing all types of knowledge that would be central to this project of repairing the effects of the fall. Bacon wrestled with the question of whether England could carry the project out without mistreating or "displanting" others.

This brief vignette of Francis Bacon's concerns about colonisation gives us a glimpse of how, if we properly engage with our past, history can help us move beyond the culture wars. We can see from Bacon that history is even more complex than the culture wars would have us believe. Bacon was not opposed to colonisation per se, yet he had serious misgivings about various aspects of how the English conducted themselves. He cannot be understood simply as an ideological apologist, still less as an oppressor.

If we know and understand something of this complexity, we can cultivate the ability to disagree peaceably with one another, both inside and outside the church. There are some good contemporary examples of Christians engaging well and disagreeing with one another on contentious issues that are often politicised but are grounded in how we deal with history. In 2019 the Australian Christian newspaper *Eternity News* ran a series of discussions on the issue of whether church gatherings ought to practice a "Welcome to Country" or "Acknowledgement of Country." In Australia, these are ways of acknowledging the original indigenous inhabitants of the land. *Eternity News* published both sides of the issue, and while there was strong disagreement the conversation was conducted in a spirit of love and open dialogue.[13]

---

12. Francis Bacon, *Valerius Terminus*, in *The Works of Francis Bacon*, vol. 3, ed. James Spedding, Robert Leslie Ellis, and Douglas Denon Heath (London: Longman, 1887), 222.

13. See the editorial "When Christians Gather Should We Make an Acknowledgement

History can also train us to empathise. If we read Bacon's writings about plantations, and indeed other accounts of colonisation, we understand both Bacon's situation and that of the people in Ireland. Moreover, if we are able to understand the complexity of history and that this complexity can lead to legitimate disagreement, and if we cultivate empathy and the ability to disagree peaceably with one another, we will also help ourselves to discern when sin was committed and repent of it without falling into the trap of seeing the past purely in terms of victims and oppressors.[14] Bacon was by no means an "oppressor." He advocated for the Irish and, to some degree, clearly empathised with them. Yet he was a powerful figure in the English state that colonised Ireland and, during his lifetime, established colonies in North America. One of the outcomes of English colonisation of Ireland, particularly in the seventeenth century, was horrific bloodshed. Does this mean nothing good came from England's expansion into Ireland? No—history is complex. But if we tend and keep history, we can develop the ability to acknowledge complexity, articulate opinions with humility, and create a foundation for fruitful dialogue with one another that rises above the culture wars.

4. Tending and Keeping History Helps Us Live as Disciples

The final reason history matters to Christians today is that we can draw upon history in ways that help us live as faithful disciples. Christian discipleship and formation are critical in an ahistoric culture that is not only ignorant of history but largely sees history

---

of Country?," *Eternity News*, November 28, 2019, https://www.eternitynews.com.au/opinion/when-christians-gather-should-we-make-an-acknowledgement-of-country/. Both sides: Mark Powell, "No: 'Not in Church,'" *Eternity News*, November 28, 2019, https://www.eternitynews.com.au/australia/no-not-in-church/ and Chris McLeod, "Yes: 'It's a Mark of Respect,'" *Eternity News*, November 28, 2019, https://www.eternitynews.com.au/opinion/yes-its-a-mark-of-respect/.

14. Two recent examples of Christians writing history that grapples with this issue are John Dickson, *Bullies and Saints: An Honest Look at the Good and Evil of Christian History* (Grand Rapids: Zondervan, 2021) and Natasha Moore with John Dickson, Simon Smart, and Justine Toh, *For the Love of God: How the Church Is Better and Worse Than You Ever Imagined* (Sydney: Centre for Public Christianity, 2019).

as irrelevant or reduces history to ideology. As we saw in an earlier chapter, the Ahistoric Age is having consequences for our discipleship: Christians are increasingly living without an inherited identity that frames our practices of formation and discipleship. Many Christians are disconnected from the church as a vertical body and primarily see themselves as united horizontally, sometimes merely by agreement on doctrinal propositions. Drawing upon history can help us because Christian formation was historically far richer than it is today. Here are five brief examples of how drawing upon history enables us to enrich our discipleship. We will explore these in more depth later in this book.

History Can Anchor Us in Orthodox, Biblical Theology

To be part of the Christian faith means living in such a way that we are guided by the authority and primacy of the Bible, yet it also means standing in the stream of what the church has established as orthodox doctrine. A good illustration of this is the doctrine of the Trinity. It would be lunacy to redefine the Trinity generation after generation. Moreover, it would invite heresy. We thus need to utilise the historic tradition of orthodox theology because it provides a mooring for our present concerns, particularly when issues of contention arise. It is enormously helpful, for example, to be able to draw upon the long-established doctrines of the Trinity, of Christ's divinity, or of the biblical understanding of marriage between one man and one woman. A historical engagement with orthodox theology helps safeguard the truth.

We are constantly enticed to change, soften, or water down the beliefs and the practices of the Christian way of life, and we are not always aware of when we might be succumbing to this temptation. Thankfully, being conscious of a long historical continuity in our doctrine and practices sharpens our vision because it enables us to recognise if we are not doing something any longer or, indeed, if we are doing something new. For example, if we are steeped in the centuries-long traditions of discipling one another, we can realise that something has gone awry if a contemporary study conducted by the Barna Group in 2022 reveals that two in five American Christians are not engaged in any kind of discipleship whatsoever.[15]

According to that same study, "in our increasingly individualized culture, 56 percent of Christians tell Barna that their spiritual life is entirely private."[16] This is a phenomenon closely related to the declining levels of Christians engaged in discipling others. We know that an "entirely private" faith is deeply problematic not just because that kind of faith is found nowhere in the Bible, but also because it is at odds with how Christians have lived and practiced their faith throughout history. The people who told the Barna survey that their spiritual life was "entirely private" have access to the Bible—this crystalises why understanding, passing down, and being steeped in our history is so important. Simple access to Scripture was clearly not enough to reveal to these Christians that there is something awry with a self-centred faith.

History Can Help Us Redeem Our Time

Time—our lack thereof and how we spend the limited time we do have—is one of the biggest issues we face in discipling ourselves and others. In previous centuries, people inhabited time very differently from the ways we do today. In chapter 7, we will see how some of the historic practices and habits of keeping time that were developed and passed down through the church over centuries can be helpful to us. For example, the millennia-old Christian traditions of observing a church calendar shaped life and worship around the key events in salvation history. Liturgical seasons gave communities rhythms, order, and a means of living out different moments in the salvation narrative in the Bible through distinctive seasons. Seasons are set apart as distinctive periods of time, markedly different both from ordinary time and from how the secular world compels us to spend our time. These kinds of historic practices can be very helpful in providing us with a

---

15. "Two in Five Christians Are Not Engaged in Discipleship," Barna, January 26, 2022, https://www.barna.com/research/christians-discipleship-community/.

16. The 56 percent statistic is found in the first paragraph of the report cited in the previous note.

model to follow in tending and keeping our time and grounding our faith through daily, weekly, and yearly rhythms.

Another example of the rich historical traditions of structuring time is that, historically, most Protestants drew upon practices of regular and disciplined worship, prayer, and personal and communal devotion to structure their time, such as observing the Sabbath or using the *Book of Common Prayer*. Ordering our time around these meaningful historical practices underscores the beautiful distinctiveness of the Christian life.

History Can Help Us Draw upon Sacredness and Beauty

Despite the rich biblical basis for engaging with beauty and the sacred, much of the contemporary church undervalues these two concepts. Indeed, in the Ahistoric contemporary West, we tend to evacuate the transcendent and sacred from the material world of our daily lives and detach beauty from any transcendent ground. In fact, most of us do not even realise that our contemporary views about the sacred and beauty are markedly different from the role they played historically in the Western church. In a later chapter, we will draw upon the prose, music, and poetry of William Law, J. S. Bach, and George Herbert to explore how beauty and sacredness can enrich our glorification and enjoyment of God.

History Can Help Us with Our Intellectual Formation and Education

Biblically, intellectual formation should be a central concern of our Christian lives. Engaging deeply with the long historical tradition of great books and ideas helps us to cultivate our character, particularly our ability to reason, think wisely, and develop empathy, by familiarizing us with the broad horizons of God's creation. Our intellectual heritage helps us cultivate the qualities and virtues we need to be Christian citizens who serve and contribute to society and public life.

Later in this book we will explore John Milton (author of *Paradise Lost*) and the hymnist Isaac Watts, for whom the formation of the intellect and the formation of Christian character go hand in hand.

Watts, for example, argued that Christians should draw upon the "vast treasuries" of the past. The more we read of the history of human experience, the more we widen our ability to appreciate and articulate the goodness and beauty, as well as the fallenness, in humanity and creation. We form ourselves to engage with the good, the true, and the beautiful. If we read well and wisely, we find in the old books a valuable treasury to help us wrestle with what the good life—life lived well for Christ—might entail.

History Can Help Us with Our Spiritual Formation

Today many Christians struggle with spiritual formation. I have heard people of different generations speak of their gnawing sense of spiritual drought and nausea when their spiritual life revolves around using a "verse of the day" app or a five-minute devotion. What happened to Christian spiritual formation? In a later chapter, we will explore two seventeenth-century examples of spiritual practices and see how they might help us. We will examine how the seventeenth-century Anglican community at the village of Little Gidding in rural Huntingdonshire gives us a glimpse of some of the spiritual practices of fellowship, hospitality, charity, singing, and worship of a family devoted to the Christian life. We will also survey the seventeenth-century theologian Joseph Hall's practices of "Protestant Meditation." These historical treasures can help us resist both the rootlessness of contemporary culture and the pervasive sense that Christians are just individuals who happen to agree on who Jesus is, consequently reducing their faith to an abstract doctrine and their Christian life to apps and entertaining worship experiences. Using history well can help us immeasurably here.

In short, history matters to us today more than ever precisely because we are immersed in an Ahistoric Age. Fortunately, we can respond by using our past wisely and biblically. History can equip Christians to engage well with culture, and it can provide models of spiritual and intellectual discipleship.

SIX

How Do We Engage
with the Past?

So far, we have examined the Ahistoric Age in contemporary Western society and how it is affecting the church. Many Christians are struggling to resist both the secular culture's facile politicisation of history and its disdainful sense that history has no relevance for us. Ahistoricism has far-reaching consequences; we are struggling to understand how to engage with history meaningfully. How can we address our disconnection from history and our sense that it has nothing to teach us? How ought Christians view history in general and their own history in particular—the story, tradition, and heritage of the church? We need a framework to give us an understanding of how to approach history as Christians. That is the task of this chapter.

Summer in Cambridge

One summer when I was studying for my doctorate at Cambridge, I spent long days immersed in the work of the seventeenth-century chemist Robert Boyle (1627–1691), one of the founders of modern science and a pioneer of the methodology of the experiment. Those who recall high school chemistry will probably be familiar with "Boyle's Law," which describes the inverse relationship between the

Robert Boyle (1627–1691)

pressure and volume of gases when the temperature is constant.[1] This law also explains the pain you feel in your ear when you are on an airplane and the air pressure changes rapidly.

Boyle was a devout Christian. An earnest and deeply pious man, he wrestled with theological questions, and both his published and unpublished works testify to his abiding and robust faith. Boyle was a committed member of the Church of England and actually refused to take holy orders on the grounds that his theological writings would have greater weight coming from a layperson. Before I even knew how to make sense of Boyle's faith, I was struck by the image and phrase he used to describe the task of natural philosophers. In his work *A Disquisition about the Final Causes of Natural Things* (1688), Boyle claimed that natural philosophers (we might now use the term *scientists*) were "priests of nature."[2] Boyle argued that the intricate ordering of the natural world had long compelled those who studied nature to acknowledge an author of the creation. Boyle saw creation through the metaphor of a temple, with the Christian natural philosopher as a priest:

> The excellent Contrivance of the great System of the World, and especially the curious Fabrick of the Bodies of Animals, and the Uses of their Sensories, and other parts, have been the great Motives,

---

1. The law was named for Boyle due to his groundbreaking research into the pressure and volume of gases, though he did not articulate the relationship as an equation.

2. Robert Boyle, *A Disquisition about the Final Causes of Natural Things: Wherein It Is Inquir'd, Whether, And (If at All) with What Cautions, a Naturalist Should Admit Them?* (London: John Taylor, 1688), 34. For an exploration of Boyle's idea, see Peter Harrison, "'Priests of the Most High God, with Respect to the Book of Nature': The Vocational Identity of the Early Modern Naturalist," in *Reading God's World*, ed. Angus Menuge (St. Louis: Concordia, 2004), 55–80.

that in all Ages and Nations induc'd Philosophers to acknowledge
a Deity, as the Author of these admirable Structures; and that the
Noblest and most Intelligent Praises, that have been paid Him by
the Priests of Nature, have been occasion'd . . . by the Transcending
Admiration, which the attentive Contemplation of the Fabrick of
the Universe and of the curious Structures of Living Creatures,
justly produc'd in them.[3]

To frame his idea, Boyle quoted Psalm 8 and proceeded to explore its
significance for the systematic study of nature:

Thou hast made him, a little lower than the Angels, and hast
crown'd him with Glory and Honour. Thou mad'st him to have
dominion over the works of thine hands, and hast put all things
under his Feet.[4]

Psalm 8 is referring to the commission given by God to humanity in
Genesis 1:27–28:

So God created humankind in his image,
in the image of God he created them;
male and female he created them.

God blessed them, and God said to them, "Be fruitful and multiply,
and fill the earth and subdue it; and have dominion over the fish
of the sea and over the birds of the air and over every living thing
that moves upon the earth."

I felt peculiar as I read Boyle's description of humanity's relationship to creation. I thought of myself as an atheist, yet the splendour
of summer in Cambridge evoked a sense that beauty might have a
transcendent ground. The wild grasses along the banks of the river

---

3. Boyle, *A Disquisition about the Final Causes of Natural Things*, 33–34.
4. Boyle, *A Disquisition about the Final Causes of Natural Things*, 82.

Cam grew verdant; fronds tumbled into the water where they tangled with reeds. Out rowing one day, my team glimpsed a mother duck with her trail of tiny ducklings paddling frantically after her. We were so filled with delight at this scene that we fell about laughing.

At that latitude, it was light before five in the morning and still twilight until almost ten at night. I spent many of those long days trying to concentrate on Boyle under the apple tree by the river in front of my room in Bodley's Court. The more I read Boyle's natural philosophy—what scholars now consider formative for the origins of modern science—the more I was compelled to read his theology. One simply could not understand what we would now call Boyle's scientific work without understanding his faith.[5] I found myself reading works with titles like *The Christian Virtuoso* and *A Discourse of Things above Reason*. I occasionally pondered what Boyle might make of the mother duck and her ducklings, or, rather, why such little creatures reduced grown men and women to giggling delight.

Boyle was particularly interested in the Genesis passages about humanity's relationship to the creation. Humans were to have dominion over creation and extend human flourishing, civilisation, and God's presence over all the world. Adam was given the job of tending and keeping the garden of Eden (Gen. 2:15). Boyle believed this commission extended to the task of studying nature. Undertaken properly, the systematic study of nature would be part of the human endeavour to repair the effects of sin on creation. It could even help alleviate the suffering of humanity. In short, studying nature glorified God. In his *Some Considerations Touching the Usefulnesse of Experimental Naturall Philosophy* Boyle wrote:

> So in the World, where there are so many inanimate and irrational Creatures, that neither understand how much they owe to their Creator, by owing him even themselves, nor are born to a condition inabling them to acknowledg it; Man, as born the Priest of Nature,

---

5. The term "science" was not used in the modern sense until the mid-nineteenth century. Boyle considered himself a natural philosopher.

and as the most oblig'd and most capable member of it, is bound
to returne Thanks and Praises to his Maker, not only for himselfe
but for the whole Creation.[6]

Even as an atheist, I found something beautiful and compelling
about Boyle's vision. Boyle's epistemology—his understanding of
knowledge's purpose, character, and methodologies—was grounded
in his theology. The study of nature ought to glorify God and serve
him through improving the conditions of human life.[7] At Cambridge
I would occasionally contemplate my own beliefs and ponder whether
there was any great purpose to my own discipline of history. Several
years would still pass before I became a Christian, but reading Boyle
that summer gave me pause for thought. I realised that Boyle's faith
provided him with something for which I longed: a compelling story
about the ultimate meaning and purpose of life, of the world, and
therefore of his own vocation. I had a gnawing sense that my atheism
could not provide a similar narrative.

Years later and now a Christian, I find myself revisiting Boyle's
idea of the scientist as priest of nature who tends and keeps creation,
studying nature for the glory of God and the care of humanity. I believe
Boyle's vision can help us with our contemporary issue of ahistoricism.
Boyle's conception of the *priestly* nature of the natural philosopher's
vocation can help underpin a framework for how Christians in our
contemporary culture ought to approach history.

Tending and Keeping the Past: The Christian Practice of History

Boyle used a priestly metaphor for the natural philosopher's vocation.
But what is priestly work? In the Old Testament, priests were given

---

6. Robert Boyle, *Some Considerations Touching the Usefulnesse of Experimental Naturall Philosophy* (London: Henry Hall, 1663), 58.

7. Sarah Irving, *Natural Science and the Origins of the British Empire* (London: Routledge, 2016).

the responsibility to take care of, tend, and guard the temple, which was the place where God's presence dwelt. Theologian G. K. Beale has argued that this priestly image and work runs all the way back to Genesis and forward to Revelation and that Adam was in fact the first priest.[8] He was given the task of extending the garden of Eden to the rest of the creation.

In Genesis 2:15, "The Lord God took the man and put him in the garden of Eden to till it and keep it." The alternative translation "tend and keep" stems from the New King James Version. Because "tend and keep" is a familiar, elegant, and memorable translation of this phrase, I will use it as a shorthand to denote the work and responsibility of priesthood. There are helpful synonyms of tending and keeping in other translations, including, for example, "work it and watch over it" (CSB) or "work it and take care of it" (NIV). G. K. Beale points out:

> The two Hebrew words for "cultivate and keep" (respectively, *'ābaḏ* and *šāmar*) are usually translated "serve and guard." When these two words occur together later in the OT without exception they have this meaning and refer either to Israelites "serving and guarding/obeying" God's word (about 10 times) or, more often to priests who "serve" God in the temple and "guard" the temple from unclean things entering it (Num 3:7–8; 8:25–26; 18:5–6; 1 Chron 23:32; Ezek 44:14).[9]

After the fall, when the first couple was banished from Eden because of their sin, God in his mercy eventually came to dwell with his people in the tabernacle during the Israelites' time in the wilderness and then in Jerusalem's temple. Israel's priests were commissioned to tend and keep, watch over and work, and guard and serve the place where God's presence dwelt. In Numbers, for example, the Levites were to "guard

---

8. G. K. Beale, *The Temple and the Church's Mission: A Biblical Theology of the Dwelling Place of God* (Downers Grove: IVP Academic, 2004) and G. K. Beale, "Adam as the First Priest in Eden as the Garden Temple," *SBJT* 22, no. 2 (2018): 9–24.

9. Beale, "Adam as the First Priest," 9–24, 10.

all the furnishings of the tent of meeting, and keep guard over the people of Israel as they minister at the tabernacle" (Num. 3:8 ESV).

A central Reformation principle asserts that because of Christ's death and the dwelling of the Holy Spirit in every Christian, we are now, in Martin Luther's words, "a priesthood of all believers." As 1 Peter 2:9 states, "But you are a chosen people, a royal priesthood, a holy nation, God's special possession, that you may declare the praises of him who called you out of darkness into his wonderful light" (NIV). Luther framed this idea in terms of a universal priesthood or the one spiritual estate of Christians:

> It is pure invention that pope, bishop, priests, and monks are called the spiritual estate while princes, lords, artisans, and farmers are called the temporal estate. This is indeed a piece of deceit and hypocrisy. Yet no one need be intimidated by it, and for this reason: all Christians are truly of the spiritual estate, and there is no difference among them except that of office. Paul says in 1 Corinthians 12[:12–13] that we are all one body, yet every member has its own work by which it serves the others. This is because we all have one baptism, one gospel, one faith, and are all Christians alike; for baptism, gospel, and faith alone make us spiritual and a Christian people.[10]

The priestly task of tending, guarding, stewarding, and spreading the wonderful light of God's presence to the whole world belongs to each Christian individually as well as collectively to the gathering of followers of Jesus (that is, the church) because we are all members of the one "spiritual estate."

Drawing upon Boyle's idea of priests of nature and the Reformational emphasis upon the priesthood of all believers, I want

---

10. Martin Luther, *Luther's Works, Vol. 44: The Christian in Society I*, ed. Jaroslav Jan Pelikan, Hilton C. Oswald, and Helmut T. Lehmann (Philadelphia: Fortress Press, 1999), 127. For an excellent and accessible article on the idea of the priesthood of all believers, see Rachel Ciano, "Luther's Doctrine of the Priesthood of All Believers: The Importance for Today," *Credo*, January 8, 2020, https://credomag.com/2020/01/luthers-doctrine-of-the-priesthood -of-all-believers-the-importance-for-today/.

to suggest that Christians are called to tend and keep time, including the past. In short, we are to be a witness to the past, cultivate it, and keep uncovering the stories and ideas that comprise the history of the world. This is a beautiful commission as well as a profound responsibility.

On the one hand, this vocation involves the work of *tending* the past, that is, uncovering the historical stories of people sometimes overlooked, bringing historical injustices to light, and recognising the sins of the past, including our own. On the other hand, our calling to be priests of history is conservative in its role of *keeping* and watching over the past. This involves protecting and passing down historical knowledge and our heritage as Christians; our stewardship covers not only the doctrines of orthodox biblical teachings, but also includes spiritual habits, practices, and traditions. This work honours the past and values our inheritance.

Mitigating the Ahistoricism of Our Age

The priestly framework of tending and keeping history can help us resist the prevailing attitudes of *irrelevance, ignorance,* and *ideology* which characterise the Ahistoric Age's approach to the past.

When we are affected by an ahistoric attitude, we tend to view the past merely in terms of its perceived irrelevance to our individual lives, which are primarily about relentless self-invention. However, when we view the past through the framework of tending and keeping, we assume that the past is not only supremely relevant but also crucial to our priestly calling as Christians to cultivate civilization. This endeavour is often referred to as the creation mandate. After all, the Christian responsibility to steward creation involves not just the care of the natural world but also the care and cultivation of culture. We cannot hope to understand civilisation properly, let alone develop and spread civilisation in ways that glorify God, if we do not understand history. If we can tend and keep the past, we will not succumb to the Ahistoric Age's assumption that the past is irrelevant.

Second, if we embrace our responsibility to tend and keep the past, we will make significant progress towards addressing our ignorance of history. The more we tend and keep the past, the more we will learn about history, building up a "vast treasury" of knowledge which we can draw upon and transmit to others. Later in this book, I outline some of the practical ways Christians can draw upon history in the areas of stewarding our time, intellectual formation and education, spiritual formation, and sacredness and beauty. By tending and cultivating the past, we expand and uncover history and stories that are part of the grand tapestry of humanity, sin, grace, and virtue. By keeping and guarding the past, we understand and preserve the history and stories that have profoundly shaped our societies and our lives.

Third, when we tend and keep the past, we protect against the Ahistoric Age's attitude of viewing the past through the lens of ideology. This reductionism is a symptom of what happens when a political or ideological framework becomes the lens through which history is viewed. Because the Christian framework of tending and keeping the past draws upon the biblical ideas of sin, redemption, and hope, it gives us a model of how to engage with historical sin humbly and biblically while retaining the hope of redemption. In chapter 8, we will see an illustration of Frederick Douglass modelling what this might look like. Douglass's biblical convictions about sin and redemption enabled him to identify sin and demand justice in line with biblical principles, while refraining from dismissing or condemning the sinner or, indeed, his own nation.

Tending and Keeping the Past in Different Walks of Life

I want briefly to suggest how some of the ways to tend and keep the past can be helpful for many of us, including academics, teachers, pastors, parents, and laypeople. For academic historians or those involved in the professional practice of history, the framework of tending and keeping the past brings a balance to the practice of history.

Everyone has a natural inclination to focus upon either the tending and cultivating approach to the past, which seeks to recover overlooked stories, or the keeping and guarding approach, which emphasises the preservation of tradition. I hope that by valuing both approaches, we might develop a posture of modesty and charity in our scholarship as well as our dialogue. We can also attend to our sources and texts with the humility and vigour that comes from understanding how our calling glorifies God.

For teachers, as well as for scholars and professionals, the priestly framework of tending and keeping the past encapsulates the significance and importance of the study of history for Christians. This framework helps communicate to students that the study of history is part of the profound responsibility and commission we have as stewards of culture and civilisation. Our students and young people are currently immersed in the endless banalities and meaninglessness of the online world. We should not underestimate how inspired they would be if they knew that what they study has genuine and profound purpose and meaning that comes from outside of themselves.

Tending and keeping the past also enables us to understand how teaching the full spectrum of history is valuable. In preparing a syllabus we are unfortunately constrained by time and often curriculum requirements set by the government or the educational institution. Nonetheless, in most systems we are able to think through how best to respect the history that has been handed down to us, enabling our students to engage with the long conversation and tradition as well as honour many of the overlooked stories that show the rich tapestry and complexity of history. For example, in teaching the history of Nazi Germany we typically discuss the political rise of the Third Reich along with its consequences and policies that led to the Second World War and the Holocaust. Yet many also teach about the complexity of German citizens' complicity with, and insurgence against, their government. For instance, we can cover not just the complicity of the German church but also the opposition of the Confessing Church of Dietrich Bonhoeffer and Karl Barth, along with the Barmen Declaration.

My suggestion for pastors is that you strive to learn about and draw upon your own tradition and heritage so you can educate and encourage your flock. By drawing upon the past, you can enrich the Christian life of your congregation as its members grow in their understanding of being part of a new people worshipping and following Jesus. Pastors might include historical examples in their sermons, offer Christian education classes on their tradition as well as general church history, or incorporate aspects of historic liturgies from their tradition. They may also tell stories of believers who have been overlooked and yet are remarkable and inspiring examples of Christian witness. Indeed, as Christians we have more in common with other Christians of vastly different ethnic groups and nationalities and backgrounds than we do with non-Christians, even if we share the same family or background. We will share eternity with these fellow Christians.

Those of us who are biological or spiritual parents can tell our children the stories into which they have been born or adopted—where we and our ancestors came from—as well as our primary and ultimate family story—the story of the church which encompasses Christians who look like us as well as those who do not. We may learn about and tell the stories of well-known figures of Christian history (for example, past saints, great theologians, and reformers and defenders of the faith) as well as the lesser-known heroes of our faith and tradition. This might include, for example, Christians from other countries, martyrs of the early church who are often forgotten, and those individuals who quietly made great impacts on our own lives and faith. We may also engage with and use historical liturgies, like the *Book of Common Prayer* or the Presbyterian *Book of Common Worship*, to help our children experience the profound depth of the historic Christian faith. We may catechise our children; special catechisms just for children have a long history. Martin Luther himself wrote one! Let us catechise ourselves, too. We may bring our children up in the richness of a Christian community that is historically grounded, well-formed and informed, and active in its faith and love for one another.

For all Christians everywhere, let us read deeply and broadly about history. Let us engage with the great and lesser-known thinkers, doctrines, and debates of the past, and approach the complexities facing our church and world. Let us use and learn from the liturgies and practices of the past to understand better how to live the Christian life. For example, we might invite a small group of friends to come over and pray the Daily Office or practice the Lectio Divina (a way of reading the Bible that dates back to the early centuries of the church). We may start groups to either engage with historic theological texts or look at catechisms from within our tradition. In my experience, nothing strengthens one's own argument and understanding more than when we research, understand, and argue the opposing point of view. We may study historic figures and movements and consider how to learn from their example, witness, and mistakes.

We could also form groups which examine the ethical or even political implications of the gospel, study how different Christians have understood these implications historically, and ponder what we may do when faced with contemporary questions. Other groups might have an apologetic or evangelistic focus. We may form "holy clubs" which focus on encouraging a pious life, just as John and Charles Wesley and the early evangelicals did in the eighteenth century, and we could also create service groups to help the poor or those in our community in need. We may practice hospitality and fellowship and lean into the historic understanding of Christian community as a small rebellion against our increasingly atomised and anonymous world. In a later chapter, we will see how a seventeenth-century extended family practiced hospitality with communal meals and reading Scripture aloud.

SEVEN

Tending the Past:
Recovering Overlooked Stories

O ur five-year old son, James, is obsessed with "Aussie Rules" football. For my non-Australian readers, Aussie Rules is a game that seems to combine elements of basketball, soccer, and American football. James will attempt to spend every waking minute kicking and catching (or "marking") the football in the backyard, eagerly co-opting friends and visitors to join him. James wears the guernsey sweater of his favourite teams and sings along to the team songs. Like all children, James needs role models. Like many children, especially young boys, he looks to sporting heroes. Recently, we discovered a historical role model for James who was an Aussie Rules footballer and passionate Christian. However, his remarkable and inspiring story is not well known.

Sir Doug Nicholls (1906–1988):
Athlete, Pastor, and Statesman

Sir Doug Nicholls was born into the Yorta Yorta people group and grew up on the Cummeragunja Aboriginal Mission in New South Wales. Converting to Christianity in 1932 after the death of his mother, he was soon baptised and began to witness to fellow footballers. Nicholls played six seasons of professional football for the team of Fitzroy (part of Melbourne, Victoria) in the mid-1930s. In 1935,

Doug was playing for Fitzroy at an away game in Perth, Western Australia. On that Sunday, he preached a sermon at both the morning and evening services of a local Church of Christ. The newspaper *The West Australian* printed excerpts from one of the sermons Doug gave at the church:

> "It is not very long ago," he went on, "that I reversed the course of my life to follow Christ. I was fortunate enough to have done well in sport in Victoria, and the result was that, being well-known and popular, I was carried away by the sporting public of Victoria, wandering about everywhere in sin, until one night I was brought to know that if my life was to count for anything worthwhile, Christ should be governing it. He has given me power to witness for Him in the sport that I have chosen. Last, but not least, He has given me a passion to be of service for Him amongst my own people."[1]

Sir Doug Nicholls (1906–1988)

Image courtesy of the National Archives of Australia. NAA: A6180, 21/2/80/1

Nicholls did indeed continue to live a life serving God. He was ordained as a Churches of Christ pastor in 1945 and established a "vigorous ministry" at a small chapel in Melbourne.[2] Doug and his wife Gladys established an Aboriginal Girls' Hostel in 1956 and were effectively the parents of the house, caring for the girls. Nicholls was also a prominent leader in the campaign for the referendum on May 27, 1967, in which the Commonwealth recognised Aboriginal Australians

---

1. "Witnessing for Christ: Aboriginal Footballer's Sermon," *The West Australian*, June 25, 1935, 19, https://trove.nla.gov.au/newspaper/article/32882406?/.

2. Richard Broome, "Sir Douglas Ralph (Doug) Nicholls (1906–1988)," *Australian Dictionary of Biography*, 2012, https://adb.anu.edu.au/biography/nicholls-sir-douglas-ralph -doug-14920/.

as citizens to be counted in the census. Finally, in 1976 Nicholls was appointed Governor of South Australia, being the first non-white person to hold this office. He was knighted by Queen Elizabeth II.

Sir Doug Nicholls—Christian, pastor, footballer, servant of his country—is indeed a perfect role model for James. Despite his name being given to the Australian Football League's indigenous round, where the league honours indigenous players, most Australians, especially younger generations, could probably not tell you much about Sir Doug Nicholls's life. Fewer still would know about his Christian faith. Stories like Sir Doug's need to be tended and kept. This chapter explores the first priestly responsibility in relation to the past, namely, the "tending" (or cultivation) of those aspects of history which are important and yet often overlooked or forgotten.

William Cooper: The Christian Advocate for Indigenous Australians

Sir Doug Nicholls's mentor, William Cooper, was also his great-uncle. Born around 1861 near Echuca on the banks of the Murray River, William Cooper was also part of the Yorta Yorta people group. At fourteen, Cooper and his siblings arrived at the Maloga Mission, which had been established in 1874 by the evangelical missionary Daniel Matthews and his wife Janet. On a number of occasions, Matthews went into the camps of white pastoralists with an axe and chopped off the chains of young indigenous women who had been tied up for use as sex slaves. He then took them back to the safety of the Maloga Mission.[3] Daniel Matthews quickly recognised that Cooper was remarkably intelligent and a quick learner and became his mentor. He and Janet (who ran the Mission's school) taught Cooper to read and write. Indeed, as a mark of his admiration and love for Matthews, Cooper later named his own son Daniel.

---

3. John Dickson, "Indigenous Rights before Their Time," Centre for Public Christianity, March 20, 2008, https://www.publicchristianity.org/indigenous-rights-before-their-time/.

After working during his late teens and early twenties for some years in a pastoralist's household and as a shearer, Cooper returned to the Mission. One Sunday in January 1884, after a church service on the Mission, Cooper approached Daniel Matthews and told him, "I must give my heart to God."[4] Cooper kept working as a rural labourer, and he developed his faith and biblical knowledge under the guidance of Methodist preacher Thomas Shadrach James (1859–1946), a convert to Christianity who had migrated to Australia from Mauritius, where he had been born to Tamil and Indian parents.

In Australia at this time, Aborigines were not legal citizens. They had no representation in any parliament and no right to vote. The story of God's people Israel, rescued from slavery and brought into the land God had promised them, resonated with Cooper because he could recognise his own people's suffering. In 1933, Cooper wrote a petition to demand representation for indigenous people in the Federal Parliament and argued for enfranchisement. After spending years travelling around Aboriginal reserves and collecting over 1800 signatures as well as marks from those who could not read or write, Cooper presented his petition to the Commonwealth government in 1937.[5]

Cooper held the British to biblical standards. The Bible taught that because Aborigines were created in God's image, they were of "one blood" with white people, to use Cooper's phrase. Therefore, Cooper's petition argued, indigenous people are entitled to the same legal rights as white Australians:

> Are you prepared to admit that, since the Creator said in his Word that all men are of "one blood" we are humans with feelings like yourselves in the eyes of Almighty God, that we can have joys and

---

4. Nancy Cato, *Mister Maloga: Daniel Matthews and His Mission, Murray River, 1864–1902* (St. Lucia, Australia: University of Queensland Press, 1976), 167.

5. A copy is held at the National Archives of Australia and is online at https://www.naa.gov.au/learn/learning-resources/learning-resource-themes/first-australians/rights-and-freedoms/petition-king-george-v-aboriginal-inhabitants-australia/. Prime Minister Joseph Lyons failed to pass Cooper's petition on to the king. It was finally presented to Queen Elizabeth II by Governor General Peter Cosgrove in 2014.

our sorrows, our likes and our dislikes, that we can feel pain, degradation, and humiliation just as you do?[6]

But the Parliament failed to deliver the petition to the king. Consequently, Cooper organised a day of mourning in 1938 on the sesquicentenary of colonisation to draw attention to the injustices and mistreatment of Aboriginal Australians.

In his later life, Cooper worked with the Anglican archbishop of Sydney, John Needham, to establish Aborigines' Sunday on the Sunday nearest to Australia Day. It was first celebrated in 1940 in a number of Protestant denominations. When describing Aborigines' Sunday, Cooper wrote, "We request that sermons be preached on this day dealing with the Aboriginal people and their need of the gospel and response to it."[7] Just as Cooper had been mentored in the faith by Daniel and Janet Matthews, and by Thomas Shadrach James, he mentored others, including his grandnephew Sir Doug Nicholls.

It is difficult to read Cooper's story—and that of Doug Nicholls, for that matter—without being moved and inspired. Cooper's story needs to be uncovered, tended, and kept. This is especially important because Australia's National Museum, which has an online tribute to Cooper, audaciously writes Cooper's Christian faith entirely out of his story and omits the biblical principles that Cooper used to articulate rights in his petition.[8] It is quite remarkable—and rather ironic—that Cooper's Christian faith, which underpinned his life and, indeed, his quest for justice, is intentionally silenced by a cultural institution which rails against the silencing of other stories. This is a Christian story, yet many Christians know more about the latest vacuous celebrity or "influencer" than about William Cooper. And,

---

6. Quoted in Meredith Lake, *The Bible in Australia: A Cultural History* (Kensington, Australia: University of New South Wales Press, 2018), 274.

7. William Cooper, Honorary Secretary, Australian Aborigines' League, Circular Letter, December 27, 1937, National Archives of Australia, A659, 1940/1/858.

8. "William Cooper Protests," National Museum Australia, September 29, 2022, https://www.nma.gov.au/defining-moments/resources/william-cooper-protests/.

sadly, many non-Christians know nothing of Cooper's faith in the God who humbles the mighty and lifts up the oppressed (Luke 1:52).

Doug Nicholls's and William Cooper's stories are illustrations of what it might look like to cultivate the past—that is, to recover forgotten or overlooked stories. Cooper's story, for instance, enables us to make sense of the past in its complexity: Cooper was a Christian who shone the biblical light on racism. Uncovering stories like these can help us by providing resources for how to deal with the past without reducing history to crude ideological battlefields. There are many such stories; Nicholls's and Cooper's are just two from the Australian context. Let us tend and cultivate their stories, and then let us keep them.

Mary Prince (1788–c. 1833): The Abolitionist

The daughter of slaves, Mary Prince was born in the British colony of Bermuda in 1788. Early in her life, she was sold with her mother to a British naval captain. He gave her as a personal slave to his granddaughter Betsey, who was around the same age as Mary. Mary's mother, meanwhile, was a domestic slave to the captain's daughter-in-law, Sarah Williams. Upon Sarah's death, Betsey's father decided to sell Mary and her sisters while retaining their mother. Mary's account of the day her mother had to accompany her three young daughters—Mary and her sisters Hannah and Dinah—as they were taken to the market and sold to different masters is a heart-wrenching scene:

> The black morning at length came; it came too soon for my poor mother and us. Whilst she was putting on us the new osnaburgs [coarse clothing] in which we were to be sold, she said, in a sorrowful voice, (I shall never forget it!) "See, I am *shrouding* my poor children; what a task for a mother!" . . .
>
> Our mother, weeping as she went, called me away with the children Hannah and Dinah, and we took the road that led to Hamble Town, which we reached about four o'clock in the afternoon. We

followed my mother to the market-place, where she placed us in a row against a large house, with our backs to the wall and our arms folded across our breasts. I, as the eldest, stood first, Hannah next to me, then Dinah; and our mother stood beside, crying over us. My heart throbbed with grief and terror so violently, that I pressed my hands quite tightly across my breast, but I could not keep it still, and it continued to leap as though it would burst out of my body. [. . .] The great God above alone knows the thoughts of the poor slave's heart, and the bitter pains which follow such separations as these.[9]

Mary was sold to Captain John Ingham. In her autobiography, she describes how Ingham flogged one young slave, Hetty, so severely while she was pregnant that she went into labour only to deliver her baby stillborn because the child had been killed by the flogging. A short while later, after Hetty had recovered a little, Ingham flogged her again, this time so severely that all her limbs swelled up, and she died.[10]

After several years, Ingham sold Mary to another master in the Turks and Caicos Islands, who then sold her to the plantation owner John Adams Wood. Mary worked as a domestic slave in Wood's house in Antigua, a British colony largely devoted to sugar plantations. In 1826, Mary married Daniel James, who had purchased his freedom, but she remained enslaved. One Christmas, another slave asked Mary to accompany her and her husband to a Methodist prayer meeting. Mary agreed. She recalled singing hymns at the meeting and hearing the first prayers she ever understood. Mary also described how she became aware of her own sin and of God's love for her. Today, it feels surprising and perhaps even jarring to read about someone so profoundly mistreated who, despite this, realised that she still stood

---

9. Mary Prince, *The History of Mary Prince, A West Indian Slave, Related By Herself* (London: F. Westley and A. H. Davis, 1831), 4. Emphasis original.

10. On Mary Prince's biography, see "Chronology," in *The History of Mary Prince*, ed. Sara Salih (London: Penguin, 2000), xxxix–xl; William L. Andrews, "Introduction," in *Six Women's Slave Narratives*, ed. Henry Louis Gates Jr. (New York: Oxford University Press, 1988), xxix–xli; and Moira Ferguson, "Introduction," in *The History of Mary Prince: A West Indian Slave*, ed. Moira Ferguson (Ann Arbor, MI: University of Michigan Press, 1997), 1–41.

before God as a broken person in need of forgiveness. Yet Mary states this clearly in her autobiography:

> I felt sorry for my sins also. I cried the whole night, but I was too much ashamed to speak. I prayed God to forgive me. This meeting had a great impression on my mind, and led my spirit to the Moravian church; so that when I got back to town, I went and prayed to have my name put down in the Missionaries' book; and I followed the church earnestly every opportunity. I did not then tell my mistress about it; for I knew that she would not give me leave to go. But I felt I *must* go. Whenever I carried the children their lunch at school, I ran round and went to hear the teachers.[11]

Contemporary historians tend to play down the importance of genuine Christian faith among non-white converts to Christianity in the context of empire, particularly those who were enslaved or who were converted through missionaries. These historians often assume that these converts did not truly believe but were just adapting Christianity for their own ends. However, a sneaky paternalism lurks behind this assumption. For example, one scholar dismissed the faith of Olaudah Equiano (1745–1797), another slave of this period who, after purchasing his freedom, joined the abolitionist group the Sons of Africa and published an autobiography. This scholar argued that "it is difficult to determine how sincere Equiano was about his conversion and baptism. The youth may have been acting under the assumption that baptism conveyed freedom upon a slave."[12]

Yet we know from the sources that Equiano was absolutely certain that baptism did no such thing, and he never discarded his Christian faith. Far from it—indeed, Equiano's faith became central to his life. In his autobiography, Equiano uses his understanding of God's saving grace, sovereign authority, and plan for humanity to frame his experiences of suffering. Emblazoned across the title page of Equiano's

---

11. Prince, *History of Mary Prince*, 16. Emphasis original.

12. A. Constanzo, ed., *The Interesting Narrative of the Life of Olaudah Equiano* (Calgary, AB: Broadview Literary Texts, 2001), 13.

autobiography are these two verses from Isaiah: "Behold, God is my salvation; I will trust, and not be afraid, for the Lord Jehovah is my strength and my song; he also is become my salvation. And in that day shall ye say, Praise the Lord, call upon his name, declare his doings among the people" (Isa. 12:2, 4). Like Equiano, Mary Prince's faith framed the way she made sense of her suffering years later when she began composing her autobiography. We ought to give Mary Prince the respect of taking her words seriously, which means accepting her conversion as genuine.

In 1828 Mary's owner John Wood and his family journeyed to London, and Mary accompanied them while her husband Daniel James remained behind. Unfortunately, Mary continued to be mistreated by Wood and his wife in London and eventually managed to seek help from the only place she knew in England.

> I went to the man (one Mash) who used to black the shoes of the family, and asked his wife to get somebody to go with me to Hatton Garden to the Moravian Missionaries: these were the only persons I knew in England. The woman sent a young girl with me to the mission house, and I saw there a gentleman called Mr. Moore. I told him my whole story, and how my owners had treated me, and asked him to take in my trunk with what few clothes I had. The missionaries were very kind to me—they were sorry for my destitute situation, and gave me leave to bring my things to be placed under their care. They were very good people, and they told me to come to the church.[13]

Mary was soon introduced to the Anti-Slavery Society, which took her case in order to see if they could free her and enable her to return to Daniel in the West Indies. Although the slave trade had been abolished in the British Empire with the Slave Trade Act of 1807, the practice of slavery was still legal. It is also important to understand the historically complex relationship between various churches and

---

13. Prince, *History of Mary Prince*, 20.

slavery in the late eighteenth- and early nineteenth-century Atlantic world. For instance, Mary Prince had joined the Moravian Church in Antigua. The Moravian missions in Antigua (and elsewhere) did keep slaves, but, paradoxically, the Moravians also ministered to slaves, including to Mary Prince. In London, Mary went straight to the Moravians when she was seeking to escape from slavery and attain her freedom. She used their connections and circles there to contact the Anti-Slavery Society.

The abolitionist lawyer George Stephen attempted to negotiate and work for Mary's freedom from slavery so she could return to Daniel in Antigua and remain free. He even petitioned the British Parliament, but without success. Wood refused to manumit Mary or to allow her to be purchased without his explicit oversight. He did, however, provide her with a letter that gave her the right to leave his household, although technically she remained his property. After working for some time, Mary became unemployed until Thomas Pringle, the secretary of the Anti-Slavery Society, hired Mary in his house as a domestic servant:

> At last I went into the service of Mr. and Mrs. Pringle, where I have been ever since, and am as comfortable as I can be while separated from my dear husband, and away from my own country and all old friends and connections. My dear mistress teaches me daily to read the word of God, and takes great pains to make me understand it. I enjoy the great privilege of being enabled to attend church three times on the Sunday; and I have met with many kind friends since I have been here, both clergymen and others.[14]

In Pringle's household, Mary met Susanna Strickland, who was also involved in the Society. (Strickland later immigrated to Upper Canada and became the well-known author Susanna Moodie.) Susanna transcribed Mary's life story, while Pringle edited it and wrote a preface. Finally, the slave narrative of a man named Louis Asa-Asa, who was sold by African slave traders around the age of twelve, transferred

---

14. Prince, *History of Mary Prince*, 23.

between a number of ships, and eventually brought to England in a French ship, was appendixed to Mary's autobiography.[15]

The History of Mary Prince, a West Indian Slave. Related by Herself. With a Supplement by the Editor. To Which Is Added, the Narrative of Asa-Asa, a Captured African, was published in 1831. Instantly successful, but arousing the ire of slavery supporters, the text sold quickly and was reprinted within months. Mary's story piqued the interest and empathy of the contemporary British public in the two years before the Slavery Abolition Act was passed in 1833, which abolished the institution of slavery in most parts of the British Empire. Alas, we know little about Mary's life after the publication of her autobiography, nor do we know the actual date of her death.

We ought to do the priestly work of recovering and cultivating stories like Mary's. We can learn much from Mary's testimony of the God who brings the least of these—the enslaved and suffering—into his kingdom. We also ought to cherish Mary's story because it gives us a window into understanding the larger issue of Christianity's relationship with the trans-Atlantic slave trade. Yes, Christianity was misused to justify slavery. But enslaved men and women also found hope in Jesus Christ, the God who became flesh and who offers redemption from sin, thus implying redemption in the world. Moreover, the moral argument of the abolitionist movement was grounded in—indeed, *made possible by*—the Bible. We ought to let Mary's own words conclude her story:

> I still live in the hope that God will find a way to give me my liberty, and give me back to my husband. I endeavour to keep down my fretting, and to leave all to Him, for he knows what is good for me better than I know myself. Yet, I must confess, I find it a hard and heavy task to do so.[16]

---

15. David Dabydeen and Shivani Sivagurunathan, "Asa-Asa, Louis," in *The Oxford Companion to Black British History*, ed. David Dabydeen, John Gilmore, and Cecily Jones (Oxford: Oxford University Press, 2007), 33.

16. Prince, *History of Mary Prince*, 23.

Anne Hart Gilbert (c. 1768–1834) and Elizabeth Hart Thwaites (c. 1772–1833): Educators of Slaves and Founders of the Female Refuge Society

The Hart sisters, Anne and Elizabeth, were born into a slaveholding free black family in late eighteenth-century Antigua. They were mixed-race descendants of English men and African women, designated "coloured" or "mulatto" in the terminology of that time. Devout Christians and followers of the Methodist movement, Anne and Elizabeth became the first educators of slaves and free blacks in Antigua and wrote powerful attacks on slavery. Together they established, ran, and taught in a number of schools and founded the Female Refuge Society in 1816. This group took care of the physical and spiritual needs of slaves and free black women and orphans in a context of endemic sex slavery and forced concubinage. Unfortunately, today the Hart sisters have been largely forgotten.

Anne and Elizabeth's father, Barry Conyers Hart, had been a slave. When he secured his freedom, he became a planter and owned several slaves himself, and by all accounts he treated them humanely. This is a good time to note something about the ethical complexities of history. If we approach history expecting to find people who fit easily into our contemporary categories, that is, who agree with us on every point, we will be disappointed and confused. For example, scholars disagree about whether the Hart sisters were outright abolitionists or more moderate opponents of slavery.[17] Nonetheless, they attacked slavery in their writings and spent their lives educating and ministering to slave women and children at considerable personal cost.

The relationship between missions, churches, and slavery in the British Empire during this time was also complex. Charles and John Wesley were staunchly opposed to slavery, but the attitudes of

---

17. See for example, Natasha Lightfoot, "The Hart Sisters of Antigua: Evangelical Activism and 'Respectable' Public Politics in the Era of Black Atlantic Slavery," in *Toward an Intellectual History of Black Women*, ed. Mia Bay, Farah Griffin, Martha Jones, and Barbara Savage (Chapel Hill, NC: University of North Carolina Press, 2015), 53–72.

The Hart sisters likely had a similar appearance and social
status as these two free women of color in the Caribbean
depicted by Agostino Brunias (ca. 1764).

Methodists in the Caribbean could vary. The story of Methodism's
arrival to Antigua is fascinating. In the late 1750s, a prominent
Antiguan planter and slaveholder, Nathaniel Gilbert, journeyed to
England and was converted to Wesleyan Methodism. Wesley also
converted two of Gilbert's slaves and persuaded Gilbert to return to
Antigua and share the gospel with the slaves there. Nathaniel Gilbert
brought Methodism to Antigua and possibly managed to see some

people—black and white—converted to Christianity. From the late eighteenth century, other Methodists were working both officially and unofficially as missionaries in Antigua, and there was a considerable movement to minister to Antiguan slaves. In fact, around the time that the Hart sisters were born, a religious awakening or revival swept through Antigua between 1772 and 1775.[18] In 1807, when the slave trade was abolished in the British Empire, the Methodists passed a resolution that forbade their clergy from owning slaves.

The Hart sisters were related to the four most prominent Methodist families on Antigua, but they had their own personal conversion experiences as young women, which they wrote about. For instance, in *History of Methodism* Elizabeth described that "in private Prayer my Soul was set at liberty [and] was suddenly turned into Praise, and with the eye of Faith I viewed a smiling Savior."[19] The class position of the Hart family meant that the girls' father was able to provide them with a sound education, which is revealed by their articulate correspondence and their citations of, and allusions to, authors and theologians such as John Milton. Moreover, each of the sisters wrote her own history of the Methodist faith.

Anne Hart married Nathaniel Gilbert's cousin, John Gilbert. Mixed-race marriages were rare for this time period, and Anne and John returned from their honeymoon to find the door of John's office vandalised in white and yellow paint, which represented their interracial marriage. John worked as a Methodist lay preacher and clerk for the Royal Navy, and Anne helped him. Anne's sister Elizabeth Hart married Charles Thwaites, a teacher in Anglican and Methodist schools. From their various letters and writings, it is clear that both sisters' marriages were true partnerships in the gospel, and John Gilbert and Charles Thwaites evidently encouraged their wives to use their considerable gifts in the service of God.

---

18. See Robert Glen, "An Early Methodist Revival in the West Indies: Insights from a Neglected Letter of 1774," *Wesley and Methodist Studies* 9, no. 1 (2017): 36–56.

19. Elizabeth Hart Thwaites, *History of Methodism*, in *Nine Black Women: An Anthology of Nineteenth-Century Writers from the United States, Canada, Bermuda, and the Caribbean*, ed. Moira Ferguson (London: Routledge, 2015), 10.

Both Anne and Elizabeth firmly held to the biblical idea of the spiritual equality of all people—black and white, slave and free, male and female—which was championed by Methodists but scandalous to white planters and those supporting slavery. Along with many prominent abolitionists, the Hart sisters believed that the building of God's kingdom on earth was closely connected to the abolition of slavery.[20] As Elizabeth wrote to a friend in 1794, one of the signs of the increase of Christ's government was "in the noble attempt about to be made for the abolition of the African Slave Trade."[21]

In 1809, Anne and Elizabeth founded the first Sunday school in the Caribbean that was open to any class or race. At that time, it was scandalous to teach slaves to read *at all*, let alone to read the Bible! This Sunday school met in the Gilberts' home. Some of the children and youth who became Christians in this Sunday school later went on to teach in that same school. In the memoir of her husband, John Gilbert, Anne recorded that "it pleased God . . . to pour out His blessings on the Sunday School particularly; its numbers greatly increased, and some young persons, who were the first objects of its care, were brought to a saving acquaintance with the truth as it is in Jesus, and I am happy to add, continue to this day, and are among its most valuable teachers."[22]

Anne also taught literacy and arithmetic in a primary school, which she directed with financial assistance from the Ladies' Society in London. In her *History of Methodism* (1804), Anne wrote that "there are hundreds of black and coloured children sent to school every year in this little Island."[23] The Hart sisters' faith was the driving force

---

20. On Methodism and antislavery in the Caribbean at this time, see John Saillant, "Antiguan Methodism and Antislavery Activity: Anne and Elizabeth Hart in the Eighteenth-Century Black Atlantic," *Church History* 69, no. 1 (2000): 86–115.

21. Elizabeth Hart Thwaites, "Letter to a Friend," in *Nine Black Women: An Anthology of Nineteenth-Century Writers from the United States, Canada, Bermuda, and the Caribbean*, ed. Moira Ferguson (London: Routledge, 2015), 21.

22. Anne Hart Gilbert, *Memoir of John Gilbert*, in *Nine Black Women: An Anthology of Nineteenth-Century Writers from the United States, Canada, Bermuda, and the Caribbean*, ed. Moira Ferguson (London: Routledge, 2015), 42.

23. Anne Hart Gilbert, *History of Methodism*, in *Nine Black Women: An Anthology of Nineteenth-Century Writers from the United States, Canada, Bermuda, and the Caribbean*, ed. Moira Ferguson (London: Routledge, 2015), 36.

behind all their endeavours. The task was made more difficult by the paucity of teachers, but Anne's faith is evident even in this concern. "We may with great propriety ask with the Apostle 'Who is sufficient for these things?' The Harvest truly is plenteous but the labourers are few. Pray ye therefore the Lord of the Harvest that he would thrust more labourers into the Harvest."[24]

The sisters' dedication to educating slave children prompted Elizabeth and her husband to travel to Montserrat to study the Lancastrian system of education, a pedagogy developed in England and then practiced in several places in the British Empire. It involved teaching children to help monitor and pass down to other children what they had recently learned. Elizabeth and Charles subsequently introduced it in their own schools.[25] In 1813, the couple voiced their plan to teach five hundred children from neighbouring plantations to read. The slaves voluntarily built a classroom and named it Bethesda. According to the scholar Moira Ferguson, the Thwaites taught between two and three hundred children and adults daily.[26]

In 1815, Elizabeth and Anne established the Female Refuge Society based in English Harbour, Antigua, which rescued and cared for women who were escaping concubinage or prostitution. We ought not gloss over the reality of what life for slaves was like, including the pervasive sexual sin committed by white planters, who routinely took black or "coloured" women and girls, married or unmarried, as their "concubines." These women were taken against their will, raped, and used for the sexual gratification of men. In the midst of this darkness, the Hart sisters' Female Refuge Society was a literal refuge.

It is sobering to read of the sacrifices the Hart sisters made so they could educate, care, and share the gospel with slaves and free mixed-race women and children. In a letter to her cousin, Miss Lynch, Elizabeth related that "there are several children who cannot yet attend

---

24. Gilbert, *History of Methodism*, 37.

25. See Moira Ferguson, *The Hart Sisters: Early African Caribbean Writers, Evangelicals, and Radicals* (Lincoln, NE: University of Nebraska Press, 1993), 15.

26. Moira Ferguson, ed., *Nine Black Women: An Anthology of Nineteenth-Century Writers from the United States, Canada, Bermuda, and the Caribbean* (London: Routledge, 2015), 8.

the school for want of clothes, and yet I have laid out upwards of twenty dollars cash from my own pocket since Christmas."[27] We also know that at one point, Elizabeth gave up eating meat in order to give to the needy the money meat would have cost.[28] It is easy to overlook the costly nature of these acts in our own age of plentiful, diverse, and readily available food, but in early nineteenth-century Antigua there were limited alternative ways for Elizabeth to gain the calories and nutrition she needed. Yet, for some period at least, she gave up meat so she could give more to those in need.

In the *Memoir of John Gilbert*, Anne recalls something of the personal and financial stress involved in opening their schools. She knew they would "find it impossible to obtain regular payments for the children, some of whom were to board with us" and that her husband's income was, at any rate, "fluctuating and precarious."[29] When Anne's husband John happened to come into a moment of financial blessing, having settled an account, he gave "the greater part of this money" to "purchasing the freedom of a young person who had some claims upon him, and who was saved from vice and wretchedness by being rescued from slavery."[30]

We glimpse the degree to which Anne and Elizabeth opened their lives and their homes in one of Anne's descriptions of what happened when the Thwaiteses' house became too small for the congregations that met there. Anne and John decided to open their house also, and John "preached or expounded the scriptures every sabbath, the Wesleyan missionaries preaching once a fortnight, on a night in the week. We soon had all our rooms, the bed chambers excepted quite full."[31] Anne also established a Juvenile Association that held their meetings in her home.

Elizabeth Hart Thwaites and Anne Hart Gilbert lived lives of costly discipleship. Their belief in the spiritual equality of all people

---

27. Ferguson, *Nine Black Women*, 24.
28. Ferguson, *Nine Black Women*, 6.
29. Gilbert, *Memoir of John Gilbert*, 39.
30. Gilbert, *Memoir of John Gilbert*, 38.
31. Gilbert, *Memoir of John Gilbert*, 41.

led them to give up what little money they had; to open their homes; and to clothe, feed, provide refuge for, educate, and preach the gospel to some of the most vulnerable and traumatised women and children. They were consequently often subjected to ridicule and threats. Yet Elizabeth rejoiced "in the certainty that there are many real converts in St. John's, both young and old."[32] Anne and Elizabeth died within a year of each other, on the eve of the legal emancipation of slaves in Antigua in August 1834.

We are so often ignorant of the costly discipleship of Christians in previous centuries. In this chapter we saw the first aspect of the priestly work of history, namely, the tending of stories often overlooked. Cultivating these kinds of histories chastens us and enlivens us. In an Ahistoric Age in which we know little about the past, and in which we are surrounded by comfort and cheap grace, let us tend these remarkable stories and learn from them.

---

32. Thwaites, *History of Methodism*, 12.

EIGHT

Keeping the Past:
Preserving a Rich Conversation

I n this chapter we explore the second of the two priestly tasks in relation to the past: the conservative work of "keeping," guarding, and passing down the past. This involves cultivating an attitude of humility—preserving and communicating Christian intellectual heritage, being eager to learn from it, and remembering that this has been an ongoing conversation with other cultures. Such an attitude is particularly important in an era that increasingly sees Christianity as evil and shameful, burdened by a universally oppressive legacy.

The Long Historical Conversation

Christians today are part of a long historical conversation, not just about theology but also about how we are to live both individually and collectively as God's people. In the past several years, Christians from various walks of life have talked to me about how difficult it is to reason through and articulate their Christian position on some thorny contemporary issues, particularly those to which there is no simple answer. How far do our duties to others extend? What are the contours of the relationship between church and state or between religion and politics? What does religious liberty look like, and what are its limits? These are complicated matters with which Christians—and Protestants, in particular—have been wrestling for centuries. This is why the insights of past thinkers such as Martin Luther, John Calvin, Theodore Beza, or Roger Williams can be enormously helpful. To put it another way, as C. S. Lewis pointed out, "If you join at eleven o'clock a conversation which began at eight you will often not see the real bearing of what is said."[1]

Today, I fear not so much that we are unaware of tardily entering the conversation, but that we are so acculturated to ahistoricism that we do not know we are even *in* a long historical conversation. I noticed, for example, that when Australian Christians discussed the issues surrounding COVID-19 lockdowns and restrictions, many did not realise that Christians have been writing for centuries about the jurisdiction of secular authority and "to what extent it should be obeyed," to quote Martin Luther (whose treatise on "Temporal Authority" was written back in 1523).[2] Luther and many others before and after him have wrestled with the Bible and made enormous contributions to a topic of perennial concern to us.

As I stated earlier, some of the most animated and engaging discussions I have at university, and with young people in church settings, are about the idea of human rights. Yet few people know where human rights came from historically, nor are they aware that human rights emerged from the belief in the inherent, precious, and equal value of human life found in the Hebrew Bible. Moreover, they generally think of "rights" purely in political terms, often primarily as a means of advancing a political agenda, and not in terms of a deeper understanding of natural rights as basic to human flourishing. This latter conception is historical and far broader than merely political.

Though concepts of rights existed in classical Greek and Roman cultures, these rights were only ever conceived of as properly belonging to those fortunate enough to be citizens. There was nothing universal about them. But the early Christians insisted that *all* lives were precious; for example, they regularly rescued infants who were

---

1. C. S. Lewis, "Preface: From the First Edition," in *On the Incarnation: Translation*, ed. and trans. John Behr (Yonkers, NY: St. Vladimir's Seminary Press, 2011), 12.

2. Martin Luther, *Luther's Works, Vol. 45: The Christian in Society II*, ed. Jaroslav Jan Pelikan, Hilton C. Oswald, and Helmut T. Lehmann (Philadelphia: Fortress Press, 1999), 81.

routinely left to die through exposure and created the first hospitals. This belief in humanity's basic value slowly developed into the idea that even the vulnerable might possess rights. Consequently, the rich intellectual tradition of natural rights has a long history. Conceptions of natural rights flourished in medieval natural law, were refined in Reformation political theology, and were secularised very haphazardly in the eighteenth century. However, the idea that these rights exist because they are "endowed by their Creator" remained at the core of even the more secular articulations, such as the U.S. Declaration of Independence. Some appalling abuses have been committed in the name of Christianity, sadly, but it is also true that Christian belief in the inherent dignity and equal value of all human life enables us to speak out convincingly about human rights. Moreover, the biblical vision of humanity lay at the core of various historical movements to end slavery; for example, the British Empire was the first empire in history to abolish slavery. The abolitionist movement was led by evangelical Christians.

However, even though many people today strongly emphasise human rights, we know very little of this history. We could enrich and deepen our ability to think through these ideas by thoroughly teaching this history in our schools and universities and introducing students to the ideas and historical movements of our past. In short, the priestly work of tending and guarding the past enables us to understand our heritage and recognise Christianity as a historical force shaping the world. It also helps us understand how fundamental ideas like natural rights have developed and secularised over time.

The Western Christian Tradition and Cultural Dialogue

Cultural interchange is a feature of almost every culture and civilisation, but the Western Christian tradition has exhibited a distinctive orientation towards the intellectual sources of the past. For instance, the French historian Remi Brague has argued that the West was distinguished by its openness to other cultures—Greek, Latin, Hebrew, and Arabic—a feature he terms its "eccentricity." In fact, Europe finds its heritage in Athens and Jerusalem.[3] The intellectual renaissances that are at the core of European and Western ascendency, Brague argues, are not merely due to their careful negotiation with other cultures, but because Christians tried to preserve the original sources. This preservation made possible epochs of renewal and reformation inspired by conversations with ancient sources. Brague identifies this willingness to borrow from sources outside of itself as a peculiar inheritance from the culture of Rome.

I would clarify, however, that it is more historically accurate to understand the willingness to negotiate critically with other cultures as a distinctly Christian idea, rooted in theology. Unlike any other ancient religion, the followers of Jesus of Nazareth were not defined by any particular ethnicity or secular group. Christians were sent to live in the world but they did not belong to it, as John's gospel emphatically holds (John 15:19). The corporate Christian life was independent of the state.[4] From the earliest days of the church, Christians have been in conscious dialogue not only with other cultures but also with their own heritage. In part, this approach has enabled Christians to distil and define orthodox teaching. In fact, Tertullian (c. 155–c. 240) first used the symbolism that Brague and others would adopt so many centuries later. "What indeed has Athens to do with Jerusalem? What concord is there between the Academy and the Church?" he asked in *The Prescription against Heretics*, consciously defining the Christian intellectual tradition against the terrain of pagan philosophy.[5]

In the second century, Justin Martyr explored the way in which some elements of the *Logos*, the Word, were found in both Greek and Roman philosophy as well as Christian theology. As Alister McGrath

3. Remi Brague, *Eccentric Culture: A Theory of Western Civilization* (South Bend, IN: St. Augustine's Press, 2009).

4. See Sarah Irving-Stonebraker, "The Forgotten History of Religious Liberty: The Richard Johnson Lecture 2020," *Journal of Religious History* 45, no. 4 (2022): 644–58.

5. Tertullian, *The Prescription against Heretics*, in *Ante-Nicene Fathers, Volume 3: Latin Christianity: Its Founder, Tertullian*, ed. Alexander Roberts, James Donaldson, and A. Cleveland Coxe, trans. Peter Holmes (Buffalo, NY: Christian Literature Company, 1885), 246.

points out, Justin Martyr argued that God scattered the seeds of the Logos throughout human societies, suggesting that non-Christian intellectual traditions may contain ideas which point—however imperfectly—to Christ.[6] Justin explained, "For whatever either law-givers or philosophers uttered well, they elaborated by finding and contemplating some part of the Word."[7] Therefore, "Whatever things were rightly said among all men, are the property of us Christians."[8]

Drawing upon the Exodus narrative a few centuries later, Augustine gave further grounding to the idea that God's people have always carefully made use of aspects of pagan ideas and culture which might contain elements of God's truth. In his work *On Christian Doctrine*, written around AD 397, Augustine argues:

> For, as the Egyptians had not only idols [. . .], but also vessels and ornaments of gold and silver, and garments, which [Israel] when going out of Egypt appropriated to themselves, designing them for a better use [. . .] in the same way all branches of heathen learning have not only false and superstitious fancies [. . .]; but they contain also liberal instruction which is better adapted to the use of the truth, and some most excellent precepts of morality; and some truths in regard even to the worship of the One God are found among them. . . . These, therefore, the Christian, when he separates himself in spirit from the miserable fellowship of these men, ought to take away from them, and to devote to their proper use in preaching the gospel.[9]

Augustine shows that the Western Christian intellectual tradition can be in dialogue with other cultures and may appropriate and adapt

---

6. Alister McGrath, *The Christian Theology Reader*, 5th ed. (Hoboken, NJ: Wiley-Blackwell, 2017), 5.

7. Justin Martyr, *The Second Apology of Justin*, in *Ante-Nicene Fathers, Volume 1: The Apostolic Fathers with Justin Martyr and Irenaeus*, ed. Alexander Roberts, James Donaldson, and A. Cleveland Coxe (Buffalo, NY: Christian Literature Company, 1885), 191.

8. Justin Martyr, *The Second Apology of Justin*, 193.

9. St. Augustine, *On Christian Doctrine*, in *Nicene and Post-Nicene Father, First Series, Volume 2: St. Augustin's City of God and Christian Doctrine*, ed. Philip Schaff, trans. J. F. Shaw (Buffalo, NY: Christian Literature Company, 1887), 554.

ideas without jeopardising its doctrinal integrity. Such a dialogue is not only geographic, but also historical. For example, C. S. Lewis's book *The Discarded Image* is a wonderful description of the various ways in which medieval Christian thought incorporated classical elements. Moreover, dialogue with the original sources, and with the church fathers—Augustine in particular—was central to the Protestant Reformation.

Indeed, the Christian conversation has been so rich and influential through the centuries precisely because of its own historical awareness. A powerful illustration of this is Francis Bacon, whom we met in chapter 5. As I mentioned there, his work was formative in the foundations of what we now call modern science. He developed his methodological insights through critical negotiation with the intellectual tradition of scholasticism, which was based upon the work of Aristotle. Bacon argued that the study of the natural world was not merely a contemplative endeavour; rather, natural philosophy should improve human life. It ought to "work for the relief of mankind's estate," as he put it.[10]

Bacon also developed a new methodology that involved the direct observation of particulars in nature and then ascended to more general knowledge. This approach is how Bacon especially distinguished his methodology, the *New Organon*, from the Aristotelian "old" Organon.[11] Not only did this explorative foray require a thoroughgoing critique of scholasticism, but it compelled Bacon to engage with both classical antiquity and the Renaissance humanists. His theology framed this endeavour:

> For by the Fall man declined from the state of innocence and from
> his kingdom over the creatures. Both things can be repaired even in
> this life to some extent, the former by religion and faith, the latter
> by the arts and sciences. For the Curse did not make the creation an
> utter and irrevocable outlaw. In virtue of the sentence 'In the sweat

---

10. Francis Bacon, *The Advancement of Learning*, in *The Works of Francis Bacon*, vol. 3, ed. James Spedding, Robert Leslie Ellis, and Douglas Denon Heath (London: Longman, 1887), 294.

11. Francis Bacon, *Cogitata et Visa*, in *The Works of Francis Bacon*, vol. 3, ed. James Spedding, Robert Leslie Ellis, and Douglas Denon Heath (London: Longman, 1887), 612.

of thy face shalt thou eat bread,' man, by manifold labours (and not by disputations, certainly, or by useless magical ceremonies), compels the creation, in time and in part, to provide him with bread, that is to serve the purposes of human life.[12]

Bacon argues here that even though sin caused humanity's spiritual and moral brokenness as well as the loss of our command over nature, we ought to be able to work to repair the effects of sin in this life. Science, Bacon says, is key to this; it can help us improve human life.

Not only were Bacon's insights foundational for what eventually became modern science, but he was also a formative influence on Robert Boyle, whom I discussed in chapter 6. Bacon was certainly part of a fertile historical conversation. We would be much better equipped to deal with questions about the supposed inherent opposition between science and Christianity if we knew this history.

Great Books and Long Historical Conversations

Knowledge of our intellectual inheritance—this multifaceted historical conversation—holds much fruit for us. C. S. Lewis recognised this truth. Many evangelicals today love Lewis's *Mere Christianity*, the book that originated from his series of wartime radio lectures, and Lewis himself looked to the seventeenth-century Puritan Richard Baxter for the term that eventually became the title of that work. Lewis discussed what he meant by "mere Christianity" in the preface he wrote to an edition of Athanasius's *On the Incarnation*. He argued, "The only safety is to have a standard of plain, central Christianity ('mere Christianity' as Baxter called it) *which puts the controversies of the moment in their proper perspective. Such a standard can be acquired only from the old books.*"[13] Lewis was right, of course.

---

12. Francis Bacon, *New Organon*, ed. Lisa Jardine and Michael Silverthorne, Cambridge Texts in the History of Philosophy (Cambridge, UK: Cambridge University Press, 2000), 221.

13. C. S. Lewis, "Preface: From the First Edition," 12. Emphasis mine.

The old books, the past, and that great conversation of history hold enormous riches for us.

I was recently appointed associate professor in a Western Civilisation program at Australian Catholic University, part of which focuses on reading the "great books" from different disciplinary perspectives. One of the reasons I love the great books, as well as great thinkers, is that they can point us to the good, the true, and the beautiful. By inviting us into a richer world, they help shape our character. Many of us are able to recollect a scene from a great work of literature that had a formative influence upon us, which we will never forget. Perhaps, for example, you will feel a lump in your throat as you recall reading about that group of young pilgrims in *Little Women* who packed away their Christmas breakfast to give to their impoverished neighbours. A personal example is the way that my three children were inspired by *Anne of Green Gables* to name a pond in our neighbourhood "the Lake of Shining Waters." So heartily did they relish reading L. M. Montgomery's classic work that Anne's imagination helped shape theirs.

As this chapter demonstrates, the Christian tradition has always engaged in dialogue with other cultures while earnestly preserving its truth. Embracing this approach enables us to read the great books of world history (including those from outside of our own Christian tradition) with the intellectual resources to assess and learn from them and their historical context. We can also define our own positions on various questions by disagreeing with the ideas we encounter. Thomas Aquinas, for example, has been central to the development of ideas about rights and the will. Not all Christians today will agree with everything Aquinas writes. But this actually reinforces why we ought to read him. Let us have the robust intellectual resources and the proper attitude of humility to read not only the great thinkers of our own traditions but also more broadly, including authors outside of our own tradition and outside of the traditional canon. We should read authors as diverse as Aristotle and Aquinas, Cicero and Hume, Luther and Calvin, Dante and Dostoevsky, Nietzsche and Mary Wollstonecraft, Virgil and Locke, Confucius and Siddhartha,

Augustine and Chesterton, Flannery O'Connor and Marilynne Robinson, and Wendell Berry and John Finnis. Reading these works places us in a dialogue, enabling us to develop the doctrinal and intellectual rigour we need in order to resist the tides of culture that undermine the historic orthodox Christian tradition.

Wrestling with great thinkers also cultivates our minds and teaches us to engage them with patience and empathy as we read slowly and carefully. This attitude cultivates a particular sensibility in us: a humble orientation towards knowledge, learning, and the past that takes delight in learning about God's world. For instance, one of my husband's most formative moments in his spiritual life occurred when he read Martin Luther's *On the Bondage of the Will* during the summer of his sophomore year at his agricultural college in rural Georgia. The past holds such riches for us.

Frederick Douglass (1818–1895): The Prophetic Abolitionist

Most people have heard of the abolitionist, author, and statesman Frederick Douglass (c. 1818–1895) and many (at least in the United States) will have read his *Narrative of the Life of Frederick Douglass, an American Slave* (1845). Douglass is an example of a well-known historical figure whose story we ought to guard and preserve. But do we know Frederick Douglass as a Christian, and can we keep and preserve his story in a way that honours it as profoundly Christian?

More broadly, we often do not recognise the degree to which the abolition of slavery is a Christian story. Several years ago, when I taught an undergraduate course which dealt with the abolition of slavery, I was surprised that my undergraduate students did not know that Christian ideas were at the core of the abolitionist movement in the British Empire. Most of them also were unaware of the central role those Christian ideas played in the abolitionist movement in the United States during the antebellum and Civil War periods. They did, however, know about how people attempted to justify slavery using

Frederick Douglass (1818–1895)

the Bible and assumed that Christianity has only been a force of oppression and domination. Accordingly, they had a very one-sided understanding of this history, which was in reality far more complex. This is one reason why Douglass's story serves as a good illustration of the kind of history we need to guard and pass down.

A slave from birth, Douglass was born on a plantation in Maryland and could only guess at his precise age. Nor did he truly know his mother, from whom he was separated as an infant and who lived on a plantation many miles away. Initially raised by his maternal grandparents, young Frederick was eventually taken away from them. He was first moved to the Wye House Plantation in Maryland when he was about six and subsequently to Baltimore, where he became the slave of Hugh and Sophia Auld. Sophia at first taught Frederick the rudiments of literacy, but then rather abruptly ceased helping him. Frederick then became an autodidact, desperate to educate himself because he believed this would be the path to freedom. At some point during his childhood, Frederick Douglass became a Christian, and he later recounted how he found hope and comfort in God as a "father and protector."[14]

Douglass spent his adolescence and early adulthood hired out by Auld to other masters. After a failed attempt to flee, he successfully escaped to New York and then settled with his wife Anna in Massachusetts. Douglass joined the African Methodist Episcopal Zion Church, was licensed as a preacher in 1839, and became active in the abolitionist

---

14. Frederick Douglass, *My Bondage and My Freedom* (New York: Miller, Orton, and Mulligan, 1855), 166.

cause. He delivered speeches along the Underground Railroad and at antislavery conventions as well as the American Anti-Slavery Society. In 1845, Douglass journeyed to England and then to Ireland and Scotland lecturing for the abolitionist cause and raising funds. During this time he met the famous abolitionist and minister Thomas Clarkson, who had been a leading campaigner against the British Empire's slave trade. Douglass also met the Irish nationalist leader Daniel O'Connell.

When Douglass returned to the USA in 1847, he had collected enough funds from his tour of the United Kingdom to begin publishing the abolitionist newspaper *The North Star*. In addition to his newspaper, he spoke frequently and published prolifically. His *Narrative of the Life of Frederick Douglass, an American Slave* was published in 1845, *My Bondage and My Freedom* in 1855, and the *Life and Times of Frederick Douglass* in 1881. Douglass also brought out a collection of his addresses and speeches.[15]

Of particular interest to us is Douglass's speech "What to a Slave Is the Fourth of July? An Address," his 1852 keynote address at an Independence Day celebration in Corinthian Hall, Rochester, New York. There, Douglass spoke with a prophetic voice decrying the treatment of slaves. This speech is remarkable not only for its moving oratory, but also because of how Douglass engages with the past and addresses historic and contemporary aspects of sin.

Douglass questioned if the Fourth of July, established and celebrated as the beginning of the nation's history, had meaning and significance for a slave. In order to make sense of the history of enslavement, he turned to the story of Israel's history in the Old Testament. He quotes Psalm 137, in which Israel sits by the waters of Babylon and weeps when she remembers Zion. Indeed, the psalmist and Douglass ask very similar questions: "How can we sing the Lord's song in a strange land? If I forget thee, O Jerusalem, let my right hand forget her cunning. If I do not remember thee, let my tongue cleave to the roof of my mouth."[16] Douglass searingly asserts:

---

15. The Library of America has two readable and affordable volumes dedicated to Douglass: one covers his autobiographies and the other contains his speeches and additional writings.

16. Frederick Douglass, "What to the Slave Is the Fourth of July? An Address," in

What, to the American slave, is your 4th of July? I answer: a day
that reveals to him, more than all other days in the year, the gross
injustice and cruelty to which he is the constant victim. To him,
your celebration is a sham; your boasted liberty, an unholy license;
your national greatness, swelling vanity; your sounds of rejoicing
are empty and heartless; your denunciation of tyrants, brass fronted
impudence; your shouts of liberty and equality, hollow mockery;
your prayers and hymns, your sermons and thanksgivings, with all
your religious parade, and solemnity, are, to him, mere bombast,
fraud, deception, impiety, and hypocrisy—a thin veil to cover up
crimes which would disgrace a nation of savages.[17]

Douglass also drew upon the idea of the *imago Dei* from Genesis to
insist upon the humanity and dignity of the slave as a person, created
in God's image. He paraphrased Genesis 1:27 to exclaim, "When the
dogs in your streets, when the fowls of the air, when the cattle on
your hills, when the fish of the sea, and the reptiles that crawl, shall
be unable to distinguish the slave from a brute, *then* will I argue with
you that the slave is a man!"[18]

Yet despite his scathing admonition of America for its sin in practicing the profound evil of slavery, Douglass did not simply dismiss
America entirely, as if there were no hope for redemption. Far from it:

Allow me to say, in conclusion, notwithstanding the dark picture I
have this day presented of the state of the nation, I do not despair of
this country. There are forces in operation, which must inevitably
work the downfall of slavery. "*The arm of the Lord is not shortened*,"
and the doom of slavery is certain.[19]

Frederick Douglass: Speeches and Writings, ed. David W. Blight (New York: Library of America, 2022), 175.

17. Douglass, "What to the Slave Is the Fourth of July?," 178.
18. Douglass, "What to the Slave Is the Fourth of July?," 176. Emphasis original.
19. Douglass, "What to the Slave Is the Fourth of July?," 190. Emphasis original.

Douglass presents a model of how to engage with the sin of the past, which is particularly pertinent to our contemporary time in which the phenomenon of cancel culture surrounds us. Significantly, Douglass's theology undergirds his ability to call out sin and demand justice in line with biblical principles; yet he refrains from dismissing the sinner (America) altogether. First, since sin is a universal condition affecting all humanity, this means that judgement and righteous anger belong to God and are pronounced by God. A democratic humility underlies this doctrine. Douglass could speak prophetically and call upon God's judgement rather than becoming the source of moral authority himself:

> Standing with God and the crushed and bleeding slave on this occasion, I will, in the name of humanity which is outraged, in the name of liberty which is fettered, in the name of the constitution and the Bible, which are disregarded and trampled upon, dare to call in question and to denounce, with all the emphasis I can command, everything that serves to perpetuate slavery—the great sin and shame of America![20]

Second, because Douglass understood the evil of slavery theologically as *sin*, there is the possibility—the hope—of redemption. Sin does not dictate the end of the story. Douglass does not condemn America; rather, he condemns its sin. Indeed, Douglass holds profound eschatological hope: "I do not despair of this country."[21] This trust in redemption enables Douglass to resist condemning and dismissing the past and the present: "The fiat of the Almighty, '*Let there be Light*,' has not yet spent its force. No abuse, no outrage whether in taste, sport or avarice, can now hide itself from the all-pervading light."[22] In short, Douglass was able to use the Bible to condemn sin, yet maintain hope for his nation.

---

20. Douglass, "What to the Slave Is the Fourth of July?," 175.
21. Douglass, "What to the Slave Is the Fourth of July?," 190.
22. Douglass, "What to the Slave Is the Fourth of July?," 191. Emphasis original.

When we keep and guard stories like Douglass's, we are resisting the ahistorical tendency to reduce the past to ideology. In our Ahistoric Age, many discussions are impoverished by an inability to make sense of evil, particularly in the past. Ironically, the processes of secularisation have created a public discourse that still retains a veneer of Christian ideas of good and evil—indeed, there are abundant claims to righteousness in the public square—yet these concepts are detached from their theological underpinnings. The idea of evil is detached from the biblical insistence that sin affects every one of us and that only God is righteous; hope for justice and the idea of the perfectibility of society (and man) are detached from eschatology. Consequently, contemporary culture is wildly disoriented, swinging between self-righteous insistence on perfectibility *now* on the one hand and utter despair on the other. But, for Douglass, sin is a universal condition, so he resists falling into the trap of insisting on his own self-righteousness and condemning the sinner (the American nation) altogether. Douglass also resists despair because the sin of slavery is not the end of the story. Douglass has hope in a God who has become flesh and dwelled with us to redeem humanity, trusting that God may also act to redeem the nation from this sin.

PART III

How History Can Help Us

NINE

Stewarding Our Time

Every year, after our family celebrates Thanksgiving and the Feast of Christ the King the following Sunday, we change the cloths on our white bookshelves around the fireplace to a beautiful royal blue with the Luther Rose patterned on them. Then we set out three purple candles and one pink candle, placing one additional white candle in the centre of our mantle. On the evening of the first Sunday of Advent, we light the first of the purple candles (our daughters, Madeleine and Charlotte, usually vie for the privilege of lighting the candle). Before evening prayer and our singing of "O Come, O Come, Emmanuel," we speak with our children about what the season of Advent means. Historically, Advent is a season of preparation—with its own distinctive spiritual practices—that prepares us for the great feast of Christmas. In Advent we remember the first advent (or "coming") of Christ into the world and the anticipation of Israel as it awaited the Messiah. But Advent also looks towards the advent yet to come, when Jesus will return and judge the living and the dead.

It may seem quaint or old-fashioned to talk about Advent. But the secular world we live in does not treat Christmas as merely a day; it treats it as a *season*. Indeed, Christmas is known as "the silly season" or "the holiday season." Holiday advent calendars (in Australia, these usually have chocolates behind each door), photos with Santa, Christmas shopping, Christmas lights, Christmas-themed parties, decorations, and the special food and drink all mark the lead up to Christmas as a distinctive period of time. I am not saying that these rituals and festivities are bad things, or that Christians ought not practice them.

Far from it! Rather, the way that secular culture treats Christmas as a *season* actually points to a profound truth: marking time with seasons is how human beings live, whether we do it in a Christian way or not. Indeed, the secular world will happily shape our time for us, discipling our hearts around its idols.[1] Even though we struggle so much against the pervasive hold of consumerism on our lives in this present age, we can learn much from the historic practices which help us shape our time around the Christian story.

In this chapter, we explore the first way history can help us today, namely, by enabling us to steward our time. The Ahistoric Age exerts a powerful influence over the way we use time; consequently, we often struggle to use our time well. But if we do the priestly work of tending and keeping the past, history can help us. Christians in the past, particularly before the advent of modernity, inhabited time very differently to how we do today, mainly because they saw themselves as a historic people continuing in the practices and beliefs that had been developed and passed down over the centuries. To illustrate this, let us delve into the diary of an eighteenth-century physician in rural England.

Claver Morris (1659–1727): A Country Physician and His Prayers

In the early eighteenth century, Claver Morris, a physician in Somerset, England, kept a diary. Its pages give us a fascinating glimpse into daily life in rural England at that time, recounting not only Morris's family life, the patients he treated, and the remedies he prescribed, but also his spiritual life. In many ways Morris was an ordinary man with a deep

---

1. For a detailed scholarly exploration of cultural liturgies, see James K. A. Smith, *Desiring the Kingdom: Worship, Worldview, and Cultural Formation* (Grand Rapids: Baker Academic, 2009); James K. A. Smith, *Imagining the Kingdom: How Worship Works* (Grand Rapids: Baker Academic, 2013); James K. A. Smith, *Awaiting the King: Reforming Public Theology* (Grand Rapids: Baker Academic, 2017); and James K. A. Smith, *You Are What You Love: The Spiritual Power of Habit* (Grand Rapids: Brazos, 2021).

faith. He attended Oxford University and practiced medicine in the town of Salisbury before moving to Wells, a village in Somerset. On one particular day in 1709, Morris relished describing how he managed to get into a friendly argument with a Catholic acquaintance on the topic of "our Separation from the Church of Rome . . . We did not shut up the dispute til half an hour after 2 a clock in the morning, & then we all went to bed."[2]

Aside from Morris's amusing descriptions of his theological arguments until the early hours of the morning, what may be most striking to contemporary readers is the extent to which Morris intentionally structured his time around centuries-old practices of regular worship, prayer, and devotion, both personal and communal. Morris would often discuss in his diary the sermons he had heard at church and sometimes referred to the events of his day in terms of their occurrence before or after Morning or Evening Prayer. We can infer from this activity, along with what we know about the practices of Anglicanism during this time period, that on most days (if not every day) Morris prayed Morning and Evening Prayer from the *Book of Common Prayer*, either at home or at his local church where the minister or a layperson led the prayer.

Developed by Archbishop Thomas Cranmer during the English Reformation, the *Book of Common Prayer* was the Church of England's (that is, the Anglican Church's) standard for liturgy, worship, and devotion. It sought to structure church services, articulate the Reformed theology of the Church of England, and form the people of England with the Protestant faith through practices of daily morning and evening prayer, Scripture reading, psalms, and the Lord's Supper, drawing upon historical tradition. For this reason, the *Book of Common Prayer* set out a lectionary, that is, a program for daily reading of the Old and New Testaments and Psalms for both personal use and in church services. It also listed which epistles and gospels were to be read on holy days (holidays) and Sundays. Finally, it contained a complete

---

2. Claver Morris, *Diary of a West Country Physician*, ed. Edmund Hobhouse (Rochester, UK: Stanhope Press, 1934), December 23, 1709, 59.

psalter, a catechism, and the Thirty-Nine Articles of Religion, which articulated the doctrine and practices of the Church of England.

It is clear from historians' research that the *Book of Common Prayer* was not just the liturgical text used in church services; it was the guide to an entire way of life.[3] And so it was for Claver Morris, who often described attending Morning and Evening Prayer services at a local church during the week and then returning and sharing a meal with family and friends, having fellowship, and sometimes engaging in devotional singing and playing music together. On an ordinary day in early December 1719, for example, he recorded drinking coffee at a friend's house after attending morning services at church.[4] When his travels as a physician led him to visit other villages and towns, Morris would often attend prayer in the local churches there. He was taking part in what was called the "Daily Office," a series of prayer liturgies that marked two regular moments of prayer throughout the day, once in the morning and again in the evening. This, in turn, was a deliberate echo of the ways in which early Christians attempted to use the worship of God to structure their time.

The 1662 *Book of Common Prayer* stipulated that Morning and Evening Prayer were to be said by the minister or a lay leader every day, ideally in the parish church so others could attend. It added that the minister "shall cause a bell to be tolled thereunto a convenient time before he begin, that the people may come to hear God's word, and to pray with him."[5] Accordingly, the sound of church bells ringing out in the early morning and in the evening punctuated daily life, calling the community to gather together to pray. The Prayer Book also helped form local communities in other ways. For instance, the rubrics of the 1662 *Book of Common Prayer* Holy Communion service stipulated that bread for the Lord's Supper ought to be the "best and

---

3. See, for example, Judith Maltby, *Prayer Book and People in Elizabethan and Early Stuart England* (Cambridge, UK: Cambridge University Press, 2009).

4. Morris, *Diary of a West Country Physician*, December 11, 1719, 74.

5. *Book of Common Prayer*, 1662, in *The Book of Common Prayer: The Texts of 1549, 1559, and 1662*, ed. Brian Cummings (Oxford: Oxford University Press, 2011), 214.

purest wheat bread that conveniently may be gotten."[6] Keeping with one of the early church's practices of feeding the poor, unconsecrated bread that the local church had was often given to the poor after Prayer Book services.[7]

Occasionally, such as in November 1721, Claver Morris and his family would attend the local church, celebrate the Lord's Supper, and then hear somebody share a "Testimonial."[8] An entry he made for Christmas Day provides an illustration of the way in which Prayer Book services, fellowship, music, and hospitality involving a good meal were woven together:

> I receiv'd the Sacrament of the Eucharist. . . . We perform'd Mr. Brodrip's Christmass Hymn. We all went to Church, & thence came back to our Musick again. Dr. Layng, Mr. Wm Baron, Mr. Keen, & Mr. Cupper, Mr. George Mattocks, & Mrs. Lemmon, & abundance of Gentlewomen also. . . . Those of the Performers who stay'd 'till about 8, Supp'd, & afterwards took a Glass of excellent October 'till about 11.[9]

Since we live in an Ahistoric Age, many of us do not know—and might even be surprised to read—that Protestants have a long history of structuring their days using historical liturgical books like the *Book of Common Prayer*. The hyperindividualism of today's culture generally makes us instinctively sceptical of the idea that there should be set times to pray or forms of prayers that might be helpful to us.[10] Yet our forebears thought otherwise.

---

6. *Book of Common Prayer*, 406, and Jeremy Gregory, "'For All Sorts and Conditions of Men': The Social Life of the *Book of Common Prayer* during the Long Eighteenth Century: Or, Bringing the History of Religion and Social History Together," *Social History*, 34, no. 1 (Feb 2009): 53, citing E. P. Thompson, "The Moral Economy of the English Crowd in the Eighteenth Century," *Past and Present* (1971): 80–83.

7. Gregory, "For All Sorts and Conditions of Men," 53.

8. Morris, *Diary of a West Country Physician*, November 29, 1721, 101–2.

9. Morris, *Diary of a West Country Physician*, December 25, 1720, 84.

10. There is a revival of interest in liturgy in some parts of the evangelical church. For an excellent exploration of how we can use liturgy today, see Tish Harrison Warren, *Prayer in the Night: For Those Who Work or Watch or Weep* (Downers Grove: InterVarsity Press: 2021);

Regular Hours of Prayer through the Day

In 1729 the Anglican minister and theologian William Law penned a book exhorting his fellow Christians to live a holy life. Law was one of the formative thinkers for the origins of evangelicalism; his book *A Serious Call to a Devout and Holy Life* was highly influential on many evangelicals, including William Wilberforce. Law urged Christians to engage in the habit of disciplined prayer and psalm singing every three hours.[11] He believed that most Christians needed "to use forms of prayer at all the regular times of prayer."[12] Law did not see set prayers as empty; rather, they served to guide one's heart, helped people articulate personal prayers, and created a posture of repentance, thankfulness, and devotion. He did explain that "if you are such a proficient in the spirit of devotion that your heart is always ready to pray in its own language, in this case I press no necessity of borrowed forms." Nonetheless, he encouraged those who found such "borrowed forms" helpful to use them.[13]

What Law meant by "regular times of prayer" was based upon the historic practice of the early church of praying at intervals of several hours throughout the day. In the Middle Ages, "books of hours" were devotional books of prayers, hymns, and psalms developed to enable laypeople to pray a version of the canonical hours of the clergy. The historian Eamon Duffy has shown that books of hours were intensely personal objects, often carried around in pockets or up shirtsleeves, and their use in the late Middle Ages testified to a shift into a more personalised form of devotion.[14] Many families also often prayed the

---

Winfield Bevins, *Ever Ancient Ever New: The Allure of Liturgy for a New Generation* (Grand Rapids: Zondervan: 2019); and Justin Whitmel Earley, *Habits of the Household: Practicing the Story of God in Everyday Family Rhythms* (Grand Rapids: Zondervan, 2023).

11. William Law, *A Serious Call to a Devout and Holy Life; The Spirit of Love*, The Classics of Western Spirituality, ed. Paul G. Stanwood and Richard J. Payne (New York; Mahwah, NJ: Paulist Press, 1978), chapters 14–23.

12. Law, *A Serious Call to a Devout and Holy Life*, 147.

13. Law, *A Serious Call to a Devout and Holy Life*, 147.

14. Eamon Duffy, *Marking the Hours: English People and Their Prayers, 1240–1570* (New Haven: Yale University Press, 2011), 55.

divine hours. For example, the
sixteenth-century German-Swiss
painter Hans Holbein depicted the
Lord High Chancellor of England
Thomas More (1478–1535) and his
entire family sitting, each praying
from their own book. The family
members are holding uniform cop-
ies of a printed book of hours.

With the advent of the
Reformation, editions of the *Book
of Common Prayer* superseded the
book of hours in England. We
know something of how the *Book*

John Evelyn (1620–1706)

of Common Prayer was used from various journals, correspondence,
and diaries of the period; we have already seen how Claver Morris
did so. John Evelyn, an author and leading figure in English intellectual life in the seventeenth century, also recorded in his diary that
he would attend Morning and Evening Prayer on Sundays (often
twice) as well as Wednesdays and Fridays.[15] Additionally, we can
catch a glimpse of services in ordinary parishes. In Leeds parish
church in 1743, for example, Morning Prayer occurred at 11 a.m. and
Evening Prayer at both 4 p.m. and 7 p.m.[16] Not only was the *Book of
Common Prayer* used by elites, but members of all classes evidently
embraced it, particularly in the eighteenth century when laypeople
began forming voluntary associations and societies. In 1612, Thomas
Comber, the bishop of Durham, wrote his *Companion to the Temple
and Closet: in a Help to Public and Private Devotion, in an Essay upon
the Daily Offices of the Church*, in which he explained the *Book of
Common Prayer*'s Daily Office. In short, the *Book of Common Prayer*
was for everyone.

As William Law, Claver Morris, and John Evelyn knew, there is

---

15. John Evelyn, *Diary*, 6 vols., ed. E. S. Beer (Oxford: Clarendon, 1955).
16. W. M. Jacob, *Lay People and Religion in the Early Eighteenth Century* (Cambridge,
UK: Cambridge University Press, 1996), 61.

no legalistic requirement to pray every several hours. Yet it is curious that the practice of regular, disciplined intervals of prayer throughout the day as a means of redeeming our time has slowly been replaced by the standard of a once-a-day "quiet time" of around twenty minutes or maybe a short prayer before meals or before bed. We need to reflect on why we have so lowered our expectations for our prayer life. I suspect this phenomenon is part of a larger problem.

Our Problem with Time

A Barna report entitled *The Bible in America: The Changing Landscape of Bible Perceptions and Engagement* revealed the findings of an extensive study over six years, conducted in partnership with the American Bible Society. The study found that "among Millennials who reported a decrease in Bible engagement, the main culprit is simply lack of time." Thirty-nine percent of millennial Christians report that the main reason they have not read the Bible as much is because they are too busy with life's responsibilities.[17] One only needs to see the wealth of books and articles on time management written from a Christian perspective to see that the problem with time affects more than just millennials.[18]

We saw in previous chapters that the Ahistoric Age shapes our culture's underlying attitudes to time. This has two major ramifications for how we treat time on a day-to-day basis in our lives. First, the Ahistoric Age's obsession with autonomy encourages us to feel completely independent from the past. Generally speaking, people in

---

17. *The Bible in America: The Changing Landscape of Bible Perceptions and Engagement* (Barna, 2016), 107.

18. See for example, David Mathis, "Four Lessons in Fruitful Time-Management," Desiring God, July 23, 2014, https://www.desiringgod.org/articles/four-lessons-in-fruitful-time -management/; Jen Pollock Michel, "There's No Such Thing as Time Management," *Christianity Today*, December 29, 2021, https://www.christianitytoday.com/ct/2021/december-web -only/michel-new-year-productivity-time-management.html/; and Jen Pollock Michel, "What Lent Teaches Me about the Vices of Time," *Christianity Today*, March 29, 2022, https://www .christianitytoday.com/ct/2022/march-web-only/michel-lent-teaches-me-vices-of-time.html/.

the West today do not think of themselves as being formed by history; life is about going on one's own individual journey. Consequently, we tend to view time as an avenue for self-realisation and self-expression. This is why a couple of the dominant ways people spend their leisure time are in exercises of self-discovery—witness the growing trend of the gap year phenomenon—or the midlife adventure to "find" oneself.[19]

Second, because the Ahistoric Age holds that there is no sacred story giving ultimate purpose to time, time consequently has no greater significance than a resource to be juggled between the various worldly demands of life. Time becomes a kind of highly prized resource to be accumulated, spent, saved, and managed according to our own needs and preferences, often to palliate the anxieties and stresses of our lives. The sheer volume of "time management" books, social science research studies, articles, and web applications devoted to "life hacks" and "efficiency" testifies to this.[20]

Many of us will undoubtedly be familiar with this tendency to treat leisure time as if it has no greater purpose than as a resource to improve our well-being—a form of therapy and comfort. We see this in the tendency to escape by "zoning out" or "switching off" and passively consuming entertainment; for example, by mindlessly scrolling newsfeeds, gaming, or binge-watching Netflix. This therapeutic emphasis on leisure is markedly different from the idea that we are seeking to enter the true rest offered to us by Christ.[21]

---

19. On the rising trend of gap years, which older people now undertake later in life, see Julia Buckley, "The Rise of the Grown-Up Gap Year," *National Geographic*, September 30, 2019, https:// www .nationalgeographic.co.uk/travel/2019/09/rise-grown-gap-year/, and Philippa Fogarty, "The Baby Boomers Taking a 'Golden' Gap Year," BBC, November 7, 2018, https://www.bbc.com/worklife/article/20181107-the-baby-boomers-taking-a-golden-gap-year/.

20. See, for example, Erich C. Dierdorff, "Time Management Is about More Than Life Hacks," *Harvard Business Review*, January 29, 2020, https://hbr.org/2020/01/time -management-is-about-more-than-life-hacks/, and Brad Aeon and Herman Aguinis, "It's About Time: New Perspectives and Insights on Time Management," *Academy of Management Perspectives* 31, no. 4 (2017), https://journals.aom.org/doi/abs/10.5465/amp.2016.0166/. Consider also that "time management" is a category of books on Amazon.com and other major retailers.

21. On how to understand the Christian sabbath now, see D. A. Carson, ed., *From Sabbath to Lord's Day: A Biblical, Historical, and Theological Investigation* (Eugene, OR: Wipf

What structures the time in our daily lives? Do we effectively, if unwittingly, treat time as a mere resource to be managed according to our own needs and preferences? The ahistoric attitude to time is a far cry from Scripture, which holds that our time does not belong to ourselves. Rather, time is a gift to be stewarded—tended and kept—for God's glory. So, can we learn something from our history that might help us better tend and keep our time?

The Rhythms and Seasons of Life as God's People

About five years ago, my husband John and I decided that we needed to be more intentional about how our family used our time, particularly for prayer and Bible reading. Our oldest daughter, Mattie, was approaching the age where she could read the Bible. We were also struck by how our days, weeks, and months seemed largely to be dictated by the common rhythms of our broader non-Christian culture, albeit with all our Christian activities inserted. Church services and activities, youth groups, small groups, prayer, and our own personal Bible reading were all interpolated into our schedules rather than forming the primary ordering principle of our time. We wondered if we could think about and inhabit our time differently. Could we invert this situation and structure our time around the primary purpose of serving and worshipping God? What if we drew upon some of the ways Christians had ordered their time in the past to tend and keep our own time? John, who has always loved the *Book of Common Prayer*, suggested that we embrace the church calendar and the Daily Office.[22]

& Stock, 1999), as well as Walter Brueggemann, *Sabbath as Resistance: Saying No to the Culture of Now* (Louisville: Westminster John Knox, 2017).

    22. Historically, different denominations have developed their own names for these rhythms. For example, the Catholic tradition calls these "divine hours" or "divine liturgies." For Anglicanism, the Daily Office and the *Book of Common Prayer* articulate these rhythms. There is no necessity to follow the Anglican tradition; however, I would suggest, following J. I. Packer, that the *Book of Common Prayer* is one of the richest and most accessible resources for Bible-believing Christians. See J. I. Packer, "Why I Am an Anglican," recorded lecture

What we did was far from perfect. Our practice has evolved and was not implemented without difficulty, but it has dramatically reoriented our time. Broadly speaking, we decided to use the historic church practices of tending and guarding our time: first, a *daily* rhythm of prayer, Bible reading, and worship; second, a *weekly* rhythm of gathering, working, resting, serving, and worshipping; and, third, a longer rhythm that forms our *years* into liturgical seasons around the biblical story of Jesus's birth, death, and resurrection.

The Daily Office

We have found the liturgies of Morning and Evening Prayer valuable in helping us tend and keep our time on a daily basis. Each of these prayer liturgies involves reading from the book of Psalms as well as both an Old and a New Testament chapter. The regularity and quantity of Bible reading means that over time you read every chapter of the Bible. Some people choose to follow set readings for the day, but we chose simply to begin our Old Testament reading with Genesis, our New Testament reading with Matthew, and our Psalms reading with Psalm 1, cycling through accordingly. Our children inevitably have questions about the Bible chapters, so we talk about these. More than once we have remarked to friends how relieving it is that this manner of reading ensures opportunities to hear our children's questions. We can talk to them about every thorny verse, as well as about the verses we cherish. We often kneel in prayer, we stand to profess our faith and say the Apostles' Creed, and we take turns in the Bible readings. This is a quiet, calm time with no technological distractions where we are immersed in the Scriptures and in prayer.

It is worth restating that we certainly do not do our devotional exercises perfectly.[23] On school mornings, we sometimes do Morning Prayer with a psalm and omit either the Old or New Testament

---

to Regent College, November 2, 2006, https://www.regentaudio.com/collections/j-i-packer /products/why-i-am-an-anglican/.

23. I also do not want to imply that Claver Morris and his seventeenth- and eighteenth-century friends got everything right when they turned to the Daily Office to structure their

readings—or, occasionally, both. John often prays Compline (that is, the Night Prayer) and sings hymns with the children when they are in bed, and sometimes Compline takes the place of Evening Prayer. Nonetheless, we have found that the Daily Office gives an order and a rhythm to our day that is markedly different from the way our culture would have us spend our time. If our neighbours were to glimpse through our library window and see us standing together reciting the Apostles' Creed, kneeling together in prayer, or sitting and reading the Bible every morning, they would undoubtedly think the whole thing bizarre. After all, this is not how most people in our culture structure their day.

Practicing the Daily Office also brings a sense of stability that comes from God. Gathering for Morning and Evening Prayer when we are lighthearted and when we are suffering helps us live out the reality that our help comes from the Lord, who is unchanging and eternal. The peace we have in God is independent of these circumstances. Ordering our lives around God's story in this fashion gives us—and our children—the knowledge that being a Christian is not just about abstract belief. Rather, it is about a way of life that frames our time and habits and compels us to live differently.

In the midst of a society that turns us inwards to discover ourselves and uses digital media to atomise us, we found that the practices of the Daily Office and the *Book of Common Prayer* took us *out* of ourselves. One striking aspect about our decision to embrace something of these historic practices for keeping time was that we lived as if we were adopted into a community which had vertical and horizontal dimensions. One day I showed our children Hans Holbein's sketch of Thomas More and his family gathering to pray together. "It's like we're part of their family!" exclaimed Charlotte, our youngest daughter. As we offer prayers that have been prayed by hundreds of generations of Christians before us, we join God's community of saints and a story that is far larger than ourselves.

---

days. Historically, not attending daily prayer was known to be a problem in eighteenth-century England.

Sketch of Thomas More and his family by
Hans Holbein the Younger, ca. 1527.

Weekly Rhythms

We also use weekly rhythms of meeting together when we meet in our small group during the week, worship at church on Sunday, and share Sunday lunch and hospitality. We found weekly rhythms important because they brought us into God's family to serve in routine ways. For a few years, we have hosted one of these small groups in our home. One evening a week, our group meets at our house to share a meal, care for one another, read the Bible, and pray together. The evening begins with breaking bread in the form of a "potluck" dinner, to use my husband's terminology. For my non-American readers, a potluck dinner involves everyone bringing a plate of food to share—so it is "potluck" what you get. We have various allergies and dietary restrictions in our group (gluten, dairy, tomato, nightshade, and cumin!), but we work around these. In fact, our group has a running joke that we have either "Stonebraker chicken" or "Stonebraker beef" every Thursday for dinner, because these are the dishes everyone can eat!

Our small group is a partial but beautiful picture of God's people, who come from all ages and multiple ethnic backgrounds. The adults in our group range in age from eighteen to seventy and the children from newborn to eleven. Our places of origin in the past year have been Australia, the USA, Tonga, Samoa, and West Africa. There are single people and married people, grandparents, and university students. In contemporary society we would not move in the same circles, let alone be spending Thursday evenings and Sundays sharing meals together, praying and reading the Bible together, supporting one another, and inviting others to join us. Our fellowship in Jesus Christ unites us. The New Testament calls us "brothers and sisters" because we are family.

Because of this, we share the joys of new babies and the suffering of illness and death, as well as the ordinary aspects of daily life. We exhort each other not merely through conversation and encouragement, but in the act of meeting together and intentionally encouraging each other to live as God intends us to live. How are we doing in our marriages? How are we doing living as a single man or woman who follows Jesus? How can we be helping each other to serve our neighbours and God's people? These are personal issues—intimate, even—and it is not always easy to talk about them in a group. It takes a good degree of trust, time, and commitment to develop the deep fellowship and friendships in which we can have these kinds of conversations.

After our Sunday morning church service, we often have a potluck lunch at our home. These lunches are an opportunity for our small group to eat together again, but this is also frequently an open invitation. We began hosting these lunches every Sunday a couple of years ago during a season of suffering for our church, as our minister, Greg, was dying of brain cancer. Meeting multiple times a week gave us another opportunity to "bear each other's burdens," as Jesus put it, to care for one another, and to live through suffering together. At 3 p.m. after lunch, those who want to can join us for Evening Prayer from the 2019 Anglican *Book of Common Prayer*. This gathering has become an invaluable way of tending and keeping our time.

The Sunday lunches and prayer after church have been one way our community has tried to live into our story as God's people, who are set apart from the rest of the world yet *always welcome in the outsider*.

We certainly do not do this perfectly by any means, and there is much more we could be doing. There have been seasons when we do the Sunday lunches every week and seasons when we have done them monthly with weekly hospitality in smaller groups of just one or two other families. Nonetheless, this rhythm is a vignette of some of the ways we are trying to live our historical story.

The story of Ruth, the Moabite woman who chose to follow her Hebrew mother-in-law Naomi back to Israel, is a beautiful example of the openness of God. Ruth's story is about a stranger welcomed into God's family. And her story, in turn, points to the larger biblical story showing that, since the fall, we humans at one time or another are *all* strangers from God. Nevertheless, we have a God who came after us and invites us to be part of his people. One important thing to remember: we are not doing all this because we think we are earning either God's favour or a place in heaven. No amount of hospitality or good works will do that. Only the life, death, and resurrection of Jesus Christ enables us to be right with God and be adopted into his family. The actual point is the opposite: we live so differently now *because* we have been saved—into a family, a people with a history.

Our small group works together to make tending and keeping our time through hospitality possible on Sunday. Since everyone brings a plate of food, we are sharing in the meal preparation. Together we talk to any newcomers, and we work together to clean up afterwards. It feels wonderful to walk into my pantry and find a bag of walnuts Anne has left there for next time, feta cheese in the fridge, and boxes of paper plates from Kim and Rob. Leftovers are sent home with whoever needs them. I'll look around at the end of the day and see Adam stacking our dishwasher in his characteristically meticulous fashion, Steve taking out the garbage, Rob wiping down the benches, and Cate packing away the food.

Something looks so beautiful here: a community of God's people living into their profoundly countercultural historical story—of living time differently. In the eyes of our secular society, such a habitual sharing of our time, our meals, our homes, and our lives in a community that crosses ages and ethnic backgrounds makes no sense. It defies what our secular culture believes about the nature of time, private property, privacy, leisure, and friendship. In contemporary society, it is virtually unheard of to invite people, especially people you only recently met at church, into your home to share a meal together, pray with them, and then invite them back the following week. But God has made us into a new people. We were once strangers and enemies of God, but through Christ God forgave us and welcomed us into fellowship with himself and his people.

Of course, one does not need a historical rhythm to practice hospitality regularly. There are people who do this wonderfully without any such set pattern. However, it is very helpful to have a way of incorporating hospitality as part of the weekly rhythms of Christian life. In my family's experience, as noble as our intentions were, we were able to put those desires into regular practice only by drawing upon the old historical tradition of the weekly ordering of time. We would practice hospitality far less without the weekly rhythm.

One Sunday, as I sat reflecting on our meal and prayer together, I glanced around the table and thought of the countless other Christians throughout the ages and even now across the world who have gathered together over meals, had fellowship, and prayed for each other. These Christian practices that tend and keep time give us a glimpse of that ultimate banquet which will take place when God remakes the heaven and the earth. At this festal table, all God's people, of all nations and ethnicities, will eat together with the God who dwells with us. Let us live into that story and invite others to come in, for there is always room at the Lord's table.

The Year: Church Seasons

For millennia, Christians have observed a church calendar that shaped life and worship around the key events in salvation history. There is strong evidence that celebrations of Easter or *Pascha* date to the end of the second century and perhaps earlier, and commemorating Christ's nativity (though not on December 25) became widespread in the late fourth or early fifth century. The church calendar and liturgical seasons evolved over centuries and in different contexts both geographically and historically across the Eastern and Western churches. The calendar has not been without its critics; some of the Reformers had misgivings about its elements, wanting assurance of apostolic origins, and some of the Puritans even wanted to ban Christmas. Despite these dissenting voices, we cannot deny that liturgical seasons gave premodern communities rhythms, order, and a means of living out different moments in the Bible's salvation narrative through distinctive seasons.

For example, Advent, as we saw earlier, is our season of anticipation and preparation for the birth of Jesus, the God who was born to dwell among us. In Advent last year, our family incorporated the practice of advent candles and an advent wreath to our daily Morning and Evening Prayer, and our small group gathered, got out instruments, and sang advent carols like "O Come, O Come, Emmanuel." From small children to seventy-year-olds, and from musically gifted to not-so-musically gifted, we sang together. Advent was truly a distinct season that prepared our hearts for the celebration of the "mass of Christ" (i.e., Christmas), the coming of the Lord Jesus to dwell with us, through its twelve days of feasting, giving thanks, and praying about the reality of God made flesh.

Additionally, Lent is a season of fasting and preparation in which we practice spiritual disciplines. It begins with the Ash Wednesday service where Christians' foreheads are marked with ashes, physically symbolising the truth that we are but dust and to dust we shall return. A pastor friend of mine once commented that there was no time when the terrible reality of death—and our desperate longing to celebrate Christ's triumph over death—was more real to him than when he marked his children's foreheads with an ashen cross during the Ash Wednesday service. At the end of Lent is Holy Week with its Maundy Thursday liturgy where, following the example of Jesus's washing of his disciples' feet, my husband washes our feet. The sombreness of Good Friday is marked, among other things, by a Tenebrae service. Tenebrae means "shadows," and the service is accordingly pensive and mournful. It concludes in darkness with a loud bang, which marks the crack of thunder and the splitting of the curtain in the temple as Christ sighed his last breath. I will never forget when we held this service in our old stone church and heard the dramatic final *bang* as the giant wooden door slammed shut. We felt disturbed and uncomfortable, and we left in silence afterwards.

Two days later, before dawn on Easter morning, our family and some members of our small group gathered in our home, our children still in pyjamas. It was completely dark when we began our service, and we sat around the candlelit kitchen table reciting the set Bible readings from the Easter Vigil in the 2019 *Book of Common Prayer*. These are excerpts that cover the entire salvation narrative, beginning at the creation and proceeding through the fall; God's revelation to Israel; God's prophetic promises; the fulfilment of all of God's promises in Jesus's life, death, and resurrection; and Jesus's promise of his final return.

As we sat together reading through this service, I remember marvelling that we were a family of God's people from different nations and tongues in twenty-first century Australia, gathering to read the entire biblical sweep of history—words that hundreds of generations before us have read together. Over the next hour or so, as we read through these passages, the day dawned and the Easter morning sun rose behind us. At sunrise we celebrated with a pancake and waffle breakfast (a true feast!) and later went to church together. This traditional and historic practice of the Easter vigil was truly distinct and, soberly, a stark contrast to the way our non-Christian neighbours celebrated Easter.

Stewarding our time using the historical rhythms and seasons of the church underlines the rich distinctiveness of the Christian life. These seasons are set apart as distinctive periods of time, which is markedly different from how the secular world compels us to spend our time. Even the period between the season of Epiphany and the season of Lent and, later in the year, the period between Trinity Sunday and Advent are set apart as "Ordinary Time." During Ordinary Time, parts of the church (and even some Christian homes) are draped in green, symbolising that this is a period to focus on our growth as disciples and to deepen our understanding of the doctrines and mysteries of the faith.

Thus, observing the church calendar is a way of bringing the story of God's mercy towards all people from the written Word into the practices of daily life—from abstract sketch to full colour.

TEN

Recovering Sacredness and Beauty

When I was growing up, my favourite time of the school year was rehearsing for the Christmas carol service at St Thomas's, North Sydney. St. Thomas's is a magnificent sandstone building completed in the late nineteenth century and built in the style of English Gothic Revival. I was not from a Christian family, but I was captivated by the idea of being in a space which could communicate that the tangible world around me was not all there was. I was transfixed by the stained glass windows with their medieval figures and scenes. I wandered among the pews, down the nave and the chancel, through the stone arches to a passageway into the vestry, and even up the spiral staircase of the bell tower. I remember poring over the tapestry kneelers; I loved the stitching on each one that recorded the year it was made. Some of them dated back to the 1930s and had been in use ever since. The music we sang, the *Hodie Christus natus est* ("Today Christ is born"), was much older, a Gregorian chant. All these elements gave me a sense of transcendence that the secular world could not provide.

One of the hallmarks of the Ahistoric Age is how secular and naturalistic it is; it evacuates the world of the transcendent and sacred. In short, it assumes the position known as metaphysical naturalism, which holds that the only things that exist are natural. There is no supernatural realm or being. In some—perhaps many—parts of the church today, we struggle to engage biblically and fruitfully with sacredness and a sense of God's transcendence. In this sense, there is a kind of functional naturalism that pervades some parts of the church. That is, while there is an intellectual profession of belief in God, the sacred, and the transcendent, the actual ordinariness and casual irreverence of worship reveals a naturalistic assumption that God is not present and active in the world, in worship, and especially not in the sacraments. However, things were not this way historically. Christians have long traditions of engaging well with transcendence. In this chapter, we journey back to seventeenth- and eighteenth-century Britain and Europe and explore the prose of William Law, the music of J. S. Bach, and the poetry of George Herbert. These three figures used sacred places, music, and beauty, respectively, to make sense of God's sacredness, praise his transcendence, and order their minds and desires. We will see how tending and keeping these historic traditions can be enormously helpful to us today in three areas: discipleship, worship, and evangelism.

William Law and a Sacred Space

In the eighteenth century, the Anglican minister William Law (1686–1761), whom we met in the previous chapter, could often be found in a small nook in his house set apart for the purposes of prayer. Surrounded by books and lit by candles, the nook lay in a peaceful silence punctuated only by the hourly chiming of Law's clock. Such a space was not uncommon in the eighteenth century. In fact, we know that John Wesley had a prayer closet a generation or so later, which has been preserved to this day. Law describes his special place of prayer as "sacred," and in his 1729 book *A Serious Call to a Devout and Holy Life* he suggests others create such a sacred space of their own:

> [I]f you were to use yourself (as far as you can) to pray always in the same place; if you were to reserve that place for devotion, and not allow yourself to do anything common in it; if you were never to be there yourself, but in times of devotion; if any little room, (or if that cannot be) if any particular part of a room was thus used, this

kind of consecration of it, as a place holy unto God, would have an effect upon your mind, and dispose you to such tempers, as would very much assist your devotion. For by having a place thus sacred in your room, it would in some measure resemble a chapel or house of God. This would dispose you to be always in the spirit of religion, when you were there; and fill you with wise and holy thoughts, when you were by yourself. Your own apartment would raise in your mind, such sentiments as you have, when you stand near an altar.[1]

When I first read these sentences, I was taken aback. The idea that we would set apart—even "consecrate," as Law puts it—a space for prayer in order to draw ourselves into understanding, appreciating, and experiencing God's presence in the world is remarkably different from our current sense of God's presence and sacredness. As a humorous aside, when my husband and I told some of our Christian friends about Law's idea and suggested that we build a chapel for this purpose one day in our backyard, they looked at us with a mixture of horror and genuine concern for our salvation!

While some Christians would not be shocked by our suggestion, others in certain evangelical traditions would be suspicious. The naturalism of our culture has so deeply infused our lives that the idea of a sacred space seems almost Roman Catholic to some. And, yet, Law was a Protestant. In fact, he was formative for the origins of modern evangelicalism. He was utterly devoted to the question of how those who are saved by God's grace are to live holy, obedient, and devout lives as they make disciples and immerse themselves in Scripture. Yet my church friends who were uncomfortable at the suggestion of our backyard chapel are far from alone in being hesitant to think about the sacred in daily life. This attitude is probably more pronounced in Australia and the UK than it is in America.

Nonetheless, a recent series of studies by Barna surveyed Americans' feelings about spaces that gave them a sense of transcendence, which

---

1. William Law, *A Serious Call to a Devout and Holy Life*, in *The Works of the Reverend William Law*, vol. 4 (London: J. Richardson, 1762), 136.

were defined as "a physical place that brings you closer to experiencing connection with something beyond the physical world." More than half of U.S. adults (55 percent) say they do not regularly visit a space they consider transcendent. Self-identified Christians are only slightly more likely to say they frequently visit transcendent spaces: 37 percent claim they do so on a regular basis.[2] Thus, the study revealed considerable uncertainty among Americans about the experience of transcendence.

I found it particularly interesting that over two-thirds of practicing Christians (67 percent) strongly agreed that churches should reflect the beauty of God, yet only 37 percent of Christians call their church building beautiful.[3] The study also revealed that some believe a connection to our past encourages a connection with transcendence: "Nearly one in five practicing Christians and non-Christians believes that 'a sense of timelessness or permanence' can make a space feel transcendent."[4]

In the contemporary West, Christians are largely abandoning orthodox, biblical teachings on spiritual realities. This testifies to the long-term trend towards secularisation. In fact, most American Christians in 2009 did not believe that either Satan or the Holy Spirit existed, that is, that they are actual beings. The study which revealed this finding, also conducted by Barna, found that a majority of American Christians agreed either somewhat or strongly with the statement that Satan "is not a living being but is a symbol of evil."[5] Moreover, the results showed that "much like their perceptions of Satan, most Christians do not believe that the Holy Spirit is a living force, either. Overall, 38% strongly agreed and 20% agreed somewhat that the Holy Spirit is 'a symbol of God's power or presence but is not a living entity.'"[6]

---

2. "Do Church Buildings Still Matter? How U.S. Adults Feel about Spiritual Spaces," Barna, November 2, 2022, https://www.barna.com/research/spiritual-spaces/.

3. *Making Space for Community: Why Church Design Matters in Ministry* (Barna, 2023).

4. *Making Space for Inspiration: Why Church Design Matters in Ministry* (Barna, 2022).

5. "Most American Christians Do Not Believe That Satan or the Holy Spirit Exist," Barna, April 13, 2009, https://www.barna.com/research/most-american-christians-do-not -believe-that-satan-or-the-holy-spirit-exist/.

6. "Most American Christians Do Not Believe That Satan or the Holy Spirit Exist."

Currently, many Christians in the West—with the notable exception of some in the charismatic traditions—are uncomfortable speaking about phenomena like angels, demons, miraculous healings, sacred spaces, and so forth. Being cautious in these matters is wise. Nevertheless, we are evidently struggling to understand and articulate spiritual realities. How is the transcendent manifest in our world? Should we anoint the sick with holy oil, for example (cf. James 5:14–15)? What would make that oil holy?

This skeptical sensibility is distinctively Western and secular; Christians in more traditional cultures do not share this perspective. For instance, a pastor friend of mine who grew up in an Indian immigrant community in South Africa speaks of how demons and evil spirits played a role in his conversion to Christianity. By contrast, in highly secular Australia evangelicals rarely speak in these terms.

In modernity, Western societies have increasingly utilised the broad categories *natural* and *supernatural*, seeing these as separate. That is, the senses of natural (or material) reality and spiritual reality are far removed from each other. Daily objects are completely mundane. For example, I often hear someone comment about a church building: "It isn't sacred; it's just bricks and mortar. There's nothing special about it; it's just a rain shelter." In other words, the natural, material, and immanent world is far removed from whatever is spiritual, sacred, or transcendent. Even though we are yearning for awe, mystery, and wonder, we unfortunately live in an age that evacuates the spiritual or transcendent from the material world of our daily lives.

However, secular cultures have not abandoned a desire for the spiritual and transcendent. Rather, as the philosopher Charles Taylor argues, this desire has migrated away from traditional Christianity.[7] The Pew Research Center, for instance, recently revealed that there is a rise of the percentage of Americans (one quarter as of 2017) who see themselves as "spiritual but not religious."[8] In 2021, Pew found that

---

7. Charles Taylor, *A Secular Age* (Cambridge, MA: Harvard University Press, 2007), 489.

8. Michael Lipka and Claire Gecewicz, "More Americans Now Say They're Spiritual but Not Religious," Pew Research Center, September 6, 2017, https://www.pewresearch.org /short-reads/2017/09/06/more-americans-now-say-theyre-spiritual-but-not-religious/.

about three in ten U.S. adults are now religiously unaffiliated.[9] At the same time, we are seeing a marked attempt to satisfy spiritual yearnings in other quasi-spiritual practices such as SoulCycle, crystals, and the "wellness" industry.[10]

Because the Ahistoric Age disconnects us from historic streams of thought, we often do not realise how the secularity of late modernity has shaped our approach to sacredness and transcendence. Our task in considering how the transcendent and sacred are present in daily life is enormously complex and necessarily theological. Such a project cannot be reduced to a simple statement. But we can learn from the ways Christians in the past have engaged with God's sacredness and the transcendent. For example, William Law and his friends had a different understanding of God's transcendence and sacredness from us. Early modern Christians did not view transcendence as experiential or abstract, but rather sought to inhabit the tensions between the immanent and transcendent in their daily lives.[11] Let us consider Law's thoughts again concerning a sacred space for prayer. He believed that such a space can cultivate our attitudes and sensibilities:

> [A sacred space] would dispose you to be always in the spirit of religion when you was there, and fill you with wise and holy thoughts when you was by yourself. Your own apartment would raise in your mind such sentiments as you have when you stand near an altar, and you would be afraid of thinking or doing anything that was foolish near that place which is the place of prayer and holy intercourse with God.[12]

What might it look like in practice to draw upon the early modern sense of sacredness? Later in this chapter, we will see how Law's approach to

---

9. Gregory A. Smith, "About Three-in-Ten U.S. Adults Are Now Religiously Unaffiliated," Pew Research Center, December 14, 2021, https://www.pewresearch.org/religion/2021/12/14/about-three-in-ten-u-s-adults-are-now-religiously-unaffiliated/.

10. On this phenomenon, see Tara Isabella Burton, *Strange Rites: New Religions for a Godless World* (New York: Public Affairs, 2020).

11. James K. A. Smith, *How Not to Be Secular: Reading Charles Taylor* (Grand Rapids: Eerdmans, 2014), 32.

12. Law, *A Serious Call to a Devout and Holy Life*, 136.

sacredness can help us. But, first, let us consider one important way early modern Christians engaged with transcendence and sacredness in the world: through beauty.

George Herbert (1593–1633): The Pastor Poet

George Herbert was born in 1593 into a literary family in a small Welsh town. He moved to England to be educated at his grandfather's house, which prepared him for admission to Trinity College, Cambridge, as a king's scholar. A gifted writer and orator, Herbert had a promising career in public life and briefly sat in the English Parliament in his early thirties.[13] However, he discerned a call to the Anglican priesthood and was ordained a deacon of the Church of England in 1626. Herbert composed poetry throughout his life, and wrote in an early letter to his mother, "My poor Abilities in Poetry shall be all, and ever consecrated to God's glory."[14]

By the early 1630s, Herbert could be found writing, praying, and diligently caring for a tiny rural community. By the time Herbert became the rector of both St. Andrew's at Bemerton and St. Peter's at Fugglestone, in Wiltshire, in the south of England, he was nearing the end of his short life; he died at the age of thirty-nine. In their home across the road from the church, Herbert and his wife Jane raised their three orphaned nieces. The Herberts regularly opened up their home to countless others in their parish and invited them into a life of prayer and fellowship.

During his final years, Herbert wrote *A Priest to the Temple, or, The Country Parson His Character, and Rule of Holy Life*, in which he

---

13. Simon Healy, "HERBERT, George (1593–1633), of Trinity College, Cambridge; later of Bemerton, Wilts," in *The History of Parliament: The House of Commons 1604–1629*, ed. Andrew Thrush and John P. Ferris (Cambridge, UK: Cambridge University Press, 2010), https://www.historyofparliamentonline.org/volume/1604-1629/member/herbert-george-1593-1633/.

14. Herbert's letter to his mother, cited in Helen Wilcox, "Herbert, George," *Oxford Dictionary of National Biography*, September 23, 2004, https://www.oxforddnb.com/display/10.1093/ref:odnb/9780198614128.001.0001/odnb-9780198614128-e-13025/.

George Herbert (1593–1633)

earnestly described the duties and life of a pastor. He was interested in "the rule of holy life" for developing the virtues that form one's character. Indeed, *The Country Parson* revealed much of Herbert's character. He possessed an earnest and humble sense of responsibility as a Christian and as a public poet. *The Country Parson* details the unglamorous devotion of pastoral care to parishioners and the way Herbert would cross the street, ring the church bell, and lead whoever entered in Morning and Evening Prayer every day.

Herbert saw his prose and poetry as part of the lived experience of his Christian life. His well-known plain style and elegance manifests the sincerity of the way he lived. The sweetness he wished to "copie out" [in his poetry] was a beauty "readie penn'd" by God.[15] In *Jordan*, for example, Herbert wrote with the simple elegance of unadorned beauty:

> Who says that fictions only and false hair
> Become a verse? Is there in truth no beauty?
> Is all good structure in a winding stair?
> May no lines pass, except they do their duty
> Not to a true, but painted chair?
>
> Is it no verse, except enchanted groves
> And sudden arbors shadow coarse-spun lines?
> Must purling streams refresh a lover's loves?
> Must all be veil'd, while he that reads, divines,
> Catching the sense at two removes?

---

15. Hermine Van Nuis, "Sincerity of Being and Simplicity of Expression: George Herbert's Ethics and Aesthetics," *Christianity and Literature* 27, no. 1 (1977): 20.

> Shepherds are honest people; let them sing:
> Riddle who list, for me, and pull for Prime:
> I envy no man's nightingale or spring;
> Nor let them punish me with loss of rhyme,
> . Who plainly say, *My God, My King*.[16]

Herbert was deeply aware of our inadequacies and fallen nature. In his dedication of his collection of poems, *The Temple*, he wrote, "Lord, my first fruits present themselves to thee; / Yet not mine neither: for from thee they came, / And must return."[17] At the same time, he also clearly saw the responsibility of the Christian poet:

> Of all the creatures both in sea and land
> Only to Man thou hast made known thy ways,
> And put the pen alone into his hand,
> And made him Secretary of thy praise.[18]

As we will see soon when we discuss how beauty can help us today in worship, discipleship, and evangelism, we can learn much from Herbert's use of beauty to praise God.

J. S. Bach (1685–1750): Musician for the Glory of God

The Lutheran composer Johann Sebastian Bach was born in 1685 in the German town of Eisenach. This locale was central to Reformation history, since it is also the home of the medieval Wartburg castle where Martin Luther took refuge in the early 1520s and produced his translation of the New Testament into German. Although Bach was

---

16. George Herbert, "Jordan (I)" in *The Country Parson, The Temple*, ed. John N. Wall Jr. and Richard J. Payne, The Classics of Western Spirituality (New York; Mahwah, NJ: Paulist Press, 1981), 171–2. Emphasis original.

17. Herbert, "Dedication," in *The Country Parson, The Temple*, 118.

18. Herbert, "Providence," in *The Country Parson, The Temple*, 238.

Johann Sebastian Bach (1685–1750)

orphaned at the age of ten, he was the youngest of eight children and grew up in the care of his oldest brother, Johann Christoph, a professional church organist. The Bach family excelled in music, and young Johann Sebastian had an obvious talent for both the violin and the organ. In his late teens, Bach began to work as a musician for various churches and became the court organist and chamber musician for the Duke of Saxe-Weimar.

Musicians employed by churches in this region needed to know their theology well, for their day-to-day work involved glorifying God through the composition, teaching, and performance of sacred music. In fact, they had to undergo an examination to take up their position. When the Leipzig town council appointed Bach as its cantor, it examined his biblical and theological knowledge.[19] Thus, Bach unsurprisingly owned an extensive theological library. We know that he had a clear sense of his calling as a musician and thought deeply about the purpose of music. He would sign his works with three letters, "S. D. G.," *Soli Deo Gloria*, and he wrote that "the aim and final reason . . . of all music . . . should be none else but the Glory of God and the recreation of the mind."[20]

We also know about Bach's faith through his surviving Lutheran Bible. This Bible, which Bach acquired in 1733, is an edition with commentary by the Lutheran theologian Abraham Calov, originally published in Wittenberg in 1681. Bach wrote his own notes beside a

---

19. Robin Leaver, "Johann Sebastian Bach: Theological Musician and Musical Theologian," *Bach* 31, no. 1 (2000): 24.

20. Hans T. David and Arthur Mendel, eds., *The Bach Reader*, rev. ed. (New York: Norton, 1972), 33.

number of Calov's commentaries. These reflect not only how seriously Bach took his faith but also display the depth and sincerity of his understanding of music as a form of worship. Next to Calov's commentary on 1 Chronicles 29:2, for example, Bach wrote, "A splendid example [showing] that, besides other forms of worship, music especially has also been ordered by God's spirit through David." Beside the text of 2 Chronicles 5:13, Bach noted, "With a devotional music God is always in his presence of grace."[21]

Today, as Andy Crouch, former executive editor of *Christianity Today* magazine, put it, the Christian faith and the arts is "a fragile friendship."[22] On the whole, Crouch added, "Christians continue to vote with their dollars for popular entertainment."[23] Indeed, we need to teach ourselves how to appreciate the arts as Christians, either as an audience or as creators of literature, classical music, or the visual arts.[24] Likewise, we can benefit from thinking through how art and beauty can help us in our Sunday worship and in our evangelism. In part, our present dilemma exists because some strands of Protestantism have been in a complicated relationship with beauty for theological and historical reasons.

Can an image represent God's transcendence without becoming an idol? This has been a particularly important question since the Reformation, and for good reason. Protestants, critical of the medieval church's emphasis upon the power of relics, the invocation of the saints, and the theology of transubstantiation, have keenly stressed the transcendence and otherness of God, emphasising God's separation from the immanent.[25] Some strands of Reformation Protestantism

---

21. Excerpts from Bach's comments reprinted in Christoph Wolff, Hans T. David, and Arthur Mendel, eds., *The New Bach Reader: A Life of Johann Sebastian Bach in Letters and Documents* (New York: Norton, 1998), 161.

22. Andy Crouch, "Faith and the Arts: A Fragile Friendship," *Christianity Today*, May 20, 2016, https://www.christianitytoday.com/ct/2016/june/faith-and-fine-arts-fragile -conversation.html/.

23. Andy Crouch, "Faith and the Arts."

24. There are some notable exceptions, such as the publication *Ekstasis* (www.ekstasis magazine.com). See also Russ Ramsey, *Rembrandt Is in the Wind: Learning to Love Art through the Eyes of Faith* (Grand Rapids: Zondervan, 2022).

25. For an overview of the arts in the context of the Protestant Reformation, see Bridget

desired to protect the image of God and preserve a proper biblical understanding of how he acts in the world. During the iconoclasm of the English Reformation, for example, many works of art were removed from churches or were ruthlessly destroyed.[26] For the most part this iconoclasm did not persist, and successive centuries have witnessed periods in which Protestants had a healthier engagement with the visual arts, as we can see in this chapter's examples. Moreover, in recent years—prompted by a sense of that "fragile friendship" between Protestants and the arts—there has been a revival of interest in how Protestants can engage well with the arts.[27] On the other hand, the history of the Roman Catholic artistic tradition is an entirely different story and does not share this particular struggle.[28]

My concern here is not to rehearse different theologies of aesthetics, but to articulate the historical case for beauty as an avenue for engaging with and appreciating God's transcendence and sacredness. This can only help us as we seek to love God and others.

Biblical Beauty

Before outlining what a Christian vision of beauty might look like in practice, we need briefly to consider its biblical origin. The nature of beauty has been a topic of discussion throughout the entire history of Western philosophy and theology. Moreover, the theology of aesthetics is enormously complex. For our purposes, it is helpful to draw upon Jonathan King's twofold working hypothesis about beauty: "First,

---

Heal, "Introduction: Art and Religious Reform in Early Modern Europe," *Art History* 40, no. 2 (2017): 246–55, https://onlinelibrary.wiley.com/doi/full/10.1111/1467-8365.12305/.

26. See Eamon Duffy, *The Stripping of the Altars* (New Haven: Yale University Press, 1992), and John Phillips, *The Reformation of Images: Destruction of Art in England, 1535–1660* (Berkeley, CA: University of California Press, 1963).

27. See Makoto Fujimura, *Art and Faith: A Theology of Making* (New Haven: Yale University Press, 2020), and Terry Glaspey, "Are the Arts a Tool, a Temptation, or a Distraction?," *Christianity Today*, December 13, 2021, https://www.christianitytoday.com/ct/2022/january-february/glaspey-books-arts-tool-temptation-or-distraction.html/.

28. See, for example, Jacques Maritain, *Art and Scholasticism* (1933; Providence, RI: Cluny, 2020).

beauty corresponds in some way to the attributes of God; second, the theodrama of God's eternal plan in creation, redemption, and consummation entails a consistent and fitting expression and outworking of this divine beauty."[29]

Beauty is an attribute of God, and God delights in his beautiful creation. Psalm 19, for example, testifies to the overflowing abundance of beauty, which is unnecessary and cannot be explained away by naturalistic description. Beauty's resistance to this kind of reduction is part of its witness to God's transcendence. As Bach and Herbert well knew, God's Word, revealed in the incarnation of God in Jesus Christ, is *beautiful*. This does not pertain to Christ's physical appearance, for, as Isaiah reminds us, Christ had no particular physical beauty. Rather, Christ's perfect character and life are beautiful, for he dwelt—tabernacled—among us. We see something of God's beauty through Christ's life, death, and resurrection.

The apprehension of beauty is distinctly human and reflects something of the image of God. Beauty is a sign—or, as N. T. Wright put it, a broken signpost—pointing to something outside of itself.[30] Beauty draws out the universal longing of our hearts; it inaugurates desire, rightly oriented, towards the creator of that beauty. God uses beauty in this way because he cares deeply about it and uses it to bless us and mediate our relationship to him. Witness, for instance, the garden imagery on the tabernacle—in the midst of the barren desert—and then the temple in the Old Testament.

The advent of modernity and secularisation, however, unravelled beauty from its transcendent grounding. If there is no sacred or transcendent realm, then art becomes primarily concerned with subjective appreciation and the genius of the artist, rather than the divine author of all beauty. A "malaise of immanence" (a moniker coined by Charles Taylor) has consequently arisen in the modern and late modern world.

---

29. Jonathan King, *The Beauty of the Lord: Theology as Aesthetics* (Bellingham, WA: Lexham, 2018), 23. Also see Nicholas Wolterstorff's book *Art in Action: Toward a Christian Aesthetic* (Grand Rapids: Eerdmans, 1987).

30. N. T. Wright, *Broken Signposts: How Christianity Makes Sense of the World* (San Francisco: HarperOne, 2020).

Beauty is distorted into ornamentation, sentimentality, sexual allure, or kitsch, since it is no longer grounded in God's transcendence. This is a vivid example of how the Ahistoric Age's focus on the immanent and present frustrates our ability to engage with the sacred and transcendent. While this historical overview has been necessarily brief, it starkly reminds Christians that if they devalue beauty, they embrace secularisation rather than the Bible.

How the Sacred and Beautiful Can Help Us

Let us now see how a historically grounded faith might rediscover and revive the importance of beauty and sacredness in three areas, namely, discipleship, worship, and evangelism.[31]

1. Discipleship

William Law's sense of God's sacredness manifest in the physical world can help us understand how to form and orient our hearts. Perhaps there are ways of creating spaces that testify to God's holiness and sacredness. Like William Law, we might find it beneficial to set apart a quiet and beautiful place where we can discipline ourselves to concentrate on prayer.

The arts are an integral way for us to disciple ourselves by drawing upon beauty and sacredness. Jeremy Begbie has argued that we participate in God's witness to his own transcendence when we make and appreciate art. He explains, "the arts can serve as compelling witnesses to the way in which the richness of meaning we encounter in the finite world always exceeds our grasp, outshines our various representations of it."[32] There are a variety of ways of engaging with the arts that

---

31. In recent years, there has been a revival of interest and the importance of beauty in the work of Hans Urs von Balthasar, Jacques Maritain, and Marilynne Robinson, among others, all of whom have much to offer.

32. Jeremy Begbie, *Redeeming Transcendence in the Arts: Bearing Witness to the Triune God* (Grand Rapids: Eerdmans, 2018), 7.

enable us to admire and praise God and put into practice the biblical command that we set our minds on things above (Col. 3:2). While I would encourage a broad engagement with the arts, we especially have much to gain from those authors, composers, and artists in the Christian tradition.

Reading aloud the poetry of George Herbert, for example, is something my family and friends do. My husband John, whose Southern hospitality knows no bounds, cooks a lunch for George Herbert's feast day, which is marked in the Anglican liturgical calendar. Family and friends first eat and pray together, then both adults and children read aloud excerpts of Herbert's poetry. This occasion uses a lunch gathering as a springboard into engaging with the beauty of Herbert's poetry and passing down the practice and tradition of glorifying God through beauty to younger generations.

Additionally, J. S. Bach's music is a window into the tradition of sacred music that dates back to the early years of the church and which has formed generations of believers. If you have never heard Gregorian chants or the masses of Thomas Tallis and William Byrd, for example, I wholeheartedly encourage you to take a deep dive and listen, either at home or by attending performances. Some time ago, for example, John and I took our three young children to a performance of Handel's *Messiah*. In a different context, earlier this year I played Thomas Tallis's "If Ye Love Me" to my students during one of my classes. The vast majority of my students had never heard anything like it, and some were even stifling tears. There are countless more recent and even contemporary examples of sacred music, such as the music of the twentieth-century Estonian composer Arvo Pärt, who converted to Orthodox Christianity in later life. Keith and Kristyn Getty have also shown how the tradition of singing hymns can be accessible to ordinary families and helpful in discipling ourselves and our children.[33]

On another occasion (also a lunch at our house), adults and children played hymns on instruments together. On this particular

---

33. Keith and Kristyn Getty, *Sing! How Worship Transforms Your Life, Family, and Church* (Nashville: Broadman and Holman, 2017).

day, many of us happened to be playing the violin (one of our family traditions) and singing "Be Thou My Vision." Let me lend a note of encouragement here: most old hymns do not require those who sing or play them to be particularly musically accomplished; their melodies are simple and beautiful. They were meant to be enjoyed by ordinary Christians.

There is not enough space here to outline all the ways in which the arts can help us today, but we cannot fail to mention literature and poetry. While many Christians have read C. S. Lewis's *The Chronicles of Narnia*, too few of us take seriously the conviction that underpinned Lewis's novels, namely, that our imagination plays a central role in enabling us to see and understand reality—especially those realities of the divine. For Lewis, "Reason is the natural organ of truth; but imagination is the organ of meaning. Imagination, producing new metaphors or revivifying old, is not the cause of truth, but its condition."[34] In short, our imagination can help us see what we normally miss when we are awake to this world but spiritually asleep.[35] Reading T. S. Eliot's *Four Quartets* early in my own conversion had this effect on me.

We can take family, friends, children, the elderly, and others we are discipling to art galleries, poetry readings, or classical music performances. These provide wonderful opportunities for caring and serving others across generations. We can also read books and poetry aloud to each other and engage in conversations about them, developing our abilities to talk about art, beauty, and the sacred. The arts need not be premodern, nor limited to Anglophone tradition. The book *Our Mob, God's Story*, for example, is a collection that illustrates the rich indigenous Australian Christian tradition. Also, my dear friends often sing a traditional Samoan hymn to their baby, just like they did with all of their other children.

---

34. C. S. Lewis, *Selected Literary Essays* (1961; San Francisco: HarperOne, 2013), 354.

35. On C. S. Lewis and the imagination, see Kevin Vanhoozer, "In Bright Shadow: Lewis on the Imagination for Theology and Discipleship," in *The Romantic Rationalist: God, Life, and Imagination in the Work of C. S. Lewis*, ed. John Piper and David Mathis (Wheaton: Crossway, 2014).

Finally, we can also create art, using some wonderful resources by other artistic Christians. Indeed, we manifest an aspect of the *imago Dei* by participating in the creation of art and encouraging others to do so. For example, a friend of ours, a missionary in West Africa, uses his textiles and paintings to glorify God and engage with the historic traditions of the local culture. In doing so, he sparks conversations with his community and has even formed a fellowship group of other Christian artists. In short, the arts are a central part of our historic Christian faith. They have formed generations of Christians throughout the ages, and it is now time to draw upon and revive their history.

2. Worship

As human beings, we have an inbuilt longing for awe and wonder; we sense that our mundane world does not exhaust reality. In ahistoric late modernity, we acutely long for something that transcends our self-centred, ordinary lives. Many in the church today, including those who attend but are not yet Christians, are yearning to understand and experience something of God's holiness. Unless churches orient these desires towards their proper object in God, they will be directed towards the myriad of idols of our age, from "spirituality" to wellness philosophies.[36] The Christian historical tradition of beauty and sacredness can help us here.

A proper orientation of our desires is important in worship. William Law's thoughts about the sacred caution us against triviality in our worship. Too often, our services remove any sense that we are worshipping a holy God who is present in our gathering. This particularly happens when we replace serious awe with casualness almost to the point of irreverence. For example, when we celebrate the Lord's Supper with non-Christian pop music and when a laid-back atmosphere replaces solemnity, we are sending a message about how seriously we take God's holiness and Christ's sacrifice. This is a good illustration of the functional naturalism I described earlier. We are

---

36. Tara Isabella Burton, *Strange Rites: New Religions for a Godless World* (New York: PublicAffairs, 2020), gives a good discussion of this phenomenon.

portraying worship as an ordinary consumer experience in which you show up at your own convenience for your own pleasure and entertainment. To illustrate, when I visited a church one Sunday I noticed that a sizeable proportion of the congregation nonchalantly wandered into the building a solid fifteen minutes into the one-hour service, during the second song. I was told that this was the normal situation.

More disturbingly, if we have no sense of God's transcendent and radical holiness in our worship, then we are communicating that this world is all there is. Meanwhile, people will continue to direct their spiritual yearnings elsewhere. While I am not arguing by any means for us to be unwelcoming, the way the church has dealt with sacredness historically, illustrated by William Law, can chasten us. This approach can prevent us from unwittingly embracing a rootless consumer faith in which God's holiness and transcendence disappear into our secular Ahistoric Age.

William Law also makes us aware that our physical surroundings impact how we pray and worship. We need to think carefully about whether we want to present an atmosphere and space intentionally modelled on that of a coffee shop or live music venue. This was the wisdom of a strand of thinking about how Christians could be "relevant" several decades ago. But, as we saw in the first chapters of this book, our cultural context has changed. More than ever, we need to emphasise that Christians are not of this world. I am not advocating a simple formula that says, "return to all things 'high church.'" After all, churches and worship need to look different in various parts of a city and in other demographics, cultures, and regions. Rather, I want to urge us to think creatively and historically about how we can draw upon sacredness and beauty.

There are many ways to set a space apart to communicate something of God's beauty and transcendence. We do not have to use an ancient building, for instance. However, I do know of a couple churches in Sydney that have done a terrific job with contemporarily renovated historic church buildings. In one such church in Sydney's inner west, white walls, high ceilings, local timber, wattle, and eucalyptus are draped as a nod to our local Australian heritage. The building's architecture and its internal space draw us out of ourselves and away from this mundane world's veil of tears and death.

A friend of mine is the minister of an Anglican church in the inner city of Sydney. This area was once the home of gritty working-class people, but is now becoming increasingly gentrified. This church is serious about evangelising the community, yet it is also intentional about using beauty to witness to God's sacredness. Such a place is perhaps one of the last areas in which you would expect a traditional liturgy of the *Book of Common Prayer* combined with an evangelistic message to prosper. Yet this has happened. A group of twenty-somethings and several much older people have become active attendees of this church's evening service. Several of the young people, who are now university students, are at the time in their lives when they need to embrace the Christian faith as their own. They pore over the work of art printed on the cover of the service book. They also immerse themselves in the liturgy, sing traditional hymns accompanied by a single acoustic guitar, and sit quietly amidst the historic beauty of the church. All these elements draw them out of the mass-produced superficiality of daily life and point them towards the sacredness and beauty of God, who broke through time in order to inhabit and transform the physical world.

3. Evangelism

Perhaps one of the most surprising aspects of beauty and the sacred is their role in evangelism. I was not won over to Christianity merely by the persuasiveness of C. S. Lewis's *Mere Christianity*, still less by the poverty of atheist ethics. In no small part both the *beauty* of the gospel and my encounter with God's sacredness in the Lord's Supper showed me that God is real and Christ did become human and die for us. Let me share a vignette from my own faith story that illustrates the enormous power of beauty and sacredness in evangelism.

When I was in my mid-twenties, I moved to Tallahassee, Florida, to take up an assistant professorship at Florida State University. I had been privately questioning my atheism over the previous year or two, ever since my attendance of Peter Singer's Uehiro Lectures back at

Oxford. Following those lectures, I had begun to read theology. I was considering the possibility that there might be a God after all, but I was still unsure. One morning in this new city and new home, I decided to go to church.

The early fall morning gave slight relief to the omnipresent Floridian humidity, and the aroma of gardenia filled the air. Downtown Tallahassee was a place of commerce and politics—two very worldly endeavours. The city seemed particularly ordinary that morning, filled with a slow-paced atmosphere, empty streets, and closed buildings. As I walked past the live oak trees draped with Spanish moss, I brushed my fingers against their curly fronds. In a moment of reverie I smiled, remembering that my mother had called these leaves "grandfather's whiskers" back home in Sydney, where once they had draped over a hanging pot on our front veranda. I glanced at the fronds again, more soberly this time. Perhaps they were only matter in motion.

The church was a stately red brick building. Few people knew me in Tallahassee, so I felt safely anonymous as I walked up the stone steps and through the red-painted door. Suddenly the somewhat mundane and lonely morning all but disappeared. The inside seemed almost otherworldly. Wooden rafters drew my eyes upwards to the vaulted ceiling. The walls were flanked by stained glass windows streaming coloured light above and beside me, and I noticed a wooden altar far ahead of me, draped in green cloth. A giant cross hung over it.

The choir sang a hymn arranged by Ralph Vaughan Williams; this brought memories of England to my mind. Their voices were haunting, and I felt a lump in my throat. That morning the congregation celebrated the Lord's Supper. I was not baptised, but I was content just to remain in my pew and observe. The words and music took me out of Tallahassee, out of myself, and into a much larger story:

> Take, eat: This is my Body, which is given for you. Do this for the remembrance of me.[37]

---

37. The Episcopal Church, *The Book of Common Prayer and Administration of the Sacraments and Other Rites and Ceremonies of the Church* (New York: Church Publishing Incorporated, 2007), 362.

Drink this, all of you: This is my Blood of the new Covenant, which is shed for you and for many for the forgiveness of sins. Whenever you drink it, do this for the remembrance of me.[38]

These strange and profound words were followed by silence as we all knelt in the pews, and bells rang as if to echo the words. The air grew hazy and full of the smell of frankincense. A stillness descended as the congregation knelt to share the bread and the cup of wine. The present moment seemed to be transcended by this story solemnly reenacted: the body of God was made flesh and broken for his people, his blood was poured out for the forgiveness of sins, and a new covenant was inaugurated. I was a stranger, yet in that moment I knew I was standing outside looking into something greater than I could fathom: something sacred and something beautiful.

One of the issues I had been grappling with since I began to question my atheism was that if atheism were true there was no ultimate meaning. If nothing exists outside of matter in motion, then nothing is transcendent and nothing is sacred. Time, and life itself, are ultimately purposeless; the only meaning that exists is what we create for ourselves. I was generally living my life in this manner, and things were going extraordinarily well for me. In my eyes, I had complete freedom. At twenty-seven, I had fulfilled my childhood dream of earning a PhD from Cambridge and a fellowship at Oxford. I had just published my first book, which had won an award, and now I had a tenure-track assistant professorship. Yet here I was, yearning for transcendence and meaning, sitting alone in church on a Sunday morning.

What had once seemed to be a courageous and exciting responsibility to invent my own meaning in life now appeared desperately shallow. As I heard about God, who poured out his blood for the forgiveness of sins and promises to remake the entire creation and redeem its brokenness, and witnessed these people taking part in this ancient liturgy, the veil on my way of life seemed to lift. There would always be another fellowship to win and another book to write—I knew this

---

38. The Episcopal Church, *The Book of Common Prayer*, 363.

full well. But the quest to create my own meaning had merely plunged me into a relentless cycle of achievement. It was a life of vain little glories and unending pursuits. Atheism had once seemed brave and empowering; now it seemed thin and frivolous.

Here in the church, during the liturgy of the Lord's Supper, I encountered God as sacred. In that moment of solemn beauty, I glimpsed the truth that this world is not all there is. But an abstract statement did not assert this truth to me that morning. Rather, the experience of God's terrifying but beautiful holiness in the Lord's Supper took me out of the present moment and out of ordinary life. There seemed to be a purpose to human history and to time, after all. Here was the ultimate story about a God who created humanity. Then after we rejected him, he pursued us by inhabiting time and this suffering world. Through his death and resurrection, he began setting right the entire creation. This story felt compelling; it seemed to make sense of human history and of all our suffering and striving. It also seemed to make sense of my own condition; I left church that morning beginning to desire God.

ELEVEN

History and Intellectual Formation

If you open a modern edition of John Calvin's *Institutes of the Christian Religion* and turn to the end, you will discover a list of the authors and texts Calvin cites. One of my favourite exercises I get my students to do—before showing them that list—is to guess how many authors Calvin refers to in the *Institutes*. I point them in the right direction by reminding them that Calvin was in dialogue not just with church fathers like Jerome and Athanasias, but also with classical authors; the *Institutes* cites eight texts by Plato and four by Plutarch, for example. When my students count the number of authors and discover there are no fewer than *seventy*, they are struck with fascination and curiosity. "Why is Calvin constantly referring to all these old authors?" they ask. Some are genuinely surprised that Calvin referred to any texts or authors at all outside of the Bible.

One of Calvin's greatest contentions with the Roman Catholic Church was his insistence upon the supreme authority of the Bible. But this did not mean for one moment that Calvin disregarded the history of Christian—and non-Christian—thought. Indeed, he had precisely the opposite attitude. Calvin articulates his theology in a long dialogue with thinkers from the classical Greco-Roman world through the early church, medieval and early modern periods. In the *Institutes* alone, Calvin engaged with Plato, Virgil, Xenophon, Ovid, Origen, Lactantius, Tertullian, and over sixty others. No wonder my students are

John Calvin (1509–1564)

surprised and curious! Indeed, Calvin's knowledge of this tradition stands in stark contrast to our own. Even though he had a high view of the authority of Scripture, Calvin drew readily upon thinkers from the past who were formative in the development of his ideas and arguments. If Christians today assume that this long historical tradition of thought holds nothing for us, are we not perhaps being slightly arrogant or even foolish?

In the Ahistoric Age, educational institutions tend to reflect the dominant ideals of autonomy and self-fulfilment. The ideals (and idols) of the age also permeate some Christian schools and colleges. For instance, glance at the websites or marketing materials for many universities and private schools today, and you will see how these institutions are advertising themselves as places where students will be empowered to become their true selves and realise their individual dreams. "It's about what's inside you, not where you've come from. Your future success starts here," reads the website of one university, whose motto is "Unlimited."[1] The focus of education has now shifted in our Ahistoric Age. Older ideas of the school or university as a place of formation in which students are introduced to their cultural heritage and guided to develop the qualities and virtues needed to be responsible and active citizens in society are falling out of fashion.[2] Instead, schools and universities are increasingly consumer-oriented; students are largely there to unleash

---

1. "Unlimited," Western Sydney University, February 9, 2024, https://www.western sydney.edu.au/unlimited/home#find/.

2. For a classic description of the university's role and purpose, see John Henry Newman's *The Idea of a University* (1852, 1858; New Haven: Yale University Press, 1996).

and display their talents and be empowered for their own individual dreams of success.[3]

Educational institutions in the Ahistoric Age tend to downplay the importance of learning about the past in topics such as the discipline of history or classic texts of literature or other humanities subjects. In 2022, the Australian Institute of Public Affairs conducted a systematic review of 791 history subjects offered across 35 Australian universities.[4] The report found that a focus on power relations, identity, and language replaced major historical episodes, ideas, and movements of Western civilisation. For example, more history subjects that teach about "Race" than "Democracy" (86 subjects compared to 33 subjects), "Identity" than the "Enlightenment" (64 subjects compared to 25 subjects), and "sexuality" than the "Reformation" (54 subjects compared to 17 subjects) were offered at Australian universities.[5] The most common themes across the 791 subjects offered in 2022 were, in order: "Gender," "Race," "Indigenous Issues," "the environment," and "film."

Aside from history being largely irrelevant, books, authors, figures, episodes, and works from the past are subjected to a narrow prism of interpretation that reduces everything to power and oppression. As we saw earlier, the Ahistoric Age finds it difficult to grapple in a nuanced way with issues of power and authority, particularly in the context of the past. To be clear, the nature of power and oppression can often be an important framework of interpretation, but it becomes a vulgar oversimplification when it is the primary way of understanding a historical figure or book. It engenders a totalising and facile outlook classing everyone in history into "oppressor" or "oppressed" categories.

---

3. For an illustration of a pedagogy of "empowerment," see Catherine Broom, "Empowering Students: Pedagogy That Benefits Educators and Learners," *Citizenship, Social and Economics Education* 14, no. 2 (2015): 79–86, https://journals.sagepub.com/doi/10.1177/2047173415597142.

4. Bella D'Abrera and Brianna McKee, *Forgetting the Past: How Post-Modernist Theory Has Replaced History in Australian Universities in 2022* (Melbourne, Australia: Institute of Public Affairs, 2022), https://ipa.org.au/ipa-today/forgetting-the-past-how-post-modernist-theory-has-replaced-history-in-australian-universities-in-2022/.

5. D'Abrera and McKee, *Forgetting the Past*, 3.

Old texts are thus only valuable for how they reveal various structures of power. A friend of mine who is a professor of English literature at an elite UK university once shared with me that many of his students instinctively approach most literary texts from the past purely through this reductive lens.

We also need to consider the question of our broader intellectual formation outside of formal education. The term *education*, from the Latin *educatio*, denotes a broad sense of training, rearing, and bringing up. In this chapter I prefer to use the term "intellectual formation," because I wish to underline the biblical principle that intellectual formation should be a central concern of our Christian lives, extending beyond formal education in schools and universities. The God who has endowed humanity with creative spirit, reason, and imagination commands us to love him with all our heart, soul, *mind*, and strength (cf. Mark 12:30; Luke 10:27). We also need to be transformed by the renewal of our minds (cf. Rom. 12:2). For this reason, our intellectual formation is not a narrow, utilitarian means to employment, but rather seeks to form us by deepening our ability to know and enjoy God, enabling us to disciple others and serve our neighbour, and empowering us to communicate the gospel. Let us turn to two historical illustrations revealing how important the long tradition of learning was to Christians in the past.

John Milton (1608–1674): Educating for the Good Society

Many of us are familiar with John Milton's magnum opus, *Paradise Lost*, which retells in blank verse the epic story of Adam and Eve's temptation, fall, and expulsion from the garden of Eden. Already in his late fifties and blind, Milton composed *Paradise Lost* through various friends and amanuenses who wrote down his dictated lines. Milton was born in 1608 to a moderately wealthy scrivener in London under the reign of James I and during the years in which the King James Bible was being developed. After training under several private tutors,

Milton attended St. Paul's Cathedral School, which was founded by John Colet, a close friend and associate of the great Renaissance humanist Desiderius Erasmus. Milton then went up to Cambridge to study at Christ's College.

John Milton (1608–1674)

Milton's education took place against the backdrop of a turbulent century in England that witnessed a series of civil wars, the execution of King Charles I, and a short-lived republic. In the lead-up to the civil wars, which began in 1642, Milton attacked episcopacy (the form of church government by bishops), which he saw as a remnant of Catholicism. In 1644, he published an anonymous tract entitled "Of Education." Eight pages long, it took the form of an open letter to the Polish–English émigré and reformer Samuel Hartlib. The reform of education was a popular topic of discussion among Protestants in the seventeenth century, who believed this was part of the broader Christian reform of society. In "Of Education," Milton outlined an academy for boys between the ages of twelve and twenty-one. This tract articulates a reformed Christian view of education by emphasising formation and character. It aims to shape Christian citizens who contribute to public life, and especially encourages them to engage with the ideas and texts of the past.

Milton's vision of the purpose of education stemmed directly from the effects of the fall: "The end then of learning is to repair the ruins of our first parents by regaining to know God aright, and out of that knowledge to love him, to imitate him, to be like him, as we may the neerest by possessing our souls of true vertue, which being united to the heavenly grace of faith makes up the highest perfection."[6]

---

6. John Milton, "Of Education," in *John Milton: Prose, Major Writings on Liberty, Politics, Religion, and Education*, ed. David Loewenstein (Chichester, UK: Wiley-Blackwell, 2013), 172.

Milton aspired to form students who would continue the reformation of English society and create what his fellow seventeenth-century Christians referred to as a "godly Commonwealth."[7]

"Of Education" clearly displays how important the study of the texts from the past were to Milton's project of forming Christian citizens for public life and service. Milton believed that learning about God's world and about theology involves studying past authors, including non-Christian authors, in addition to the Bible. The study of law, for example, would proceed historically, beginning with "*Moses*; and as farre as humane prudence can be trusted, in those extoll'd remains of Grecian Law-givers, *Lycurgus, Solon, Zaleucus, Charondas*, and thence to all the Romane *Edicts* . . . and so down to the *Saxon* and common laws of England, and the Statutes."[8]

Milton strongly encouraged Christians preparing for a life of service to be excited about and love knowledge and learning, because these desires integrally formed their character. Milton wished students to be nothing less than "enflam'd with the study of learning, and the admiration of vertue."[9] The important thinkers and books of the past were thus central in his endeavour. Milton planned to win his students "early to the love of vertue and true labour" and suggested that "some easie and delightfull book of Education would be read to them," listing Cebes, Plutarch, and some Socratic dialogues.[10]

Isaac Watts (1674–1748): Learn from the Vast Treasuries of the Past

Anyone who has sung "Joy to the World," "Our God Our Help in Ages Past," or "When I Survey the Wondrous Cross" has sung the

---

7. Renaissance humanism must not be confused with today's secular humanism. Renaissance humanism emphasised the languages and the *studia humanitatis*: history, grammar, rhetoric, poetry, and moral philosophy.

8. Milton, "Of Education," 177. Emphasis original.

9. Milton, "Of Education," 174.

10. Milton, "Of Education," 174.

words of Isaac Watts, one of the most renowned hymn writers in the English language. Watts was born in 1674, the same year John Milton died. After the restoration of the English monarchy in 1660, a series of parliamentary acts were introduced to promote civil peace and some measure of religious conformity by preventing Catholics and those Protestants who did not adhere to the established Church of England from holding public office. Such Protestants were

Isaac Watts (1674–1748)

referred to as dissenters or nonconformists. Isaac was born into a family of dissenters, and his father, a clothier, was imprisoned for his nonconformity three times, in 1674, 1678, and 1683.

The young Isaac was clearly both intellectually astute and principled. After his father had been released from prison for the second time, he began to teach his four-year-old son Latin. We know from an early biographer of Watts that when Isaac's father was forced to live by himself away from his family, he sent his children, at Isaac's request, a detailed and lengthy letter about his faith, giving extensive advice to his children about how to live. Perhaps Isaac's early experience of his father's guidance and education in the context of religious persecution led him to advocate that every Christian, young and old, ought to be concerned with "the improvement of the mind." Watts was also adamant that girls be educated.

Watts believed that every Christian's "necessary duty" was "to improve his understanding, to inform his judgment, to treasure up useful knowledge, and to acquire the skill of good reasoning."[11] He published a number of helpful books in this area, including *The Art of*

---

11. Isaac Watts, *The Improvement of the Mind: Or a Supplement to the Art of Logic, in Two Parts, to Which Is Added a Discourse on the Education of Children and Youth* (Boston: David West, 1793), 2.

Reading and Writing English (1721), *Catechisms* (1730), and *Short View of the Whole Scripture History*, as well as a textbook on *Logick: or, the Right Use of Reason in the Enquiry after Truth* (1725). The textbook's sequel, entitled *On the Improvement of the Mind* (1741), was an advice book intended for a general audience. After Watts's death, his posthumously published *A Discourse on the Education of Children and Youth* was often published as an addendum to *On the Improvement of the Mind*.

For Watts, the formation of the intellect and the formation of Christian character go hand in hand, as a close association exists between one's capacity to reason and make good judgements and one's capacity for moral action: "Our mistakes in judgment may plunge us into much folly and guilt in practice. By acting without thought or reason, we dishonour the God that made us reasonable creatures."[12] Like Milton, Watts believed our moral and intellectual failings stem from our fallen human nature, which gives rise to "weaknesses, mistakes, and frailties which are derived from our original apostacy and fall from a state of innocence; how much our powers of understanding are yet more darkened . . . and imposed on by our senses, our fancies, and our unruly passions."[13]

How do we form Christian character? This is no simple task, but Watts believed that reading wisely and well from the books of the past was particularly helpful: "It is meditation and studious thought, it is the exercise of your own reason and judgment upon all you read, that gives good sense even to the best genius, and affords your understanding the truest improvement."[14] He also encouraged associating with like-minded people:

> Read the accounts of those vast treasures of knowledge, which some
> of the dead have possessed, and some of the living do possess . . .
> Acquaint yourselves with some persons of great learning, that by
> converse among them, and comparing yourselves with them, you
> may acquire a mean opinion of your own attainments, and may be

---

12. Watts, *The Improvement of the Mind*, 2.
13. Watts, *The Improvement of the Mind*, 4.
14. Watts, *The Improvement of the Mind*, 7.

thereby animated with new zeal, to equal them as far as possible, or to exceed: thus let your diligence be quickened by a generous and laudable emulation.[15]

Furthermore, Watts suggested that cultivating the discipline of history was helpful: "The narratives of the various occurrences in nations, as well as in the lives of particular persons . . . will furnish the soul . . . with a treatise of knowledge, whence to derive useful observations, inferences and rules of conduct."[16] Such treatises of knowledge were just as important for children as for adults. Watts's particular interest in the education of children saw him eager to see them taught "to value their understanding as a noble faculty" and to pursue its enrichment "with a variety of knowledge." Otherwise, "like an uncultivated field, they will ever be barren and fruitless, or produce weeds and briers, instead of herbs and corn."[17]

Even though many of Milton's and Watts's insights are indeed valuable, I am not arguing that they got everything "right" or that we should embrace all they suggested. After all, they were writing in their own contexts with their own purposes in mind. Rather, both men offer us a glimpse of some of the ways Christians have engaged with the long historical tradition of learning and found it enormously fruitful. Their insights can stimulate our minds and inspire us to undertake our own journey into that rich tradition.

The Long Tradition of Learning

John Calvin, John Milton, and Isaac Watts were all in dialogue with thinkers and ideas from the past, and this venerable tradition of learning grounded in history can help us in our intellectual formation today. Let me spend a moment outlining what I mean by this tradition. Many classic works date back to the ancient world and have been

---

15. Watts, *The Improvement of the Mind*, 6.
16. Watts, *The Improvement of the Mind*, 90.
17. Watts, *The Improvement of the Mind*, 64.

considered some of the most important exemplars of literature, history, philosophy, poetry, music, the visual arts, and so forth. Nevertheless, the "canon" of what are often considered great or classic works is not set in stone, and many people have had worthwhile discussions about what texts have been and ought to be considered part of this tradition.

These texts are considered valuable because they articulate with depth something of the profundity—the fullness and limits—of the human condition. They bear up well under multiple readings or multiple listenings. Even though we may repeatedly listen to one of J. S. Bach's fugues, keep rereading George Eliot's *Middlemarch*, or study Aristotle's *Nicomachean Ethics* several times, we do not exhaust these works. Furthermore, as we saw with Calvin in his *Institutes*, we do not need to limit ourselves to the Christian tradition. Indeed, we need to be well-equipped to know how to engage fruitfully—like Calvin, Watts, Milton, and others did—with works both within and outside of the Christian tradition. This mindset echoes what C. S. Lewis and so many others have said about the importance of reading the old books, and it overlaps with what some call a "liberal arts" education or a "classical" education.

The term *tradition* is a good way to describe the body of ideas within these works. Throughout millennia other authors and creators have consciously placed themselves in dialogue with this tradition, since it encapsulates key contributions to some of the most important themes with which humans have grappled. For example, difficult questions have been asked about many topics such as:

1. What does it mean to be human?
2. How can we know anything?
3. What is the purpose of suffering?
4. How many varieties of love are there?
5. What is the nature of beauty?
6. How can we live a just and moral life?
7. How can we establish and maintain families and friendships?
8. What constitutes the ideal society and good government?

These ideas emerge in ancient Near Eastern myths, medieval epics, Shakespeare's plays, nineteenth-century novels, and contemporary works. In the Ahistoric Age, however, our obsession with the present especially impoverishes us because it blinds us to these long conversations.

Engaging with the long tradition of learning can help us in two ways. First, it equips us to address the most important questions of our current world. We are wrestling just as much today as ever with questions of meaning, good and evil, the nature of truth, love, and so forth. If we are ignorant of how people from previous centuries have discussed these issues, we flounder when we try to tackle them. As we will see in the following two illustrations, the resources this tradition provides us with are not just helpful in apologetics; they also strengthen our own faith. Personally, I find that my faith is fortified when I read and engage with this long intellectual tradition because the truth, richness, and uniqueness of Christian responses to these perennial "big questions" of human life are cast in relief.

Second, our engagement with this tradition forms our character and shapes us for the Christian life. As Isaac Watts knew, improving our minds strengthens our ability to reason, judge, discern truth and wisdom, and act morally. When we read well, we are not passively absorbing the book. Indeed, this type of reading is quite unlike the passivity of internet browsing and consuming. It enables us to develop the qualities of empathy, discernment, and judgement, which are essential for cultivating both sound reasoning and the discipline of our passions. The better we are at reading and engaging with this long tradition, the better we become at empathetically and imaginatively inhabiting the world of another person across centuries and civilisations. The more we have read of human experience, the more we widen our ability to appreciate and articulate not only the goodness and glory but also the fallenness and brokenness in humanity and in creation. We thus form ourselves to engage with the good, the true, and the beautiful.

Finally, this mission of engagement is best pursued, at least in part, in fellowship as we converse with friends at church, family members, classmates, and our wider communities. Do not think for a moment that these books are merely for the elite and therefore inaccessible. As C. S. Lewis pointed out when he advocated reading the old books, these works are great because their authors are far more intelligible than modern commentators.[18] The Christian approach to intellectual formation is that same spirit which characterises God's kingdom: a humble open invitation which welcomes everyone.

A Practical Illustration: The Good Society

One of the fundamental questions we all engage with at some point is what human society ought to look like. If you have ever talked with friends or family, or perhaps discussed in a public forum, about thorny and complex but pertinent issues like social obligations to the poor or the alien or the relationship between religious freedom and the government, then you have wrestled with what the good society—this side of heaven—ought to look like. This question has occupied theologians as well as non-Christian philosophers and authors for over two millennia. We can be better equipped to engage with such an issue if we complement a biblical approach with knowledge of this long tradition of discussion.

Some years ago, I taught a graduate seminar on the idea of "utopia" in Western thought. We began with Plato's *Republic* and worked our way through sample texts covering two thousand years of utopian literature and philosophy. Some questions we covered were: What *is* justice? Is justice possible in our human societies? What is the relationship between politics and ethics? As my students wrestled with these big questions every week and read what important thinkers throughout history had written, they soon began having thoughtful conversations

---

18. C. S. Lewis, "On Reading Old Books," in *God in the Dock: Essays on Theology and Ethics* (Grand Rapids: Eerdmans, 2001), 200–207. A very helpful book is Susan Wise Bauer, *The Well-Educated Mind: A Guide to the Classical Education You Never Had* (New York: W. W. Norton, 2015).

with each other. They were beginning to think through concepts of individual rights, the rule of law, and democracy, which they genuinely cared about as central to a good society. My students knew well that none of these particular terms are mentioned in the Bible, and they greatly benefited from a deeper understanding of where these concepts had come from, how they have been justified, and what they have looked like in practice.

When my students began to grapple with the idea of "rights" and why they mattered, for example, they learned that medieval legal thinkers, including Thomas Aquinas, had drawn upon classical philosophical ideas of natural law and reshaped them around Christian ideas of the universality, equality, and dignity of all human life. Once my students began studying this long intellectual tradition—which also involved reading the Magna Carta, John Locke, the history of the American and French Revolutions, and the history of the denial of rights to women and citizens of colour in different countries—they were much better equipped to think through and articulate what they meant by the term *rights* and how rights were essential to what society ought to look like.

Many other perennial issues relate to the question of what constitutes a good society, but another good example for us to examine is what it might look like for society to care for those whom Jesus called "the least of these." Many thinkers throughout history, such as St. Francis of Assisi, Thomas More (in his *Utopia*), and William Temple have had enormously varied discussions about what this might look like in practice. As we seek to understand this complex issue, we might learn the history of charity, hospitals, and alms houses in Elizabethan England or read works of literature such as Charles Dickens's novels, the autobiography of Olaudah Equiano, Harriet Beecher Stowe's *Uncle Tom's Cabin*, and *The Diary of Anne Frank*. All these immeasurably helpful sources of information broaden our understanding of the plight of the most vulnerable and marginalised throughout history and show us the various ways in which people have tried, with varying degrees of success, to provide for them.

A Practical Illustration: The Good Life

Not long after I became a Christian in my late twenties, I began to think carefully about the question "how do I live life *well* for Christ?" A little while afterwards, I was reading The Heidelberg Catechism, written in 1563, and the first question and response struck me: "What is your only hope in life and in death?" "*That I am not my own but belong with body and soul, both in life and in death, to my faithful Saviour Jesus Christ.*" But what does the answer look like in practice? If we read widely and wisely, we can find a treasury in the old books which helps us wrestle with what the good life—life lived well for Christ—might entail. Augustine's *Confessions*, Dante's *Divine Comedy*, and John Bunyan's *Pilgrim's Progress*, for example, are rich depictions of the Christian life—its trials and sin yet also its grace. Through the centuries, literature in a variety of genres (from epic to prose, plays, poetry, and novels) has also engaged with ideas about aspects of the Christian life lived well, albeit in more oblique ways than in Augustine's, Dante's, and Bunyan's works. For example, Louisa May Alcott's *Little Women* and Fyodor Dostoevsky's *The Brothers Karamazov* grapple in very different ways with a myriad of questions about how to pursue the good through a virtuous life. We also gain much by encountering the consequences of human brokenness and sin in literature. We meet characters who are flawed and selfish yet are painstakingly and meticulously transformed through suffering, such as Gwendolen Harleth in George Eliot's *Daniel Deronda*.

When we read the Italian Renaissance philosopher Pico della Mirandola's speech "On the Dignity of Man," William Faulkner's novel *Absalom, Absalom!*, or John Steinbeck's *East of Eden*, we can think deeply about the nature of free will in the human condition, the sins of the past and how they affect the present, and the possibilities of humanity's ability to choose the good. We see instances of terrible sin and shortcomings from which we can learn, along with moments of grace and glimpses of suffering and mercy. However, we are not reading these books as instruction manuals. These characters are not simple archetypes, and some of them are not Christian. Rather, we read them in such a way that engages our conscience, our knowledge of Scripture, and of humanity. These books prompt us to wrestle with sin, grace, and everything else involved in living well for Christ.

Great or well-known books of the past are not the only sources that can help us. History also provides examples of Christians who lived lives of service to the gospel and to their neighbour at immense cost to themselves. We often need to read about these saints in histories or biographies written later, since they often left only unpublished diaries. For example, Catherine Booth (1829–1890), the "Mother of the Salvation Army," tirelessly and publicly worked to rescue young girls and women from prostitution and sex trafficking, which were rife in nineteenth-century London. When the age of consent for girls was originally just twelve, and then raised to only thirteen in 1875, Booth campaigned to raise it to sixteen. At considerable personal cost, she also argued that women's supposed intellectual and moral inferiority was entirely unscriptural and defended the biblical truth of the ontological equality of men and women.[19]

We can also study many other examples of faithful Christians, from the martyrs of the ancient and medieval world to the campaigners for the abolition of the slave trade like William Wilberforce (1759–1833), Thomas Clarkson (1760–1846), and Hannah More (1745–1833). I read recently about the missionary Gladys Aylward (1902–1970), who rescued over one hundred orphaned children in China from Japanese soldiers in 1938. She single-handedly accompanied the children on an audacious trek across remote mountains, nearly dying but saving their lives. In that same time period, the pastor Dietrich Bonhoeffer (1906–1945), who had cautioned German Christians against idolising the führer Adolf Hitler, was put in a concentration camp and later executed for his resistance to the Nazi regime and the Holocaust. We thankfully have Bonhoeffer's classic texts *Life Together* and *The Cost*

---

19. See Rachel Ciano, "Catherine Booth: Perfect Equality," in Rachel Ciano and Ian Maddock, *Ten Dead Gals You Should Know: Leaving an Enduring Legacy* (Fearn, UK: Christian Focus, 2023). All ten of the women in this book are remarkable examples of different aspects of the Christian life.

of Discipleship, which are enormously helpful in thinking through the difference between costly and cheap grace.

The long tradition of learning helps us understand the many non-Christian conceptions of the good life. If we are to speak effectively to others about the beautiful hope we have in Christ, we need to understand the alternative visions of the good life that compete with God, just like Paul did when he spoke to the Athenian Areopagus (Acts 17:16–34). Many contemporary ideas of the good life—for example, pursuing one's own well-being and happiness—have ancient roots. If we read the old books, we can develop the ability to detect and identify these ideas in our contemporary culture when we meet them. For instance, there are strong vestiges of Epicurean ideas in today's culture which encourage us to free ourselves from pain and maximise our pleasure. In fact, the entire well-being industry has arguably imbibed a greatly simplified version of some aspects of Epicureanism. The Epicurean tradition has been passed down through the centuries by figures such as the nineteenth-century utilitarian philosophers Jeremy Bentham and John Stuart Mill. The idea that the good life has minimal suffering and much pleasure is clearly attractive, so we need to know the basic principles and history of this view and others like it without oversimplifying them. We can identify these ideas, engage with them, and present (to ourselves and others) a compelling Christian vision.

Aristotle, Plato, and Cicero contributed to ongoing discussions about the relationship between living justly and the good life. Aristotle used the concept of *eudaimonia*, which is usually translated as "happiness." But what *is* happiness? Is it merely a matter for the inner soul or is it related to material conditions? Indeed, Christians need to ask: What is our initial definition of happiness? Unless we understand the lengthy intellectual and historical tradition behind this topic, we cannot robustly and winsomely articulate the Christian position on happiness. We cannot remind ourselves of its truth and goodness, let alone disciple others on it. Is a happy life a goal Christians ought to pursue? We also need to understand how the biblical idea of happiness and joy differs from classical philosophical conceptions of happiness.

After all, our non-Christian friends and neighbours do not think of the biblical background of happiness when they talk about this topic. Ideas about "love," as well as types of "love," are another example we could examine.

In short, reading widely in the long tradition of learning equips us to speak with informed and articulate humility to our fellow Christians and non-Christians about some of the most important questions in life. This is true not only for the way we approach our personal conversations, but also for our interactions in church and in the public square.

Historically, Christians sought to form themselves intellectually by engaging with a long tradition of learning that ran from the ancient world to the present time. If we approach the past as priestly work, tending and keeping this tradition, we can be helped in two significant ways. First, working alongside our biblical knowledge, this tradition equips us to interact with culture by giving us resources to speak about some of the most important questions in life. Second, this tradition cultivates our character, particularly our abilities to reason, think wisely, and empathise, as we engage with the broad horizons of God's creation. In short, tending and keeping this historical tradition improves our minds so that we can glorify God and serve others in the midst of an age that has unmoored education from any sense of a higher purpose.

TWELVE

History and Spiritual Formation

I n his law firm, my husband John regularly gathers with his colleagues and friends and prays the Commination, which is one of the offices of the *Book of Common Prayer*, modelled on a spiritual discipline dating back to the early church. The Commination involves reciting a series of prayers spoken antiphonally (that is, in a call and response style), including scriptural texts such as the Ten Commandments and Psalm 51. These prayers echo God's anger and judgement against sinners and then encourage earnest and true repentance: to turn to Christ alone as the source of our salvation. One particularly helpful feature of the Commination is how it compels us to repent of sin together. Our culture encourages us to follow "the devices and desires of our own heart," so it is all too easy for us to neglect both repentance and the command of James 5:16 to confess our sins to one another.[1]

The ancient discipline of spiritual formation is something of a lost treasure. In our current Ahistoric Age, many Christians are largely ignorant of the long traditions of spiritual formation. Indeed, some Christians—particularly evangelicals—also tend to be instinctively suspicious how our traditions and heritage could help us today. Many in the church are now realising that our spiritual formation is impoverished. Spiritual disciplines are shoehorned into our schedules,

---

1. The phrase "devices and desires of our own heart" is taken from the prayer of general confession in Morning and Evening Prayer in the *Book of Common Prayer*, beginning in 1552 (the second *Book of Common Prayer*) and continuing to this day.

sometimes with the aid of technology that minimises our time commitment and maximises convenience.

Yet spiritual formation was historically so much richer than simply inserting some prayer and Bible reading into our schedules. In previous centuries, individual Christians, churches, and private families practiced a wide variety of formative spiritual disciplines. In this chapter, we will explore how tending and keeping history can help us with spiritual formation. Let us journey back to seventeenth-century England and examine two case studies of spiritual formation, starting with the small Church of England community at the village of Little Gidding.

Little Gidding

You may know of Little Gidding today if you have read T. S. Eliot's *Four Quartets*. Eliot named one of these quartets after the village in Huntingdonshire. In the seventeenth century, Little Gidding was a community of about thirty people that flourished between about 1625 and the early 1640s, roughly coterminous with the reign of Charles I. It was formed and led by Nicholas Ferrar (1593–1637), a deputy of the Virginia Company who served briefly in Parliament. Nicholas was born into a merchant family. His mother, Mary Wodenoth Ferrar (1551–1634), was educated, erudite, and devout. She was a formative influence upon her son's faith and was effectively a matriarch at Little Gidding.

After her husband's death in 1620 and the collapse of the Virginia Company in 1624, Mary, then in her seventies, purchased the manor at Little Gidding, which at that time stood in virtual ruins. Mary, her sons Nicholas and John, John's family, and her daughter Susannah and her family moved into the manor after renovating it. There, they established a community devoted to the worship of God and service to their surrounding community. Nicholas, a bachelor, was ordained as a deacon in the Church of England so that he could lead the family in worship at the chapel.

I remember when I first came across the published work and the manuscripts of the Ferrar family, which included a variety of genres of writing such as John's biography of his brother, poetry, letters, a dialogue called *The Winding-Sheet*, a *Collection of Short Moral Histories*, and a number of tracts about practical endeavours such as beekeeping and silk production.[2] I was in Cambridge researching my PhD thesis and was not yet a Christian, but this community intrigued and fascinated me by their combination of practical interests in useful knowledge with their piety and devotion. The Ferrar family evidently followed a programme of prayer throughout the day as well as an antiphonal recitation of the Psalter, in its entirety, every day (modelled in part on the *Book of Common Prayer*). Nicholas's nieces held important roles in the management of the household and also embarked upon a project to construct gospel harmonies that combined the four gospel accounts of Jesus's life into one narrative.[3]

Little Gidding was something of a sanctuary from the corruptions of the world, but it was certainly not a retreat from the Reformation project of transforming the world in the image of Christ. It was commonplace among seventeenth-century English Protestants to portray Adam's prelapsarian dominion in the garden of Eden as exercising his encyclopaedic knowledge of the natural world. This was his ability, as Genesis 2:20 put it, to give names "to all cattle, and to the birds of the air, and to every animal of the field." The fall, therefore, had profound effects upon the human intellect and cognition: Adam and Eve lost their exhaustive knowledge of the world and, with it, their dominion over the creation. The Ferrar community shared with the Protestant culture of that time a burgeoning interest in the kinds of knowledge that would help repair the effects of sin on humanity and the creation. This reformation of the world was not just moral and spiritual, therefore, but also intellectual. It involved the exploration of natural history, agriculture, husbandry, and other kinds of

---

2. A selection of the Hartlib papers have been reprinted in B. Blackstone, ed., *The Ferrar Papers* (Cambridge, UK: Cambridge University Press, 1939). Some of the more obscure and otherwise unpublished manuscripts and letters can be found in the digital database *The Hartlib Papers*, 2nd ed. (Sheffield, UK: HROnline, 2002).

3. On the harmonies, see Joyce Ransome, "Monotessaron: The Harmonies of Little Gidding," *The Seventeenth Century* 20 (1975): 22–52.

useful knowledge. Incidentally, this emphasis upon regaining the lost knowledge of nature played no small role in the origins of modern science.[4]

The Ferrars, for example, were particularly interested in the cultivation of silk. John Ferrar published eight pamphlets encouraging planters in the Virginia colony to cultivate silkworms. At Little Gidding, John's daughter Virginia cultivated and studied silkworms and wrote poetry extolling the virtue and utility of silk cultivation. Here we can see how moral and intellectual improvement went hand in hand with the gospel. The Ferrars also funded plans for evangelical projects to make disciples out of the American Indians in Virginia, such as an Indian college to educate indigenous Americans in 1619.[5]

The community at Little Gidding also had an abiding commitment to serve the poor in the surrounding villages. In John Ferrar's admiring biography of his brother Nicholas, he detailed how Mary and the adult women cared for the sick. They made "Oyles, [and] salves" and engaged in "distilling of Waters" as well as making plasters and cloths for bandages. They furnished a surgeon's chest in a special room in the manor dedicated for medical purposes, where they "cured all Such Persons as daily came for one thing or other to be helped of Some things that ayled them."[6] John also describes how the women would "make the Sick & weak good Broaths [broths], & to give them Kitchen Phisick, which was a main thing for all poore peoples recovery of health."[7]

---

4. See Sarah Irving, *Natural Science and the Origins of the British Empire* (London: Pickering and Chatto, 2008).

5. Peter Peckard, ed., *Memoirs of the Life of Mr. Nicholas Ferrar* (Cambridge, UK: Cambridge University Press, 1740), 107.

6. John Ferrar, *A Life of Nicholas Ferrar*, in *The Ferrar Papers*, ed. B. Blackstone (Cambridge, UK: Cambridge University Press, 2015), 31. To read some of the dialogues at Little Gidding, see A. M. Williams, ed., *Conversations at Little Gidding: Dialogues by Members of the Ferrar Family* (Cambridge, UK: Cambridge University Press, 1970). Some of the original texts written at Little Gidding have been reproduced from the University of Michigan Libraries Collection. See Nicholas Ferrar, *The Story Books of Little Gidding: Being the Religious Dialogues Recited in the Great Room, 1631–1632, from the Original Manuscript of Nicholas Ferrar* (New York: E. P. Dutton, 1899).

7. Ferrar, *A Life of Nicholas Ferrar*, 32.

Additionally, matriarch Mary Ferrar established an "Alms-house or Lodging-room for 4 poor Widows, in one part of the House, where they were competently provided for, & were looked upon as part of the Family, going daily to Church."[8] The community distributed alms three times a week, when "poore House-keepers that dwelt in the Townes rownd about little Gidding came in the Morning at six a Clock." At that time Nicholas spoke "the comfortable Words" to them, and then sent out the family's broth to those who were sick in the towns and could not come to the manor at Little Gidding. These "comfortable Words" were biblical verses that gave assurance of God's promise of forgiveness and salvation. In summer, the poor were also given milk from the family's cows.[9]

We should not look back at Little Gidding through rose-tinted sentimentality. We can, however, consider this community to be one historical resource from which we can derive instruction and inspiration. Let us explore two spiritual practices from Little Gidding which we can draw upon, modify, and appropriate: the night vigil and mealtime reading.

The Night Vigil

Every night of the week in Little Gidding, several family members kept a vigil during which they would remain awake and spend the hours "in the Saying of David's Psalms, & some other Meditations of Prayer, Prayses & Thanksgiving to GOD."[10] Participation was purely voluntary, for these gatherings sought to kindle earnest and fervent desire of the heart. In his biography of his brother Nicholas, John Ferrar gives a fascinating glimpse of these night vigils. As we read his words, we can almost see the candlelight and the fireplaces in winter, stoked now and then for warmth and light during the long hours.

John Ferrar quickly pointed out that, despite the ascetic nature of this discipline and its echoes of monastic practice, we ought not be scandalised. Night vigils (or watches, as he sometimes called them)

---

8. Ferrar, *A Life of Nicholas Ferrar*, 32.
9. Ferrar, *A Life of Nicholas Ferrar*, 32–33.
10. Ferrar, *A Life of Nicholas Ferrar*, 55.

were biblical. He knew the story of Jesus in Gethsemane well and noted other instances in the Scriptures in which people prayed during the night, such as David, who said, "At Midnight will I rise & give Thanks unto thee." Also, "Paul & Silas prayed at Midnight & Sang prayses."[11] John indicated that these night vigils were partly encouraged by Nicholas's dear friendship and fellowship with the poet and minister George Herbert, whom we met in chapter 10.[12]

The vigils began at 9 p.m. and continued until 1 a.m. Usually, those who undertook this practice would recite all of David's psalms during the four hours, typically antiphonally, since people usually kept a vigil in pairs. Then they would return to their beds and sleep till 6 a.m., when they rose as usual for the day. Many of the family members, including resident servants, were able to read and evidently memorised many of the Psalms. Sometimes they also spent the period worshipping through playing the organ, singing hymns, and reciting the Psalms.[13] Nicholas spent two (and sometimes three) nights a week in these vigils.

This is an intriguing window into a practice largely forgotten in contemporary Protestant circles in today's Ahistoric Age. The history of the night vigil dates back to the very early church. In fact, we have evidence that within a few generations of Christ's death, Christians were routinely gathering to pray during the night. As early as AD 112, Pliny the Younger, a Roman magistrate and governor whose persecution of Christians included torturing two women who were deacons, reported to Emperor Trajan that those accused of being Christians in his province met regularly while it was still dark:

> They were accustomed to meet on a fixed day before dawn and sing responsively a hymn to Christ as to a god, and to bind themselves by oath, not to some crime, but not to commit fraud, theft, or adultery, not falsify their trust, nor to refuse to return a trust when called upon to do so. When this was over, it was their custom to

---

11. Ferrar, *A Life of Nicholas Ferrar*, 55.
12. Ferrar, *A Life of Nicholas Ferrar*, 55.
13. Ferrar, *A Life of Nicholas Ferrar*, 56.

depart and to assemble again to partake of food—but ordinary and innocent food.[14]

When the church father Tertullian cautioned against marrying a non-Christian, he described the difficulties that a Christian wife married to a non-Christian husband would experience. From his description, we gain insight into some of the normal and expected practices of Christians. What non-Christian husband, Tertullian wondered, would tolerate his wife departing from his side at night to gather with other Christians and pray? He elaborated, "Who will willingly bear her to be parted from his side, by the meetings at night, if her duty so call? Finally, who will without heed endure her being away all night at the solemnities of Easter?"[15]

In the medieval church, the tradition of praying during the night formed part of the liturgy of the hours, and it was common for monks to recite the psalter at set hours—or watches—during these vigils. This practice was not completely neglected after the Reformation, either. The Church of England's 1662 *Book of Common Prayer* listed a table of vigils, fasts, and days of abstinence to be observed during the year. This setup assumed that one would hold a vigil and/or fast before sixteen holy days.[16]

So, how could the spiritual discipline of a night vigil help us today? In the dead of night, when our ordinary surroundings recede into darkness, the world becomes strange and foreign. We feel quiet and withdrawn. Our bodies are tired and crave the comfort of sleep, and we are acutely aware of our physical frailty and neediness. However, when we discipline ourselves to remain awake and pray, we are cultivating our ability to resist the bodily temptation to sleep and can more deeply

---

14. Pliny the Younger, *Letters*, 10.96–97, https://faculty.georgetown.edu/jod/texts/pliny.html.

15. Tertullian, *Tertullian: Apologetic and Practical Treatises*, trans. C. Dodgson (Oxford; London: John Henry Parker; J. G. F. and J. Rivington, 1842), 426.

16. *The 1662 Book of Common Prayer: International Edition*, ed. Samuel L. Bray and Drew Nathaniel Keane (Downers Grove: IVP Academic, 2021), xxiv–xxv.

recognise our dependence upon God for every need. A similar process happens when we fast.

This bodily discipline requires us to attend to what is truly real—that is, to remain *awake* not just physically, but spiritually. This is why people have kept vigil by the deathbed of loved ones for countless generations; remaining awake is about intentionally choosing to focus on what truly matters when our lesser and baser needs would have us do otherwise. If we are awake to Christ, we are truly awake. Of course we can be spiritually awake at any time, but the night vigil especially reminds us, through Christ's practice of spending hours at night praying to his Father, that spiritual alertness is valuable.

A night vigil is a practice we could adopt in any number of ways, perhaps as a small group or alone. Some might find that the darkness, solitude, and strangeness of being awake to pray when all others are asleep—and, indeed, when one would normally sleep—focuses them and reorients their heart towards God. After all, we have heightened sensitivities at night. The hours do not need to be 9 p.m.–1 a.m., nor must our devotion consist solely in reciting Psalms, singing hymns, or prayer. Perhaps rising shortly before 4 a.m. and spending two hours reading the Bible and praying Morning Prayer and the Great Litany from the *Book of Common Prayer* might be helpful. Others might find it helpful to rise from sleep for a few hours during the night to pray, for example, between 1 a.m. and 3 a.m., and then to return to bed for a few hours. Or, perhaps, we might gather with brothers and sisters to pray during the night at Easter or at other significant times in the Christian calendar. As I described in chapter 9, on Easter Sunday my family and some of our friends gather before sunrise for a candlelit vigil. It feels profoundly sobering, humbling, and moving to read the Bible and pray as the sunrise gradually replaces the candlelight on Easter morning.

Reading Aloud at Mealtimes

The Ferrar family also practiced the spiritual discipline of reading aloud at mealtimes. John Ferrar described the way in which the main meal on Sundays (which was called "dinner," even though it was eaten during the day) began with everyone standing and singing a hymn and hearing the organ playing. They then sat down to eat, while one of the children or youth "read a Chapter in the Bible, . . . that so [their] Eares & heartes might not want the best Spirituall food."[17] The evening meal, supper, began similarly. According to Ferrar, "At Supper time, [which] was commonly in Summer about 5, & Winter 6, the Bell rung, they all came again into the Great Parlour, & the Organs began to play, . . . & all satt downe, & a while after one read a Chapter" of the Bible. Then, the young person who had read earlier, "went to the Desk, & read a Story out of the Book of Martyrs."[18]

This mealtime reading, often accompanied by hymn singing, was different from the other times during the day when the family read the Bible and sang. In other words, this practice was not a way of merely scheduling Bible reading so that it coincided with the mealtime; it was more than that, setting apart the meal as a special devotional time. Furthermore, when John Ferrar mentioned the *Book of Martyrs*, he was referring to the famous book first published in 1563 by the English historian John Foxe that compiled stories of Protestant martyrs. This was another way the Ferrars were tending and keeping the past: passing down stories about the church and about martyrs through many generations.

John Ferrar commented that the family had decided that "there shall always be something read during Meal times" because it helped to combine the "refreshment" of the bodies as well as the mind, making the reading edifying and delightful.[19] Aside from the Bible, the Ferrars often read works of history as well as other genres of writing that would "not only furnish ye minde with variety of knowledge in all kinds, but also stir up the Affections to the embracement of virtue." The children—both boys and girls—almost always read. Readings from the Gospels then followed the readings from these books.[20]

---

17. Ferrar, *A Life of Nicholas Ferrar*, 40.
18. Ferrar, *A Life of Nicholas Ferrar*, 40.
19. Ferrar, *A Life of Nicholas Ferrar*, 46.
20. Ferrar, *A Life of Nicholas Ferrar*, 47.

For the "better retaining in memory," summaries of each book were written, usually compiled by the parents but transcribed by the children. Every noon, just before the daily meal, they would repeat what was formerly read. At the end of the day when supper was over, the reading had ceased, and grace was said, one of the children who had read earlier repeated a story from heart.[21] Memorising and recounting stories was one way the Ferrars formed their children. This exercise taught the children "something of worth, exciting to Virtue, & the hatred of Vice; & by this the young ones learned to speak gracefully & courageously."[22]

Adopting a version of this practice of reading aloud at mealtimes could be enormously helpful today as we battle declining literacy rates and daily see how few of us, particularly those in younger generations, are avid readers who relish books and continually seek enrichment from them. According to Pew research data, roughly a quarter of American adults say they have not read a book in any format—print, electronic, or audio—either in whole or in part in the past year. That 2021 statistic was triple the percentage in 1978, when there were no audio or digital books at all.[23]

The practice of eating meals together is also diminishing quickly. You have probably observed some of your companions on their phones or iPads while eating; they are retreating into a highly individualistic and private online world of comfort and entertainment, stress and work, or distraction and vanity. Every meal has a liturgy whether we realise it or not, as many have recognised. If this liturgy involves technology, perhaps we ought to think again about its structure.[24]

Apart from merely putting away the technology, the tradition of breaking bread together while reading aloud from a well-chosen book

21. Ferrar, *A Life of Nicholas Ferrar*, 48–49.

22. Ferrar, *A Life of Nicholas Ferrar*, 49.

23. Steven Mintz, "Is Literacy Declining?," Inside Higher Ed, January 18, 2022, https://www.insidehighered.com/blogs/higher-ed-gamma/literacy-declining/, cites the Pew research data. See also, "What Does It Mean to Be 'Literate'—And Is It under Threat?," ABC Listen, February 1, 2023, https://www.abc.net.au/listen/programs/theminefield/the-minefield/14138898/.

24. An excellent resource to guide us with technology is Andy Crouch, *The Tech-Wise Family: Everyday Steps for Putting Technology in Its Proper Place* (Grand Rapids: Baker, 2017).

is an opportunity to orient ourselves to God and to each other. We ought to think of this as a spiritual discipline since it requires intentional commitment. We are being trained. The practice of reading aloud as part of a communal meal can shield us against retreating into technology or letting our minds sink to their baser instincts of distraction and self-absorption. Not only the content of the books themselves is helpful, but also the act of hearing and engaging our minds in ideas and language that edify and bring us out of the ordinary. Perhaps the books we choose will shed light on some situation or topic. Perhaps they will enliven us with beauty and transport us into a distant, wonderful land.

Reading at mealtimes also enables us to *share* the experience of engaging with a book. This is a communal spiritual discipline of the mind; we can encourage and build each other up as we read. We are brought outside of ourselves and given shared subjects and ideas to discuss. Not only would reading the Bible at mealtimes be particularly helpful, but we can use other books as well. We can read over meals with our biological families as well as when we eat and have hospitality with other brothers and sisters in Christ.

Like with the night vigil, we do not need to replicate precisely the Ferrars' method. Perhaps we might read one of Jesus's parables, or perhaps recite one or two of the Psalms. Maybe some households will sing or play a hymn together and then read during or immediately after the meal. Recently, for example, my family finished a mealtime ritual of reading Frederick Marryat's 1847 novel *The Children of the New Forest*. When we focus our thoughts on edifying texts and great books, we participate in the Holy Spirit's transformation of our minds. We engage our minds in higher things, and we can then talk about what we have read with our companions as we break bread together.

Joseph Hall and Protestant Meditation

When many people hear the word *meditation* today, they often think of Eastern spirituality. But Christians had their own distinct meditative tradition centuries before Eastern spirituality became fashionable in the West. For instance, the Church of England bishop Joseph Hall (1574–1656) wrote a number of books about what he called "Protestant Meditation." Hall fervently believed that meditation could help all Christians in their spiritual formation. This Protestant tradition has largely been forgotten or neglected in the Ahistoric Age, yet it holds riches for us.

Joseph Hall (1574–1656)

Joseph Hall was a contemporary of the Ferrar family, and his story shows how challenging it is to live wisely in turbulent times. He was both a Church of England bishop and a Calvinist, an occasionally uneasy combination during this tumultuous period of English history. Born into a well-connected family, the young Joseph soon showed himself to have considerable intellectual promise. He attended Emmanuel College, Cambridge, graduated with a BA in 1593, and was elected lecturer in rhetoric at the university in 1596. I first came across Hall when I was researching my doctoral dissertation and read his satirical account of an imagined voyage to the Antipodes entitled *Mundus Alter et Idem* (1605; "a different world and the same"). This book was later translated into English as *A Discovery of a New World*, later serving as an inspiration and model for Jonathan Swift's *Gulliver's Travels* in the eighteenth century.

Hall was ordained in 1600 and served as minister of Hawstead in Suffolk. He was appointed chaplain to the court of Prince Henry, the eldest son of King James, and served until the prince's death in 1612. A prominent member of the English church, Hall served as one of the delegates to the international Synod of Dort, where he delivered a sermon. Despite his prominence, Hall came under suspicion for how Reformed his theology was, not least because he received such a warm welcome when he travelled to Scotland with King James in 1617. Hall did not intentionally court controversy, however, and what we know of his character indicates that he acted with integrity despite being a participant in the religious debates of that time. His support of the episcopacy was controversial among more radical Puritans, but his Calvinist theology and insistence on purifying the church from the excesses of ceremonialism troubled some high church supporters of the archbishop of Canterbury, William Laud. Hall was appointed bishop of Exeter in 1627, where he served until 1641 when he became bishop of Norwich on the eve of the English Civil War. Hall was briefly imprisoned in the Tower of London for petitioning to be allowed to serve in Parliament as a bishop when presbyterians and independents gained power during the civil war.[25]

Despite all this turmoil, Hall advocated for toleration among Protestants in matters indifferent and anticipated to some degree the latitudinarian movement that accepted some doctrinal diversity within the Church of England. In 1626, he penned a tract entitled *Via Media* which attempted to mediate between Calvinists and Arminians. What we know of Hall's personal life is limited, but he evidently adored his wife, Elizabeth, and their eight children. In subsequent generations, Hall was admired by the poet Alexander Pope (1688–1744) and the satirist and novelist Laurence Sterne (1713–1768), two key writers of the eighteenth century.

I continue to be fascinated by Hall's work on "Protestant Meditation" more than a decade after I first encountered him. In 1606 Hall published *The Arte of Divine Meditation*, which was so popular that it was reprinted in both 1607 and 1609 and then multiple times over the following decades, sometimes as part of other works. He also wrote *Meditations and Vows* (1603) and *Occasional Meditations* (1630). The well-known Puritan Richard Baxter praised Hall's work on meditation and encouraged others to read it. Thus, as we can see, meditation is a very practical form of piety with a long history, yet in the Protestant church we have largely lost this tradition.

---

25. On Hall's life, see Richard A. McCabe, "Hall, Joseph (1574–1656)," Oxford Dictionary of National Biography, September 23, 2004, https://www.oxforddnb.com/display /10.1093/ref:odnb/9780198614128.001.0001/odnb-9780198614128-e-11976.

The tradition of meditation dates back to the early centuries of the church and was particularly encouraged by patristic writers such as St. Augustine, who was a major influence on Hall. This diverse tradition developed in the ascetic practices of various monastic communities, particularly as part of *lectio divina* ("divine reading"), which involved reading, meditation, prayer, and contemplation. The Rule of St. Benedict, for example, included the meditative reading of Scripture. In the Middle Ages, various authors embraced meditation as a form of piety, including Anselm of Canterbury.[26] Meditation was also a central part of the *devotio moderna*, which was a religious reform movement during the fourteenth and fifteenth centuries. This movement emphasised renewing spiritual practices and piety and significantly influenced St. Ignatius of Loyola, who published his *Spiritual Exercises* in 1548.

Protestants did not abandon the practice of meditation, despite its prevalence in monastic communities. Rather, many of them developed and reshaped meditation around their theology. J. I. Packer, for example, has shown the importance of meditation to the Puritans' vision of the Christian life: a number of them wrote manuals about meditation and incorporated it as a part of their spiritual discipline.[27] Whereas in the Catholic tradition these kinds of spiritual exercises were primarily aimed at the clergy and religious orders, Joseph Hall, like other Protestants, believed that meditation could be a helpful part of all Christians' spiritual lives. Hall aimed to produce a work that would be "profitable for all Christians." In the end, as Todd Baucum points out, "meditation would be an unquestioned and common practice among Protestants well into the eighteenth century in both the English church and in the American colonies."[28]

Hall's form of meditation was essentially a method of orienting the soul to, and igniting its love for, God. As Hall put it, "every Christian

---

26. Benedicta Ward, "Introduction," in Anselm of Aosta, *The Prayers and Meditations of St. Anselm*, trans. Benedicta Ward (Harmondsworth, UK: Penguin, 1973), 37–38.

27. J. I. Packer, *The Quest for Godliness: The Puritan Vision of the Christian Life* (Wheaton: Crossway, 1990).

28. Todd Baucum, *The Puritan Imagination: Bishop Joseph Hall's Use of Meditation* (Eugene, OR: Wipf and Stock, 2022), 196–97.

had neede of fire put to his affections."[29] Hall used the popular imagery of spiritual ascent, but this language does not for one moment
mean that we are ascending any scale of righteousness or salvation.
Rather, meditation is a response to God's grace—an outworking of the
Holy Spirit enabling us through contemplation to draw our minds and
souls upwards towards closer union with Christ. With the Holy Spirit's
leading and help, meditation engages the body, senses, imagination,
and mind in a sustained reflection on a particular subject. Our contemplation of a particular topic for the meditation proceeds through
ordered steps so that our affections are stirred and strengthened and
our hearts delight in the deeper experience of God. In Hall's words,
at one stage in meditation, "our hearts shal be so full that we cannot
chuse but sing, and wee cannot but sing melodiously."[30]

Hall makes it clear that his method is but one among others that
might be helpful. First, he gives some preliminary and practical considerations. Hall encourages his reader to think through the place,
the time, and the posture of the body. Ideally, the place would be one
set apart—in other words, sacred. "*Solitarinesse of Place* is fittest for
Meditation," Hall writes, and the place could be a garden, somewhere
in the wilderness, or perhaps a chapel.[31] We will not always meditate
in the same position; sometimes we will "fall grovelling on our faces,
somtimes we bow our knees, sometimes stand on our feete, somtimes
we lift up our handes, sometimes cast down our eyes." Hall emphasised
that God does not care about the exact type of gesture or position, but
rather desires it to be "reverent."[32]

Once we are in the right place, preparing ourselves for meditation
involves clearing our hearts of the preoccupations of worldly life and
praying to confess our sins. This requires "an honest sincerity of the
heart" and "willingly repenting when we have sinned."[33] Hall then

---

29. Joseph Hall, *The Arte of Divine Meditation: Profitable for All Christians to Knowe and Practise* (London: Humphrey Lownes, 1606), 8.

30. Hall, *The Arte of Divine Meditation*, 108.

31. Hall, *The Arte of Divine Meditation*, 49. Emphasis original.

32. Hall, *The Arte of Divine Meditation*, 60–61.

33. Hall, *The Arte of Divine Meditation*, 27.

proceeds to set out a particular series of steps for meditation. We decide on a topic for meditation as we consider what we need deliberately to think through. Common subjects for meditation among Protestants included the majesty of God, sin, death, the beauty of Christ, judgement, hell, the glory of heaven, or even particular scriptural doctrines.

Hall's method for meditation begins in our understanding and ends in our affections. In other words, meditation begins in our brains as we contemplate a topic and we bring this process to conclusion in our hearts as our affections are stirred. It thus helps to think of meditation as something our souls are doing.

The first half of Hall's method is intellectual: the soul engages in an ordered contemplation of one's chosen subject. One attends to the subject's definition, meaning, and significance, thinking these through carefully. Here is an example of a topic and the questions we might consider during this part of the meditation: What is the resurrection? What is its significance? What place does Christ's resurrection have in God's story? What is the resurrection of all Christians on the final day? What does the resurrection tell us about God and his plan for salvation? We can be guided here by scriptural passages about the resurrection.

The second part of Hall's process of meditation, broadly speaking, shifts attention from our understanding to our affections. In this section, we stir up our longings for God and for heaven. During the course of meditation, we are able to glimpse, through the Holy Spirit guiding our intellect and our imagination, something of the promised joy and glory of heaven and union with Christ. However, we are reminded that we are not yet there. We contemplate the mortality, frailty, transience, and sufferings of this earthly life and its nature as a pilgrimage. This juxtaposition between joy made complete and infinite and our "not yet" present reality propels our hearts. We then descend the mountain, reminded of our pilgrimage and that distant land of heaven. Our journey prompts us to beckon, anticipate, and watch for Christ's return, our hearts "enflam'd" (as Hall put it) by the assurance that we can trust God's promises and covenant.

The tradition of meditation can particularly help us today by, in Hall's words, "quicken[ing us] out of this dull and lazy security."[34] Meditation arouses our affections. This spiritual practice is not about increasing our knowledge of information as such, and herein lies its help for spiritual formation. Global culture today is increasingly shaped by the excessive abundance of information. Having lots of information is not bad in and of itself, but we consequently tend to isolate propositional truth from goodness and beauty, especially neglecting the latter of these two transcendentals. Moreover, contemporary culture tends to understand and treat the mind as if it is separate and divided from the body and, even more so, the soul. Meditation, however, recognises that we are souls in bodies; there is a connection between the soul, the conscious mind, the desires of the will, and the heart's affections.

Indeed, using a process of meditation is scriptural. The Psalms regularly encourage us to meditate on God's mighty works. Paul encourages us to think about and ponder whatever is true, honourable, just, and worthy of praise (Phil. 4:8). The psalmist meditates day and night on God's instructions (Ps. 1:2–3) and reflects with careful contemplation upon his mighty deeds in Psalm 77. In Psalms 45, 49, and 73, among others, we find the psalmist meditating on human joys, frailty, and sorrow. Joshua is taught to meditate on the book of the law (Josh. 1:8). Careful reflection, pondering, and prayerful contemplation are part of a long and rich tradition. Of course, we can adopt and modify Hall as we see fit. Hall himself wrote that "Every man aboundeth in his owne sense" and could use different paths to the same end.[35] The historical tradition of meditation that engages the different faculties—the imagination, the senses, the will, and the mind—could be as helpful to our spiritual formation today as it has been for other saints through millennia.

"*Protestant* meditation? Who knew?" exclaimed a friend of mine when I told him about Hall's writings. Such is our surprise and excited

---

34. Hall, *The Arte of Divine Meditation*, 192.
35. Hall, *The Arte of Divine Meditation*, 186–87.

curiosity when we encounter a long heritage largely forgotten in the Ahistoric Age. Yet we need this kind of spiritual formation more than ever in today's world. I smiled when I read Joseph Hall's list of all the daily preoccupations in the seventeenth century: *"What have I yet? How may I gette more? . . . What shall I leave for posterity?"*[36] Humanity has not changed one bit! If we can be priests of history, tending and keeping the past, we will find that historical treasures like the night vigil, reading aloud at mealtimes, and meditation can help us enormously with our spiritual formation.

---

36. Hall, *The Arte of Divine Meditation*, 189–90. Emphasis original.

Conclusion

History and the Renewal of the Church

I'm just . . . *disconnected*," a friend of mine said, pausing before emphasising the last word. I was chatting after church with some of the young adults, and she had exercised her characteristic candour and insight to touch upon a vital concern. This was a moment of realisation for me. I hear about the same sense of disconnection from my students at university. So many people are disconnected. But from what? The usual answers are community and relationships, and those are certainly part of the explanation. But this disconnection is emblematic of a broader issue at the heart of contemporary culture: we are disconnected from our history.

This book asserts that contemporary Western culture has now entered an Ahistoric Age. At heart, we have lost the ability to engage meaningfully with the past.

I am particularly concerned that ahistoricism is seeping into many parts of the church, leaving Christians rootless, unmoored from their history, and largely unequipped to grapple with the ethical complexities of the past. We are thus rendered even more susceptible to the idols of non-Christian culture. The Ahistoric Age also has dire consequences for discipleship: Christians are increasingly living without an inherited identity that frames the practices of formation and discipleship.

So, what can we do about this? How can we address our disconnection from history and our sense that history has nothing to teach us?

This book is both a critique of culture and a positive vision of a way forward. After exploring how Western societies lost their connection to history and outlining why history matters to Christians, I presented a framework for a Christian approach to history both within and outside of the academy. Christians are called to be "priests of history" who do the work of "tending and keeping" the past. Approaching the past through this priestly vocation involves, firstly, the work of tending and cultivating, which entails uncovering overlooked histories, bringing historical injustices to light, and recognising the sins of the past, including our own; and, secondly, the conservative work of keeping, guarding, protecting, and passing down historical knowledge and practices, habits, and traditions.

In the last section of this book, I explored a number of historical figures, ideas, and practices to show how tending and keeping the past can help us in four areas today: to redeem our time, to engage with sacredness and beauty, to enrich our intellectual formation, and to cultivate our spiritual formation.

The Promise of History

My friend's sense of disconnectedness epitomises contemporary culture, and it also describes my own situation before I came to faith in Christ. In the Ahistoric Age people are rootless, atomised, and consistently told to dispense with the past and go and invent themselves. But, as I discovered in my own searching, Christians do not need to be disconnected from the past. Rather, God invites us to be part of a much larger *historical* story. We are a redeemed people, a people forgiven of sins, and a people called to the ministry of reconciliation (2 Cor. 5:18).

As I mentioned in the introduction, history is a rich storehouse and a "vast treasury," in Isaac Watts's words, if we can use it with wisdom. If Christians can be priests of history who tend and keep the past, we can inhabit our story as God's people and renew the church. We can not only strengthen and revive our spiritual and intellectual formation, but we can also equip ourselves to communicate the truth, goodness, and beauty of Jesus Christ to a confused and rootless world. Now that we have spent much of this book exploring historical figures, I feel it is only fitting to conclude with my own testimony.

A Historian's Testimony

My story unsettles a number of popular but misguided assumptions about people who convert from atheism to Christianity, not least because I came to faith at a high point of my life. Far from needing a "crutch," so to speak, I had everything I always wanted. Moreover, far from being led "blind" into faith, my conversion to Christianity emerged from an explicit engagement with atheism.

I grew up in Sydney, Australia, in a non-Christian home with parents who loved each other and their children dearly. My family took seriously the engagement with truth and ideas; my father was a renowned scholar of Australian labour history and a professor of government at the University of Sydney. Family mealtimes were often a forum for discussing history, politics, and issues of social justice. The rhythms of university life punctuated my childhood. My brother and I loved spending some of the summer school holidays going on the train to "the Uni" with our father. We researched school projects at the University's Fisher Library and had the privilege of feeling grown up when our father took us for lunches at the Student Union. The Victorian Gothic sandstone quadrangle of the University of Sydney symbolised the world of learning and ideas. To me the world was a wondrous and complex place, and I was keenly aware that the human mind needed to grapple with our existence in all its fraught complexity. My parents, accordingly, encouraged me to learn and to pursue the truth.

When I was eight, my family travelled to England and to America due to my father taking up sabbatical appointments, including at the University of Texas at Austin. While we were in England, we spent time at Darwin College, Cambridge. This trip was formative; I saw the remains of medieval castles and towns old enough to be in the Domesday book of William the Conqueror. From that moment onwards, the past captured my imagination. Just before my ninth birthday, I decided that I wanted to study history at the University of Cambridge when I grew up. This ambition gave me a firm sense of who I was and what my life was all about. I knew it would take considerable drive to go all the way from Australia to become a student at Cambridge. I believed I did not need a god to tell me who I was or how to make sense of the world. I knew what my life was all about. Surely, Christianity was just a crutch—I didn't need it.

My ambition to study at Cambridge propelled me through school. I took multiple prizes as an undergraduate at the University of Sydney and finished with the University Medal and a Commonwealth Scholarship to undertake my doctorate in history at Cambridge. My childhood dream was coming true. I arrived at Cambridge as a student of King's College just before my twenty-third birthday. Years earlier, as tourists from the other side of the world, my brother and I had posed for a photograph in front of Bodley's Court, a stately stone building on the river Cam. Directly behind us in the photo was the room that, almost fifteen years later, would become my bedroom.

The Question of History: Cambridge

At King's College, Cambridge, I began work on my doctoral dissertation, which focussed on the relationship between seventeenth-century natural philosophy and the origins of the British Empire. This involved studying the work of some of the founders of what we now call modern science, including Robert Boyle, one of the forefathers of modern chemistry; Robert Hooke, who did pioneering work on the microscope; and their colleagues who developed the experimental method. As I read the work of these natural philosophers, however, what I discovered began to unsettle an assumption I held about Christianity. I originally believed Christianity and science were fundamentally in conflict.

Robert Boyle's work, in particular, showed me that such an anti-thetical statement about Christianity and science would have made no sense to him. To my bemusement, Boyle seemed preoccupied with questions of Christian faith and reason. I was struck by his attitude towards studying nature. He believed he was engaging in a study of God's creation, understanding the complexity and order that God had given to the world. At first, I dismissed Boyle's frequent references to the Bible and figures like Adam and Eve as intellectual window dressing. But I increasingly saw that Boyle's entire epistemology—his understanding of knowledge and its character, methodologies, and purposes—was shaped by his Christian faith.

Likewise, when I read Robert Hooke's treatise *Micrographia* (1666), which was one of the pioneering works on the development of the microscope, I came across this curious passage in the preface in which Hooke describes the microscope as a means of compensating for the corruption wrought upon the human senses by the fall: "By the addition of such *artificial Instruments* and *methods*, there may be, in some manner, a reparation made for the mischiefs, and imperfection, mankind has drawn upon it self . . . both from a deriv'd corruption, innate and born with him." Hooke's Christian faith lay at the very core of his work on the development of the microscope. His faith spurred him to help humanity "recover some degree of those former perfections [and] rectifying the operations of the *Sense*, the *Memory*, and *Reason*" which it had once possessed but lost at the fall.[1]

While working hard on my dissertation, I became friends with some Christian fellow students. They were seriously intellectually engaged, and their faith meant that they lived differently. Their witness and kindness made a powerful impression upon me, breaking down my own intellectual snobbery and suspicion of Christians. They continued to be faithful friends even though I was the last person whom they thought would ever become a Christian. One of these friends, Rebecca McLaughlin, has described me (quite truthfully) at the time as "politely hostile to the Christian faith."[2]

---

1. Robert Hooke, *Micrographia* (London: James Allestry, 1665), a. Emphasis original.
2. Rebecca McLaughlin, *Confronting Christianity: 12 Hard Questions for the World's Largest Religion* (Wheaton: Crossway, 2019), 65.

The Big Questions: Oxford

Towards the end of my doctoral studies at Cambridge, I was elected to a Junior Research Fellowship at the University of Oxford. A few months into my fellowship, my atheism faced an intellectual challenge from a surprising source. My friends and I learned that one of the most famous atheist philosophers, Peter Singer, was visiting Oxford to give that year's Uehiro Lectures on the subject of human value and ethics (a foretaste of his subsequent 2009 book *The Life You Can Save*). Singer was thoughtful and calm, and droll yet quick-witted; I remember feeling proud as I heard his Australian accent in the lecture hall at Oxford. He had an impressive intellectual honesty. With logical consistency, Singer pursued the implications of atheism for ethics, even when they led to uncomfortable positions. I left Singer's lectures feeling a profound intellectual vertigo.

I was now compelled to confront one of my most deeply held beliefs: the innate equality of all people. I assumed that this belief was something all reasonable people agreed upon and that my atheism was entirely consistent with it. One of Singer's foundational claims, however, suggested that the innate preciousness and equal value of human beings is actually a Christian myth.

Atheism was also failing me in another, more personal way. In my mind, I was free to create the meaning and significance of my life because God didn't exist. I was in my mid-twenties, and I had been living according to this mentality, relishing one success after another. I had everything I had always wanted.

However, as I described in the introduction of this book, one grey Oxford winter's day I found myself alone in the Wolfson College library. I noticed that my usual desk was in front of the theology section. With an awkward reluctance, I opened a book of sermons. I was curious, but I was still expecting to read some pious, self-righteous vagaries. Yet these sermons were intellectually robust. They pointed me to a number of biblical passages that presented a very different account of human life and human value. One was Psalm 139:13: "For it was you who formed my inward parts; you knit me together in my mother's womb." I also saw another verse I had read for my doctoral studies but never properly thought about: "Let us make humankind in our image, according to our likeness" (Gen. 1:26).

I saw a stark contrast between atheism and these glimpses of a biblical view of human life. Those who were weak and those who were strong, able-bodied and disabled, black and white, and male and female were all created by God *in his image*. If God created all humanity in his image, then all people were inherent and equally precious. What a beautiful idea—but could it be true?

A few months later, near the end of my time at Oxford, I was invited to a dinner for the International Society for Science and Religion. I sat next to Andrew Briggs, a professor of nanomaterials, who happened to be a Christian. During dinner, Briggs asked me whether I believed in God. I fumbled—perhaps I was an agnostic? He responded, "Do you really want to sit on the fence forever?" This question made me realise that if issues about human value and ethics mattered to me, an uncertain response about God's existence was unsatisfactory.

The Question of God: Tallahassee

Soon afterwards, I moved to Tallahassee, Florida, to take up an assistant professorship at Florida State University. One of my new friends there gave me a copy of C. S. Lewis's *Mere Christianity*. I was struck by how reasonable Lewis's arguments were, and that book chipped away at some of my narrow-mindedness.

As I described more fully in chapter 10, one morning I finally decided to go to church. As I saw the congregation celebrate the Lord's Supper, the words and music brought me into a much larger and more profound story. Even though I was a stranger, I knew I was gazing upon a wonderfully sacred and exquisite scene. While the congregation knelt in prayer, the minister repeated the ancient words of Jesus:

Take, eat: This is my Body, which is given for you. Do this for the remembrance of me.[3]

---

3. The Episcopal Church, *The Book of Common Prayer and Administration of the*

Drink this, all of you: This is my Blood of the new Covenant, which
is shed for you and for many for the forgiveness of sins. Whenever
you drink it, do this for the remembrance of me.[4]

Those profound words have echoed through generations for thousands of years with the promise of forgiveness of sins and reconciliation
with God because of what Jesus has done. I had seemingly encountered
what one of my favourite poets, T. S. Eliot, once called the "still point
of the turning world."[5]

If atheism were true, this beautiful and mysterious ceremony was
utterly meaningless. Nothing would be transcendent or sacred; the
only meaning in life would be what we create for ourselves. I was now
twenty-seven and had crafted my own life according to this ideology.
I had fulfilled my childhood dreams—yet here I was yearning for
transcendence and ultimate meaning, sitting alone in a church on a
Sunday morning.

Atheism could not provide adequate answers to the big questions
of life, and it could not make sense of the human predicament of living
in a world that does not satisfy our deepest longings. This dilemma
always lay before my eyes, both in my work as a historian and in my
personal experience. The promise of inventing my own meaning in
life revealed itself to be utterly shallow when compared to the story of
God's redemptive work through Christ.

As I sat in this beautiful church, I began to have hope. History and
time could have purpose and meaning through the astounding biblical
story of creation, sin, and redemption. Not only did this story help
human history make sense, but it also illuminated my own condition.

Yet I noticed something else that morning. As the Lord's Supper
was being celebrated, I encountered God as *sacred*. My universe was
flat, as it were, without anything transcendent; there was nothing

Sacraments and Other Rites and Ceremonies of the Church (New York: Church Publishing
Incorporated, 2007), 362.

4. The Episcopal Church, *The Book of Common Prayer*, 363.

5. T. S. Eliot, "Burnt Norton," in *Four Quartets* (1944; London: Faber and Faber, 2001), 7.

beyond this life. But here, in church, I realised that Christianity is not just intellectual; it is not only a set of truths that can be expressed as propositions which you believe or don't believe. Rather, Christianity marries truth to an entire way of life. The liturgy invited me into this new life, to be part of this new creation of a people whom God formed *in* history.

I now began to attend church regularly, and I spent a lot of time reading theology and the Bible. I found the story of Jacob wrestling with God in Genesis chapter 32 especially compelling; it seemed to be an apt description of my own grappling with the idea of God. God wants anything *but* the unthinking faith I had once assumed characterised Christianity. God wants us to wrestle with him; to struggle through doubt and faith as well as sorrow and hope. Moreover, God wants broken people, not self-righteous ones.

The more I learned about God's love for us in Jesus, the more I found myself overwhelmed. I realised that God had always known me and always loved me. He wanted me to stop running after everything else in life except him. I also acutely perceived that I was a deeply sinful person in need of God's forgiveness. I had lived a life rejecting God and arrogantly ridiculing and poking fun of the very idea of God. Yet God showed me grace. He gave me this grace at the horrific cost of taking the punishment that my sin deserved onto himself in Jesus Christ.

Interestingly, the issue of Jesus's historicity did not loom large for me in my coming to faith. I never doubted that Jesus of Nazareth existed, and even in my non-Christian home we acknowledged that Jesus had lived as a real historical person. I knew there was no serious scholarly debate about this; I distinctly remember my historian father, who is still not a Christian, saying as much. The real question was whether Jesus was God; whether he was who he said he was. In the years since becoming a Christian, I have read widely about the historicity of the resurrection and the origin of the biblical manuscripts.[6]

---

6. One of the most helpful and concise books for a popular audience is John Dickson's *Is Jesus History?* (Epsom, UK: The Good Book Company, 2019). See also N. T. Wright, *The*

There is more to the story of my coming to faith, but, in short, I believed the Bible's explanation of who God is and who we are. I wanted to follow the God who made me, loves me, and died for me. So, one night I knelt in my closet in my apartment. In prayer, I admitted that I had lived a life turning away from God but was now asking Jesus to become my Lord and Saviour. I was not doing this because God would then enable me to avoid suffering or disappointment or to achieve all my dreams, but rather because God himself *is* life. Indeed, life with him is life with abundance: "I came that they may have life, and have it abundantly" (John 10:10). The love of God was unlike anything I had expected, and I could not comprehend it. When he became fully human in Jesus, God behaved decidedly unlike a god. Why deign to walk through death's dark valley or hold the weeping limbs of lepers if you are God? Why submit to humiliation and death on a cross in order to save those who hate you?

Becoming a Christian is not something one does to attain a better or easier life. God does not promise us health, wealth, or less suffering. And salvation is not about us earning our way to some place in the clouds through good works. Rather, I learned that Jesus's resurrection initiated the kingdom of God, which will "bring good news to the poor . . . proclaim release to the captives and recovery of sight to the blind, to let the oppressed go free, to proclaim the year of the Lord's favor" (Luke 4:18–19). To live as a Christian is a call to be part of this new creation. Now, as a follower of Jesus, I am compelled to live a different life—to serve others and call them to come and follow Jesus—the crucified King and risen Lord. We have a sure hope that God is transforming this broken, unjust world into a new creation where there will no longer be any death, suffering, or pain. God himself will wipe every tear from every eye (cf. Rev. 21:4).

Resurrection of the Son of God (Minneapolis: Fortress Press, 2003); Craig Blomberg, *The Historical Reliability of the New Testament* (Nashville: B&H Academic, 2016); F. F. Bruce, *The New Testament Documents: Are They Reliable?* (Grand Rapids: Eerdmans, 1943); Peter J. Williams, *Can We Trust the Gospels?* (Wheaton: Crossway, 2018); and Richard Bauckham, *Jesus and the Eyewitnesses: The Gospels as Eyewitness Testimony* (Grand Rapids: Eerdmans, 2017).

Part of my own path towards Christian faith involved recognising that Christianity is not only true, but also good and beautiful. Regardless of what you have done and how you have lived, the invitation to be reconciled with God in Jesus is for all people—black and white, male and female. This invitation is for all races and classes. It calls you to be part of a historical community. This invitation is for *you*.

Acknowledgements

I am deeply grateful to the friends and brothers and sisters in Christ who took the time to read earlier versions of my book to give me their thoughts and encouragement. I would like to thank John Anderson, Taylor and Kristina Charles, Rachel Ciano, John Dickson, Sophie Dickson, Mark Earngey, Johanna Harris, Belinda and L.-T. Hopper, Michael Jensen, Simon Kennedy, Simon Manchester, Chris and Helen Mann, Miranda McLaughlin, Rebecca McLaughlin, Steve and Alex Meredith, Laura Rademaker, Pre and Holly Shunmugam, Molly Worthen, and Daniel and Romy Zahra. To our church small group who met at our house and who have prayed for me and for this project—thank you for being a loving Christian community for us. I will always give thanks for our minister, the late Greg Peisley. He and his wife Susan modelled a life of loving Jesus and boldly encouraged me and so many others to "go and make disciples of all nations" (Matt. 28:19).

Several early conversations with Collin Hansen helped me refine the central issues of this book. I am thankful for Collin's generosity and encouragement, and I am also grateful to Megan Hill and the team at The Gospel Coalition for helping me think through how to structure the book.

I would particularly like to thank the team at Zondervan for all that they have done to publish this book. Ever since I first met with Ryan Pazdur, Kyle Rohane, Alexis De Weese, and Katya Covrett, the Zondervan team has been supportive, helpful, and prayerful for this work. I would like to thank Ryan Pazdur for his insightful comments and suggestions on the original manuscript and proposal. I am grateful to my acquisitions editor, Kyle Rohane, for his careful reading of the full manuscript and for his suggestions about ways to strengthen my argument. Daniel Saxton first noticed this manuscript in Zondervan's unsolicited submissions email inbox and also edited the text meticulously—thank you, Daniel. I also want to express my gratitude to Alexis De Weese and her team for the elegant cover design and for marketing this book.

I am truly blessed to be part of the Western Civilisation Program at Australian Catholic University. I would like to thank The Ramsay Centre for Western Civilisation and Australian Catholic University for their generous and courageous support of the humanities, of history, and of Western Civilisation in a climate that increasingly undervalues these three disciplines.

I am so thankful to three dear friends. These women model how to serve God through one's intellect. Rebecca McLaughlin has been urging me to write a book about my faith for years, and she has been praying for me since I was that polite but hostile atheist at Cambridge. Rachel Ciano and Johanna Harris are brilliant scholars of history and literature and are role models for so many. I cherish our friendship.

My parents, Sue and Terry Irving, are an endless source of encouragement, love, and inspiration. I have been discussing history and ideas with them for as long as I remember. My father showed me that history is something that we participate in making, not just writing about in books. I want to thank him for reading this manuscript and asking me the most challenging questions, for modelling a life of writing history, and for showing me grace and love even when we disagree. My mother (and my grandmother, Norma, before her) showed me what it means to steward the history of a family—to pass down the heritage, wisdom, and identity that forms deep roots through generations. I also want to thank my parents-in-law, Teri and Garry Stonebraker, for inviting me with such love into their own family and its rich traditions and history.

Finally, Johnathan Stonebraker made it possible for me to write this book. He embodies what it means to be a husband according to

Ephesians 5 and Psalm 128—giving himself up so I can use my gifts and so our family can flourish. He read and reread every word of this book, and we discussed every idea together. Our children—Madeleine, Charlotte, and James—have inherited our love of learning about the history of the Christian faith. I am so thankful to them for their abiding encouragement, and for teaching me things I did not know about the American Revolution.